Love Colors

Also by Pamala Oslie

Life Colors: What the Colors in Your Aura Reveal

Make Your Dreams Come True:
Simple Steps for Changing the Beliefs That Limit You

Love Colors

a new approach to
love, relationships, and auras

Pamala Oslie

New World Library
Novato, California

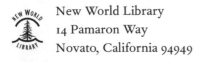

New World Library
14 Pamaron Way
Novato, California 94949

Text design and typography by Tona Pearce Myers
Author photograph by Connie Adams

Library of Congress Cataloging-in-Publication Data
Oslie, Pamala.
Love colors : a new approach to love, relationships, and auras / Pamala Oslie.
   p.   cm.
ISBN 978-1-57731-575-9 (pbk. : alk. paper)
1. Aura. 2. Typology (Psychology)—Miscellanea. 3. Love—Miscellanea.
I. Title.
BF1389.A8O853 2007
133.8'92—dc22   2006100318

First printing, March 2007
ISBN-10: 1-57731-575-8
ISBN-13: 978-1-57731-575-9
Printed in Canada on acid-free, partially recycled paper

g New World Library is a proud member of the Green Press Initiative.

Distributed by Publishers Group West

10   9   8   7   6   5   4   3   2   1

We are each a unique expression of Divine Love.

Love is who we are,
and the desire to know and experience love is our nature.

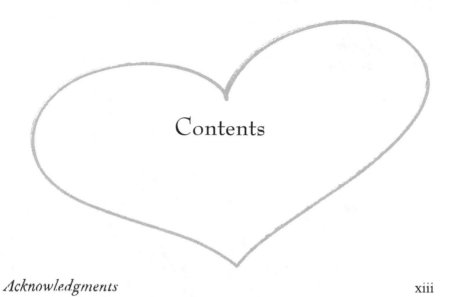

Contents

Part Two. Where Are They?

Acknowledgments

I sincerely appreciate my family, friends, and clients, who share their love with me, and who patiently supported me as I created *Love Colors*.

Thank you Khelly Miller, Caitlin Crest, Mary Judge, and Kat for your wonderful contributions to this book. Thank you also to my editor, Georgia Hughes, who believed in *Love Colors*. And to Bonita Hurd, as well as Kristen Cashman, Kim Corbin, Mary Ann Casler, Munro Magruder, Tona Pearce Myers, and all the other wonderful people at New World Library, who dedicated so much of their time and energy to make this book a reality.

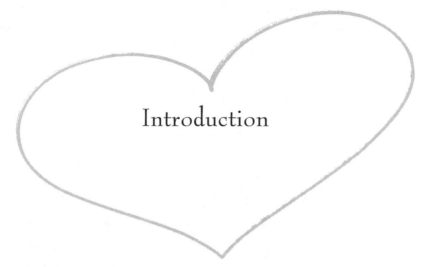

Introduction

It doesn't seem to matter what culture, faith, or background we come from: most of us yearn to experience love. We long to share our lives, to have a deep, soulful connection with another person. We feel a strong pull to unite, an inner need that goes far beyond a mere physical drive to reproduce. Do we feel incomplete without another person by our side? Or is there another purpose, a higher purpose, behind our desire to experience love? Do we long for a loving relationship simply because we have been conditioned to believe in romantic fairy tales and happy endings? There does seem to be a part of us that resonates with these stories, though. We recognize that feeling of love — the warm sensation and joy that two people experience when they truly care for one another. We want to believe in the magic that brings two lovers together, and to believe that living happily ever after is possible. Maybe our souls know that love, and our desire to feel love, is the true nature of our being.

Throughout my years as a psychic consultant, I have spoken with thousands of clients from all over the world, and without a doubt the most prevalent questions that people have — and the biggest challenges most face — revolve around relationships. A tremendous number of people feel that finding a partner is taking too long, or they fear that love will never come their way. Many are dissatisfied with their current relationship and want out, or they are working too hard to maintain what they have. Too many people have lost their belief in themselves or have lost faith in love. Some fear that they are unlovable or do not deserve love, which makes finding real and lasting love even more of a challenge.

We are amazing beings who have the ability to create anything our hearts desire, and our beliefs about ourselves and about life create our experiences. For many of us, distorted, limiting beliefs about ourselves, and our subconscious fears about relationships, are sabotaging our ability to receive the love we so deeply desire. To find and sustain true love, it is important to first recognize and value who we are — wonderful souls who deserve love. And second, we must believe that love is possible, probable, and real. Once we realize how magnificent and lovable we truly are, and that love is a real possibility, attracting and allowing love into our lives can be as easy as breathing.

Love Colors was written to help us connect with love and create the relationship of our dreams. It is meant to serve as a guide to uncover what our hearts truly desire so we can actually attract the right partner into our lives. The book is designed to help us remember who we are, clearly define what we are looking for, understand what type of person may actually be best for us, discover where we may meet this person, uncover beliefs that may be standing in our way, and learn new ways to create long-lasting, fulfilling partnerships. Learning about the different Love Colors is a great way to begin understanding who we are and to identify the qualities we are looking for in a partner.

What Is a Love Color?

Have you ever wondered why you are drawn to some people and not others? Have you seen a pattern in the type of people you are consistently attracted to? Do you feel a certain "vibe" from some people that fascinates you, and a vibe from others that makes you want to pull away? If so, you are most certainly sensing their auras. The different colors in our auras, or energy fields, reveal important information about our personalities, goals, priorities, and relationship styles.

The one or two bands of color in our auras that are closest to our bodies are our life colors (in this book about relationships, I refer to them as our Love Colors). There are many different Love Colors — some are compatible with our personal aura colors, and some are contrary. This book describes the different personality of each color and explains why relationships between people with the different colors may or may not work out, and why some relationships may be more challenging than others.

I describe the different colors' positive qualities and their more challenging traits, their greatest potentials as well as their downsides. In order to paint a full picture for you, I have written about possible extreme behaviors as well as the more common qualities of each color. Most people you meet will not exhibit the more serious attributes, but I include these nonetheless to help you avoid potential disasters.

Love Colors is intended not to limit you — you are free to choose any partner you want — only to help you identify those who may be better suited to your personality. Understanding the unique qualities and personality of each color may help you create a shortcut to finding your ideal relationship and help you avoid the ordeal of trial and error with incompatible people. The book also explores ways you can enhance your relationships and create harmony and happiness by understanding and respecting your own and others' different needs and desires.

How to Use This Book

Chapter 1 discusses the first steps to take to create your ideal relationship. Also listed are possible reasons why your past relationships may have been unsuccessful. To help you better understand your own personality and relationship style, chapter 2 presents the Love Colors personality test, which will help you discover which one or two colors best describe you. (Most people have two Love Colors.) After taking the test, you can read more about these particular colors in chapter 3. You may also want to read the brief descriptions of all the different colors in this chapter to see if you are attracted to any particular personality type as a potential life partner. Since most people have two Love Colors, notice which two personality types you are drawn to. Then go to chapter 4 to see which Love Colors are either moderately or most compatible with your own colors. This can also help you recognize which personalities could be best aligned with your ideal dream. Reading about the colors that are least compatible with your colors can help you understand why relationships with certain personalities may be more challenging for you.

Since you probably don't see auras yourself, and it could be uncomfortable to ask everyone you meet to take the Love Colors test, you will need another way to help you identify which Love Colors a person is. Chapter 5 reveals some of the more obvious signs and behaviors of each color so you can easily recognize them. Chapter 6 shows you where you are likely to find the different Love Color personalities — where they work, where they hang out, and what their favorite hobbies and pastimes are. This chapter also offers suggestions on how to go about meeting your favorite Love Colors.

Chapter 7 discusses the important inner steps you can take to create a healthy relationship. Being emotionally, spiritually, and psychologically healthy plays an important role in creating long-lasting, harmonious, and loving relationships.

Whether you are looking for your potential mate or you are already involved with a partner, chapter 8 can help you understand what you can look forward to in a relationship with particular Love Colors — their positive qualities, their challenging behaviors, and the strengths and weaknesses of their relationship styles. Chapter 9 gives advice on how to create a fulfilling, mutually respectful relationship with the Love Colors you choose. Included in the chapter are details about what will make you and your partner happy and what will cause trouble in your relationship, what each admires in a mate and which behaviors may disappoint you or drive you apart.

Chapter 10 sheds light on each Love Color's more serious flaws and problem behaviors that could potentially destroy your relationship. It discusses how to know if your relationship is in trouble, and how and when to move on from that particular individual.

I hope the information in *Love Colors* will help you understand yourself and your love interest, and help you honor your true desires so you can create fulfillment in your life. My sincerest wish for you is that you easily connect with, and joyfully experience, great love in your life.

What Is an Aura?

The aura is the electromagnetic or energy field that radiates from all matter, although some matter is so dense and vibrates so slowly that detecting its aura is often difficult. Throughout the ages, artists have depicted auras as halos or glowing lights that appear around the heads or bodies of highly evolved, enlightened spiritual masters and saints. Apparently, the auras around these beings were so powerful that others could easily see, feel, or sense them. Auras can now be scientifically detected by means of various electronic instruments and Kirlian photography.

Like many other people, I see the aura as a glowing light that radiates out from the body in all directions like light from a lightbulb. This light, or aura, can emanate six feet or more from the person's body. The aura has many different layers, or bands, of light as it extends out from the body. Each band is a different color, as in a rainbow. Every person is unique. One person may have a band of blue light closest to the body that completely surrounds her or him, and then a band of yellow light outside of the blue. There are numerous colored bands in a person's aura; each color reveals a different quality about the person. Some people may have five different bands of colors in their aura; others may have ten or more bands.

The one or two bands closest to the body are the Love Colors, and these bands typically do not change throughout a person's lifetime. The outer bands in the aura change constantly, depending on what is going on in a person's life at different times. The width of the bands varies, depending on how a person is living the personality trait of each particular color. For example, people who have a Yellow Love Color and are always playful, outgoing, and happy typically have a very wide yellow band in their aura. People who have a Yellow Love Color but are usually quiet and reserved will likely have a narrower band of yellow.

The aura also reveals — by the intensity and vibrancy of the color, as well as by its size — whether a person is healthy or ill, happy or frustrated. One person's aura may be bright, vibrant, and expanded, showing openness, well-being, positive self-esteem, and good health; another's may be faded and contracted, showing fear, illness, lack of self-esteem, hopelessness, or a perceived need for protection. A dark, densely colored aura usually reveals depression, frustration, or self-pity. The different colors of an aura are created in much the same manner as sounds are created. With sounds, the faster the vibration, the higher the frequency — and the higher the sound. The high C note on a piano vibrates at a faster rate than a bass note. Similarly, as the waves of energy that make up the aura change their speed of vibration, the colors change. In the aura, a slower vibration creates red and orange. Faster vibrations create blue, violet, and indigo. A bass note is not better or worse than a high note. It is just a different sound. Likewise, orange in the aura is not better or worse than blue.

The particular Love Colors in your aura reveal the overall theme and purpose you have chosen in this lifetime — whether that is to live a life of service, leadership, creativity, travel and exploration, research, and so on. No life choice is better or worse than another; it is just a different experience. This does not mean that you are limited to a particular life purpose, goal, or way of processing information, however. We have free will and are free to grow and change in any way we choose. Life would be mundane and uninspiring if we all had the same colors, just as a song would be monotonous if it were composed of only one note. Although we may each have different Love Colors — with different methods, goals, and life purposes — we are a part of and contribute to the whole human rainbow of Love Colors.

Part One

Getting Started

Chapter 1

Creating Harmonious Relationships Begins with Knowing Yourself

Why does it seem to be more and more challenging to find a perfect mate or maintain a happy and compatible relationship? Was love always this difficult? Haven't we heard stories of people being truly fulfilled and happy in love? Is love a myth? There are more people on the planet than ever before, and traveling the world has never been easier. Not only that; now we can use technologies like the Internet to connect with others. So what is the problem? Why does it seem to be more complicated than ever to meet the right person and live happily ever after?

Before we probe that question, there may be other questions to consider. Perhaps the real questions are: Am I *being* the "right" one? Am *I* happy with who I am? Do I have issues and fears that are preventing me from finding the love I desire? Do I truly know what I desire in a relationship?

Possibly we haven't met the right person or created harmony in our current relationship because we don't know who we are, or don't know how to do our part to create a happy and healthy relationship. Or maybe we like who we are, but we don't believe we can create the relationship we want.

I have friends who believed with all their hearts that their life partners would just show up at the door, that they would not have to do anything special, go out of their way, or change who they were to meet their mates. And amazingly, they were right.

I have clients who desperately wanted to be married, and who searched and searched in vain to find a compatible life partner. Inevitably, with this desperate need to find a companion, they met someone, got married, and then realized they still were not happy. The majority of these clients are now divorced and, once again, out in the world searching for love.

I know many other people who stay in unfulfilling, unhappy, and even unhealthy relationships because they are too frightened to be alone.

These are examples of three different attitudes and three different outcomes. Each example reveals what these people think about themselves. Obviously relationships are possible. People are creating them every day. So what is the problem?

Our current beliefs about ourselves, and our fears about relationships, are creating the problems. If we have unresolved fears and doubts, we sabotage our potential to create a wonderful relationship. How can we be part of a healthy, fulfilling relationship if we don't trust or like ourselves? How can we offer the best of ourselves to another when we secretly fear we are not at our best? How can we feel safe getting into a relationship when we fear it may be the wrong one and therefore could cause us pain? How can we trust ourselves, and therefore our choices, if we fear repeating our past mistakes? How can we create a wonderful relationship if we have given up on the magic of love or have forgotten how lovable we truly are?

We have all heard that we must first be happy with ourselves, but we don't like that. Why can't someone just show up, love us unconditionally, and in doing so make our lives wonderful? The reason this won't work is that it takes two healthy, happy partners to create a healthy, happy relationship.

The first step to finding and sustaining a wonderful relationship is to know, love, and value ourselves. It is important to believe we are lovable, or we won't be able to accept or trust love. The second step is to believe in love, trust that the desire in our hearts is there for a reason, and believe that love is not only possible but real and on the way to us now. So it is important to begin the process of finding or creating a fulfilling relationship by examining ourselves. Let's first uncover some of the beliefs we may be carrying before we look at how to change our lives. We can start by looking at our past relationship choices. Discovering the hidden beliefs, fears, and motives that cause us to keep creating the same unhealthy relationships is the first step to changing.

Understanding Past Relationships

Consider your past relationships. Can you pinpoint a particular reason why most of them did not work out? And if you are currently in an unhappy, unfulfilling relationship, is it not working out for similar reasons?

If you believe something was wrong with you in those relationships, then discover what those qualities — the ones that strike you as "inferior" or "unsatisfying" — are so you can either change them or realize that they are not the truth about you. This is not to say that there is actually something wrong with you. However, if *you* believe there is something wrong with you, it *becomes* an issue. Our fears and self-judgments can keep us from being healthy partners and from completely accepting love into our lives.

Do you believe, for example, that you were too weak and needy in your past relationships or too strong and demanding? Do you think you were too lazy and unmotivated or too aggressive? Were you too insecure or too arrogant? Were you too selfish and self-centered or too doting and suffocating? Or are you just really good at choosing the "wrong type of person" over and over again? If you believe you still possess any of these qualities, you may create the same unhappy experience and outcome with the next partner.

Perhaps you have changed since then. Maybe your relationship experiences motivated you to become a better person — or at least a person you like and appreciate more. If you feel you have improved, congratulations for learning from your relationships. You gained valuable insights and wisdom from your experiences. You can trust *you* to take care of yourself.

As you read this book, you may discover that there is nothing wrong with your particular personality traits. They may be exactly right for you, and the problem may be that you have simply not allowed yourself to be with the partner who perfectly matches your qualities. If you believe your relationships failed because of your partners' faults and weaknesses, then you can change your habit of being attracted to that type of person. Did you learn not to be attracted to that type again? If not, we are back to the original question: Do you think there is something "wrong" with you? If you feel that the failure of past relationships damaged you or made you afraid to get involved with someone again, then ask yourself: Do you think there is something "wrong" with you that would cause you to make those same choices and therefore be hurt again?

If you believe there *is* something wrong with you, you may continuously sabotage your relationships or prevent yourself from finding a relationship at all. If you secretly fear that your flaws or problems could hurt another person, you might flee from emotional intimacy every time an opportunity for love presents itself. Or, if you have a fear of commitment, you might be choosing the wrong type of partner over and over again so that it is easier for you to leave. The people you choose may be conveniently unavailable, unable to commit themselves to you, making it easier for you to remain single. Relationships can be our greatest mirrors and can bring our deepest issues to the surface. Sometimes it can seem easier to be single than to face ourselves in relationships.

We often go against our true natures by trying to live up to standards and expectations set by others. Many of us suppress our true natures because we feel we aren't good enough, and then we attempt to behave like someone else. But if we cannot be real with ourselves, then we probably won't be real with our partners either. We waste precious time trying to hide our defects, fearing no one will want us, or our partners will abandon us, if the truth is revealed. Conversely, we find ourselves disappointed when a partner's flaws start to emerge.

If you hide the real you, you probably will not choose the most compatible partner. You may instead choose someone you think "should" be right for you. And if you are desperate for a relationship, you will probably attract a person who is less than what you want. If you hope that someone else will make you feel happy and complete, then you will expect that person to always make you feel safe and loved. If you base your security and well-being on their behavior, when they disappoint you — and they probably will — your perceived happiness will not survive, because this happiness was not created by something deep within you. No matter how much someone loves you, if you don't love yourself, if you haven't learned to perceive yourself as wonderful and trust that each event in your life is ultimately beneficial to you, the love that someone else gives you, and the short-lived fun things that occur in your life, will never be enough to fill the void that the lack of self-love has created. While outside events and other people may spark moments of happiness in you, those good feelings will be fleeting unless you maintain deep within you a sense of well-being, self-love, and a connection to your Source — whatever you believe that Source is.

If you are secure in yourself, if you *know* you are wonderful and lovable, then you have a better chance of attracting a healthy partner into your life. And when your partner has a bad day, you will not fall apart. Your joy will not be contingent upon the behavior or whims of another person.

Sometimes we are drawn to people who have qualities we admire, but we fear we lack those same qualities ourselves. We may be drawn to someone who is optimistic and self-confident, but we see ourselves as weak and fearful. Rather than face our insecurities and live up to our own full potential, we hope someone else will create our dreams for us so we can feel complete and satisfied. If you doubt you can become rich and famous by means of your own talents, or if you do not believe you can create your own exciting life, you may be drawn to someone who is already exciting, rich, and famous. Seeking someone who is living out your dreams may not be the best way to create a healthy, balanced relationship, however. Instead, you and your partner may feel a sense of inequality between the two of you. One may seem to be superior, and the other may feel inferior. If you desire to be in a healthy relationship, it is better to become that which you desire.

Sometimes we end up with certain partners by default: someone we meet shows an interest in us, there is a physical attraction, and things just develop from there. Occasionally, such relationships work out, but more often than not, we discover that we have connected to the same type of person we have always chosen in the past. Once the excitement of the new relationship wears off, the same turmoil and lack of fulfillment surface.

Often, we choose partners who remind us of our parents. If we have unresolved issues with a parent, we may unconsciously choose a partner we think may help us heal the wounds we may have as a result. If we weren't "perfect" enough to earn love from a parent, maybe we can work harder and earn love from someone very similar — in this case, a partner. This person may be emotionally unavailable or critical or abusive just like that parent was, and although we do not like this behavior, it is familiar territory so we know what to expect. Knowing the personalities of the different Love Colors and purposely choosing the colors that are most compatible with our own may help us break the habit of choosing a substitute parent.

Steps to Change Your Life and Move Forward

If you are ready to change your past patterns and finally create a truly fulfilling relationship, you can take the following steps to begin the process of attracting love into your life. Chapter 7 offers additional suggestions to help you shift your relationship patterns.

BE AUTHENTIC. Once you are truthful with yourself about who you really are, and you allow yourself to live authentically, you greatly increase your probability of attracting and keeping your most harmonious Love Colors. You don't have to be perfect before love can come into your life. You need only to realize and accept that you are already the perfect lovable you. Reading about the different Love Color personalities will help you recognize and understand your true nature and enable you to give yourself permission to live authentically.

TRUST YOURSELF. The key characteristic of people who are happy and successful is that they believe in themselves. And chances are they learned to believe in themselves — which means anyone can do the same. Wouldn't you rather be with someone who is self-confident and who enjoys life? It's a good bet that your partner will feel the same way.

BECOME WHAT YOU LOVE. Develop in yourself the qualities that you desire in another person. Are you asking and expecting your partner to have qualities that you are afraid to develop in yourself? This type of inequality rarely creates a successful or harmonious partnership.

Deep inside, most of us desire partners who are a better, more confident version of ourselves. As you read *Love Colors*, notice the qualities that most colors prefer in a companion — they are qualities that reflect those Love Colors' own positive nature. If we believe we are compassionate, friendly, and nice, we usually prefer those qualities in our mates as well. If we are healthy and active and enjoy life, we love to be with others who are healthy and active too. If you are attracted to people who are self-confident and self-actualized, do you believe they would want to be with partners who are insecure?

This doesn't mean you have to become strong and macho in order to attract a macho partner. It does mean, however, that such a person will probably desire someone who exhibits inner strength and self-confidence. Again, most of us desire to be with people who are the same as, or better than, ourselves.

TRUST YOUR INTUITION. If you learn to trust and follow your inner voice, you may end up being in the right place at the right time to meet the wonderful partner who is right for you, or you may sense how to create balance in your current relationship. Once you learn to have faith in yourself, you will also learn to listen to and trust your inner voice.

BE OPEN AND TRUST LOVE. Trust that you are a great person, and that if you are hurt in a relationship you will survive to love again. Suffering the loss of love isn't pleasant — it can be downright painful — but it doesn't have to be the end of happiness forever. Allowing yourself to trust, to be open and available, to be willing to love and fully give yourself to another, will eventually give you the ultimate reward of true intimacy. There are so many wonderful people in the world who are ready to be in a happy relationship. Allow one of them into your life.

FACE YOUR FEARS. To remove the emotional blocks that may be preventing you from entering into a satisfying partnership, begin by identifying and then exploring what frightens you in relationships. If you cannot face your fears and heal them, you will most likely bring them into your relationship. Chapter 7 may assist you in this process and help you become emotionally healthier, so that you can achieve greatness in your relationships.

REDEFINE YOURSELF. If you change how you define yourself and how your perceive yourself, you can change your relationship experiences. You may be limiting yourself by your definitions of who you are — weak, lonely, unhappy, inadequate, unhealthy, lazy, unlovable, uninteresting. You don't have to stay the same throughout your life. You have the ability to choose your own thoughts, beliefs, and behaviors. If others can succeed and be happy in life, so can you. You can keep what you love and appreciate about yourself and let go of the rest. If you haven't examined and changed either your behavior or your perceptions and attitudes about yourself, then it may be time to do so — unless you are willing to attract the same type of unsatisfying relationships into your life. Believe you can change.

KNOW WHAT YOU TRULY DESIRE. One of the most important steps in creating your ideal and most fulfilling relationship is to be honest with yourself about what you truly desire. If you are not sure what type of person you really want, and you have not fully considered the consequences of your choices, this may be why you have not yet created your ideal relationship.

What Do You Want?

It's natural to assume you want good chemistry in your relationship — to be physically attracted to your mate. But there are other considerations that are essential to address if you are to create and maintain a long-term, satisfying union. Before you declare your intention to meet your perfect mate and then rush out into the world to find him or her, or before you try to change your current partner or decide to leave your existing relationship, it's important to ask yourself some soul-searching questions: Do you know deep within your heart what you truly desire

— what type of partner makes your heart sing? Do you know your true priorities? Are you being completely honest with yourself about the qualities you enjoy and the activities you really have no interest in?

Many of us imagine partners based on what we see in the movies — cute and helpless, rugged and strong, dangerous and romantic, or unavailable. If this has been your tendency, you may want to consider the long-term consequences of your fantasies. Are you being true to yourself, or are you searching for someone else's idea of perfection?

Do you want a partner who is stable and predictable, a reliable provider who loves to come home every night? Are you a homebody? Do you want the house in the suburbs, the well-mannered children, and an adoring partner who will be a wonderful father or mother for your children? Some Love Colors are better suited to this lifestyle than others. Certain Love Colors are quiet, practical, and conventional, but will you feel fulfilled with this type of person, or will you become restless and bored? Did your parents tell you this is what you need in your life to be happy? Or do these qualities truly mesh with your own personality?

Do you shy away from taking risks? If so, then certain Love Color personalities will strike you as troublesome and unsettling. Some thrive on adventure and challenges and can become quickly dissatisfied with the ordinary. While you may find this type of individual thrilling and stimulating at the beginning of the relationship, will you really be able to handle unpredictable or impulsive behavior in your marriage?

Do you want to be with someone who will support you so you can have the freedom to explore your creativity or start your own business? Certain Love Colors do not like taking chances, so they may object to, or even try to stop you from, chasing risky or seemingly unrealistic dreams. Do you want a partner who is comfortable dealing with finances? Some Love Color personalities are not interested in dealing with money, so you may end up having to be the responsible partner yourself.

Do you prefer to enjoy life's simple pleasures and want to be with someone who is easygoing and easily pleased? Or do you want to be with someone who is highly motivated and goal oriented? Do you love having expensive possessions? Is this a strong priority? Do you understand that the type of partner who can provide such things may also be the type who is not home much? This person may appear to put money or work ahead of you and the family. Are you independent and self-confident enough to enjoy this type of relationship?

Do you enjoy extra time and space for yourself? Do you value your independence and therefore need someone who will be busy with his or her own life? Or do you need a lot of companionship, reassurance, and validation from a mate? Some Love Colors refuse to change their behavior or to walk on eggshells to soothe someone's insecurities. If your feelings are easily hurt, watch out for this type of Love Color.

Do you prefer being with someone who challenges you to live up to your potential, someone who will inspire you to take chances and accomplish your greatest dreams? Or do you want a partner who will allow you to stay quietly at home so you do not need to interact with the outside world? Do you want a mate who loves to travel, or does traveling frighten you? Certain Love Colors need to travel and expect their partners to travel with them.

Do you need to be with someone who is open and communicative? Or do you prefer the strong, silent type? Some of the Love Colors enjoy discussing feelings and life plans, while others tend to keep their feelings to themselves.

Your personal preferences, whatever they may be, are valid. Just be aware of what they really are. Once you identify and understand your own Love Colors, and you recognize which qualities you desire in a partner, you can continue on the road to relationship fulfillment. The following chapters can help you with this process.

Love Colors is designed to guide you in bringing forth your own authenticity, to help you choose your dates, and your mate, from a deep sense of knowing yourself and from clear insight into others' behaviors and traits. This book is intended to help you create a relationship from strength, knowledge, and wisdom. Best wishes to you as you journey with self-awareness into your own personal world of love and relationships.

Chapter 2

Identifying Your Love Colors
with the Love Colors Personality Quiz

To discover your most compatible life partner, you will first want to know your own Love Colors and then identify the colors of your ideal companion. The Love Colors personality quiz can help you do that.

Your Love Colors, the one or two bands of color closest to your body, reveal your personality, priorities, methods of processing life, relationship styles, and primary purpose for being on the planet. There are two ways this book can help you determine your Love Colors. The first method is to answer the questions in the questionnaire that follows. The second is to read through the descriptions of the Love Colors and see which of them most accurately describe your personality. If you pay close attention to all the descriptions, you may intuitively feel which one or two colors best describe the real you. Most people have two Love Colors, called "combination colors." Combination colors are discussed more thoroughly in chapter 3. As you read through the different Love Color descriptions, also notice if you are drawn to any particular color personalities: these may describe your potential life partner.

Frequently there are only subtle differences between some of the Love Colors. For example, people who are Blues, Yellows, or Violets are all emotional but they vary in intensity. They all have a desire to help people, but each does so in a different way. Yellows prefer to fix things for people — their bodies, cars, or kitchen sinks. Blues usually counsel people individually, while Violets prefer to lead, educate, and inspire the masses.

Occasionally, we suppress our natural Love Colors because of family pressures or expectations. For example, people with the carefree and energetic Yellow Love Color may have been forced by domineering or repressed parents to behave in a more disciplined fashion. These Yellows may have been told as children that it was not appropriate to be silly, playful, or irresponsible. Consequently, many of these sensitive Yellows lost their natural enthusiasm, their creative impulses, and their sense of humor. Parents frequently raise their children in ways that are based on their own beliefs and their own colors. They do the best they can, given that they are not usually aware of their children's colors and true personalities. If you know you were suppressed or taught to behave in a manner that was not true to your nature, be sure to give your true answers in the quiz, not the responses you think you should give.

Before taking the quiz, which begins on the next page, read all the questions in each category. This will give you a general feeling for the personality type of each Love Color. Then answer all the questions in the questionnaire.

Again, be sure to respond with the answers you feel are truly your own, not with answers that indicate what you feel is expected of you or who you think you should be. Also, taking the test during a time of emotional distress or trauma may skew your answers. Therefore, I recommend that you avoid taking the test during such a time.

Love Color #1

YES   SOMETIMES   NO

❏   ❏   ❏   I believe that life is physical and biological, not spiritual.

❏   ❏   ❏   I prefer to focus on the three-dimensional world — on things I can physically touch, taste, see, hear, or smell — rather than discuss spiritual or philosophical topics.

❏   ❏   ❏   I tend to be strong, honest, and blunt.

❏   ❏   ❏   I often have a quick temper, but I get over it quickly and do not hold grudges.

❏   ❏   ❏   I prefer work that is physical and has immediate, tangible results.

❏   ❏   ❏   I enjoy taking physical action on projects rather than discussing ideas and plans.

❏   ❏   ❏   The primary focus and purpose of my life is to work hard, but to experience all of life's physical pleasures.

❏   ❏   ❏   I tend to be a loner.

❏   ❏   ❏   I tend to express myself through my sexuality and my physical body more than through my intellect or emotions.

❏   ❏   ❏   I have a hard time expressing my feelings to others.

❏   ❏   ❏   I am usually powerful, self-confident, independent, and practical.

❏   ❏   ❏   I am persistent and hardworking and usually keep the rest of the team going.

____   ____   ____   (Total each column here.)

Love Color #2

YES   SOMETIMES   NO

❏   ❏   ❏   I tend to be a physical daredevil.

❏   ❏   ❏   I relish dangerous, physical challenges — the riskier, the better.

❏   ❏   ❏   Having a regular job and a family is boring to me.

❏   ❏   ❏   I prefer occupations that allow me to experience raw, physical courage. I would love to work as a stunt double.

❏   ❏   ❏   I tend to use money for daring adventures such as mountain climbing or car racing, rather than for safe investments.

❏   ❏   ❏   I prefer to spend time alone or in the company of other daredevils.

❏   ❏   ❏   Experiencing physical pain does not frighten or deter me.

❏   ❏   ❏   I prefer high-risk, individual sports rather than team sports.

❏   ❏   ❏   I enjoy the challenge of going beyond physical limitations.

❏   ❏   ❏   I don't need to talk about my feelings with anyone.

❏   ❏   ❏   People often see me as self-absorbed and aloof.

❏   ❏   ❏   Discussing spiritual beliefs and concepts does not interest me.

_____   _____   _____   (Total each column here.)

Love Color #3

YES   SOMETIMES   NO

YES	SOMETIMES	NO	
❏	❏	❏	I tend to be flamboyant and eccentric.
❏	❏	❏	My clothes, home, actions, and thoughts tend to be bizarre, outrageous, twisted, and shocking.
❏	❏	❏	Acting perverse and outrageous is fun and does not embarrass me.
❏	❏	❏	I see life as an Alice in Wonderland–type adventure.
❏	❏	❏	I am not interested in spiritual concepts or helping the planet, only in experiencing the strangeness of the physical world.
❏	❏	❏	I do not usually conform to society's rules or laws.
❏	❏	❏	Although I love parties and social events, I have trouble keeping friends because my behavior sometimes shocks people.
❏	❏	❏	I am a loner.
❏	❏	❏	I am a quick thinker, but people rarely understand my ideas.
❏	❏	❏	I enjoy outrageous artistic expression.
❏	❏	❏	I do not usually take responsibility for friends or family.
❏	❏	❏	I feel more comfortable living in a big city where I can hide out in the crowds.

_____ _____ _____   (Total each column here.)

Love Color #4

YES	SOMETIMES	NO	
❏	❏	❏	Having fun is a strong priority for me.
❏	❏	❏	I have a great sense of humor and love to laugh.
❏	❏	❏	I am optimistic and upbeat, always wearing a smile.
❏	❏	❏	I tend to look younger than my age.
❏	❏	❏	I tend to be rebellious. I hate being told what to do.
❏	❏	❏	I need to work out, dance, or do some other type of physical exercise regularly.
❏	❏	❏	I tend to fidget or have high energy.
❏	❏	❏	I like to be creative or to work with my hands.
❏	❏	❏	When there is conflict, my first impulse is to retreat or run away.
❏	❏	❏	I am sensitive to criticism and anger. My feelings can be easily hurt.
❏	❏	❏	I have, or have had, a tendency to regularly overdo at least one of the following: drugs, alcohol, cigarettes, caffeine, sex, exercise, chocolates or other sweets, food, television, or computer games.
❏	❏	❏	I believe that sex should be fun.

_____ _____ _____   (Total each column here.)

Love Color #5

YES	SOMETIMES	NO	
❏	❏	❏	I prefer a secure, stable job that provides regular paychecks.
❏	❏	❏	I am not an emotional person.
❏	❏	❏	I am uncomfortable listening to people's problems.
❏	❏	❏	I prefer to see the data and logic behind ideas.
❏	❏	❏	I prefer to work on the details of a project or assignment.
❏	❏	❏	I enjoy working with mechanical or electronic gadgets and machines — computers, calculators, appliances, and electronic games.
❏	❏	❏	I am an analytical, logical, and sequential thinker.
❏	❏	❏	My attitude is: "Seeing is believing."
❏	❏	❏	I am practical with money and prefer secure investments.
❏	❏	❏	I usually follow the rules and abide by the laws. I prefer structure.
❏	❏	❏	I tend to take a long time to make a decision. (Take as long as you want to answer this question.)
❏	❏	❏	I typically follow a regular routine.

____   ____   ____   (Total each column here.)

Love Color #6

YES	SOMETIMES	NO	
❑	❑	❑	I enjoy analyzing and measuring the environment.
❑	❑	❑	I am able to judge weight, distance, and volume through my inner physical senses. (I can tell how much something weighs by holding it in my hand.)
❑	❑	❑	I am a logical and practical thinker.
❑	❑	❑	I am slow to develop friends and usually spend my time alone.
❑	❑	❑	I am fascinated by such things as the control panels in airplanes or submarines.
❑	❑	❑	I am a responsible, dedicated employee who follows directions well.
❑	❑	❑	I perceive reality as logical and three-dimensional.
❑	❑	❑	I am a very private person and keep my feelings to myself.
❑	❑	❑	I am quiet and reserved but independent and strong.
❑	❑	❑	I prefer stable jobs and reliable paychecks.
❑	❑	❑	I tend to be serious and self-controlled.
❑	❑	❑	When raising children, I am, or would be, a rational disciplinarian.

____   ____   ____   (Total each column here.)

Love Color #7

YES SOMETIMES NO

❏ ❏ ❏ I prefer to work in a detail-oriented supporting role, such as that of secretary, bookkeeper, homemaker, or medical assistant.

❏ ❏ ❏ I am a sensitive, calm, patient, and rational thinker.

❏ ❏ ❏ Having a sense of security and stability in my home is important to me.

❏ ❏ ❏ I tend to be a patient listener.

❏ ❏ ❏ I tend to be quiet, reserved, and often shy.

❏ ❏ ❏ I prefer to understand the logic in a situation; however, I am also emotionally supportive of people's needs.

❏ ❏ ❏ I believe that service to humanity is true spirituality.

❏ ❏ ❏ I usually put my family's needs before my own.

❏ ❏ ❏ I prefer to work in a structured environment.

❏ ❏ ❏ I usually work out my emotional upsets in a calm, logical, and quiet manner.

❏ ❏ ❏ Home and family are two of my most important priorities.

❏ ❏ ❏ I feel that supporting community activities and attending functions such as PTA meetings are important.

____ ____ ____ (Total each column here.)

Love Color #8

YES   SOMETIMES   NO

❏   ❏   ❏   I prefer jobs that allow me to work with all
                    the details of a project.

❏   ❏   ❏   I can see all the details that need to be taken
                    care of, but I have difficulty deciding which
                    ones need to be done first.

❏   ❏   ❏   I usually see numerous solutions to a problem.

❏   ❏   ❏   I frequently feel scattered, often forget
                    appointments, or overbook my schedule with
                    conflicting appointments.

❏   ❏   ❏   I prefer the security of a paycheck.

❏   ❏   ❏   I tend to theorize about emotions rather than
                    actually experiencing them.

❏   ❏   ❏   I have many acquaintances but few close
                    friends.

❏   ❏   ❏   I enjoy social functions where I can talk with a
                    lot of people.

❏   ❏   ❏   I love humanity, but I am often uncomfortable
                    maintaining an intimate relationship.

❏   ❏   ❏   I get so busy and things get so hectic that I
                    often forget to pay my bills.

❏   ❏   ❏   My possessions are not very important to me,
                    so I have trouble taking care of them.

❏   ❏   ❏   I am constantly misplacing things.

──── ──── ────   (Total each column here.)

Love Color #9

YES	SOMETIMES	NO	
❑	❑	❑	I can be a workaholic, have a hard time relaxing, and am often in a hurry.
❑	❑	❑	I tend to be a perfectionist and am usually demanding of myself and others. I can be blunt and critical.
❑	❑	❑	I like things to be organized, efficient, and well planned. I frequently write lists.
❑	❑	❑	My three strongest priorities are to make a lot of money, to accomplish my financial and business goals, and to be respected by other powerful and intelligent people. (These are more important to me than helping others or improving the planet. See Love Color #11.)
❑	❑	❑	I enjoy being in charge and delegating responsibilities.
❑	❑	❑	I can be strong-willed and tenacious.
❑	❑	❑	I have a strong desire to learn and to be intellectually stimulated.
❑	❑	❑	I enjoy the challenge of developing plans and ideas rather than doing detailed work.
❑	❑	❑	I have high standards in relationships and tend to be easily bored by most people.
❑	❑	❑	I can become impatient and frustrated with people if they are not motivated and ambitious.
❑	❑	❑	I can intimidate people.

—— —— —— (Total each column here.)

Love Color #10

YES	SOMETIMES	NO	
❑	❑	❑	People frequently turn to me with their emotional problems, and I usually listen lovingly and counsel them.
❑	❑	❑	I am emotional and can easily be moved to tears.
❑	❑	❑	One of my strongest priorities is to be in a loving, monogamous relationship.
❑	❑	❑	I have difficulty letting go of relationships.
❑	❑	❑	Spirituality, love, and people are the most important elements in my life.
❑	❑	❑	Money is not my first priority.
❑	❑	❑	I tend to help and take care of everyone.
❑	❑	❑	I feel guilty if I say no to someone.
❑	❑	❑	I frequently have cold hands and feet.
❑	❑	❑	When there is conflict, I want everyone to love one another.
❑	❑	❑	I tend to feel very empathetic toward other people.
❑	❑	❑	I tend to be intuitive, sometimes even psychic.

——   ——   ——   (Total each column here.)

Love Color #11

YES SOMETIMES NO

YES	SOMETIMES	NO	
❏	❏	❏	I feel that I have a message to get across to people.
❏	❏	❏	I have a strong desire to help improve the planet.
❏	❏	❏	I have always felt that I was going to be famous or do something important.
❏	❏	❏	I have had a desire to perform for audiences.
❏	❏	❏	If I had a lot of money, I would travel or become involved in humanitarian causes.
❏	❏	❏	Freedom and independence are major priorities for me.
❏	❏	❏	I would much rather be self-employed.
❏	❏	❏	I am highly interested in cosmic and universal concepts.
❏	❏	❏	I frequently end up in a leadership position or at least at the center of attention.
❏	❏	❏	I have often felt different from others.
❏	❏	❏	I am passionate about sex.
❏	❏	❏	I can become involved in too many projects at the same time.

—— —— —— (Total each column here.)

Love Color #12

YES	SOMETIMES	NO	
❏	❏	❏	My appearance can seem androgynous or asexual.
❏	❏	❏	I have difficulty relating to my physical body.
❏	❏	❏	I have a highly sensitive physical, emotional, and psychological system.
❏	❏	❏	I am highly intuitive or psychic.
❏	❏	❏	I have clear memories of past lives or can see spiritual beings in other dimensions.
❏	❏	❏	Computers and other technologies are second nature to me.
❏	❏	❏	I have difficulty relating to the world in its current condition and often feel that I don't belong here.
❏	❏	❏	I know there is spiritual energy in all things.
❏	❏	❏	I am extremely sensitive and compassionate, yet strong and independent.
❏	❏	❏	I constantly question and challenge old, dogmatic beliefs and methods.
❏	❏	❏	I cannot be forced to operate against my beliefs even if doing so would make others happy. Guilt and punishment do not work on me.
❏	❏	❏	I feel more creative and spiritually advanced than others.

——— ——— ———   (Total each column here.)

Love Color #13

YES   SOMETIMES   NO

❑   ❑   ❑   I enjoy fantasy and make-believe more than the real world.

❑   ❑   ❑   I am quiet, sensitive, and spiritual.

❑   ❑   ❑   I am often forgetful and frequently spacey.

❑   ❑   ❑   I seem to be out of my body more than I am in it.

❑   ❑   ❑   People accuse me of being irresponsible and unrealistic.

❑   ❑   ❑   I have difficulty dealing with everyday responsibilities.

❑   ❑   ❑   I have a difficult time managing money.

❑   ❑   ❑   I tend to spend a lot of time alone, daydreaming.

❑   ❑   ❑   I prefer pretty, gentle, and fine artistic things, and I am uncomfortable with dirt, bugs, and harsh environments.

❑   ❑   ❑   I am an imaginative and creative thinker; however, I usually have trouble following through with my ideas.

❑   ❑   ❑   I tend to want others to take care of all the problems in my life.

❑   ❑   ❑   I prefer to work in a relaxed, low-stress environment.

——   ——   ——   (Total each column here.)

Love Color #14

YES   SOMETIMES   NO

❑   ❑   ❑   I am extremely sensitive and can be over-whelmed when around too many people.

❑   ❑   ❑   I often feel I have quiet, inner healing powers.

❑   ❑   ❑   Frequently, I am frightened and unsure of what I am supposed to do on the planet.

❑   ❑   ❑   I usually feel uncomfortable in social situations.

❑   ❑   ❑   My personality changes to match others around me.

❑   ❑   ❑   I tend to be withdrawn, quiet, and insecure.

❑   ❑   ❑   I feel safer and more secure when others make all the decisions.

❑   ❑   ❑   I need to spend a lot of time alone in quiet meditation to replenish myself.

❑   ❑   ❑   I often choose to work in a quiet, calm, and peaceful environment.

❑   ❑   ❑   Physical reality often feels cold, harsh, and threatening to me.

❑   ❑   ❑   My spirituality and my serene inner connection with God are the most important aspects of my life.

❑   ❑   ❑   I frequently spend quiet time reading or being in my garden.

———   ———   ———   (Total each column here.)

Identifying Your Love Colors

To discover your Love Colors, tally up the number of yes responses under each Love Color in the questionnaire. Below, note the category, or Love Color number, in which you have the highest number of yes responses. This is your first Love Color. Then note the category in which you have the second-highest number of yes responses.

Love Color with highest number of yes answers: #_____

Love Color with second-highest number of yes answers: #_____

Love Colors Key

#1 = Red	#8 = Abstract Tan
#2 = Orange	#9 = Green
#3 = Magenta	#10 = Blue
#4 = Yellow	#11 = Violet
#5 = Logical Tan	#12 = Indigo
#6 = Environmental Tan	#13 = Lavender
#7 = Sensitive Tan	#14 = Crystal

If the number of responses in the second category is close to that in the first category, you probably have two Love Colors, or combination colors; both colors are your Love Colors. If, however, your second category has far fewer yes responses than your first, you probably have one Love Color.

If three (or four) colors rate high numbers, you probably have added colors to your aura that have become part of your personality (I explain this concept in detail on page 36). Read the descriptions of each of those colors to see which two feel most like the real you. The third color is probably the Love Color personality you have learned.

After tallying the quiz, read the sections on your high-scoring Love Colors to confirm that they feel right to you. If you relate to the descriptions in those sections, then you have most likely discovered your true Love Colors. If those particular colors don't seem to describe the real you, you will either need to take the quiz again or read about each of the different colors to see which ones are a better fit. Ultimately, you are your own best judge.

Red Overlay

Finally, the following is a test to see if you have a Red Overlay. The Red Overlay is not a Love Color. If you answer yes to three or more questions below, chances are you have a Red Overlay.

YES   SOMETIMES   NO

❏   ❏   ❏   I frequently experience intense, often uncontrollable anger or rage.

❏   ❏   ❏   My life seems to be a constant struggle.

❏   ❏   ❏   I consistently experience conflict and frustration regarding relationships, health, money, or career.

I experienced the following as a child:

❏   ❏   ❏   a) emotional, physical, or mental abandonment or rejection (i.e., I was an unwanted child, I was adopted, I had an alcoholic, absent, or emotionally unavailable parent)

❏   ❏   ❏   b) emotional, physical, or mental abuse

❏   ❏   ❏   c) a life-threatening situation in which I feared I might die

——   ——   ——   (Total each column here.)

Red overlay   yes_____   no_____

In chapter 10 of this book, you can read how the Red Overlay affects relationships. And in my earlier book, *Life Colors*, you can find more in-depth information about the Red Overlay and how to release it.

Now that you have identified your Love Color or combination Love Colors, the following chapters can help you discover your relationship styles and your compatibility with other Love Colors.

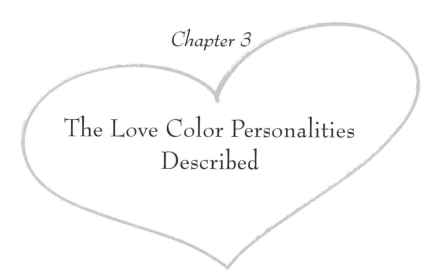

Chapter 3

The Love Color Personalities Described

Now that you have discovered your personal Love Colors, you can learn more about them by reading the following descriptions. You may also sense which of the various Love Colors you would enjoy as a partner.

The Love Colors are categorized into three families: the physical colors, the mental colors, and the emotional colors. People with physical colors tend to process information predominantly through their physical bodies, through touch. These colors are Red, Orange, Magenta, and Yellow.

People with mental colors tend to process life intellectually, by first gathering information, then analyzing it. These colors are Logical Tan, Environmental Tan, Sensitive Tan, Abstract Tan, and Green.

People with emotional colors tend to process life primarily through their emotions and intuition. These colors include Blue, Violet, Indigo, Lavender, and Crystal.

Some Love Colors are found predominantly in males; others are found predominantly in females. The use of "he" or "she" throughout the book, however, is usually arbitrary.

I believe that we have all chosen our Love Colors. Choosing to come into this life with particular Love Colors does not mean, however, that we cannot also experience the qualities, purposes, priorities, and methods of other Love Colors. We have free will and can choose to have any experiences we want. People cannot usually ignore or discard the attributes of their original Love Colors, however, without experiencing a sense of disconnection, confusion, and disharmony within themselves. Most people need to fulfill their original Love Colors before they can expand to include the other colors: that is, they must first love and accept who they are before they can satisfactorily experience the qualities of the other colors.

Some people are born with one Love Color; others are born with two, which are called combination colors. Combination colors show up as the two bands of color consistently positioned closest to the body. Having two Love Colors can be powerful if they complement each other; they give an additional dimension to one's abilities. If they are not complementary, they can create inner conflict. The reasons why some people choose to come into this world with the personality traits of two different Love Colors differ with each individual. Some people may choose two because the qualities of the second color add more power, energy, fun, or creativity to their lives and help them achieve their goals. Another reason could be to ensure balance, practicality, responsibility, or self-reliance.

Frequently, people add another significant band of color to their auras at some point during their lifetime — often unconsciously — and this color becomes a part of their personality. People often add this extra band because they have been intentionally trying to adopt personality traits and qualities of that particular color. For example, it is common for people with the powerful, independent Violet Love Color to think they should instead be the well-mannered, people-pleasing Blue so their parents will love and accept them. They begin behaving like a Blue, which adds this color to their aura. You do not need to know whether you were born with a certain Love Color or added it later in life, as long as you are happy and the color benefits you. For example, if you came here as a Blue and have added Yellow to your aura, and the addition is having a positive influence on your life, then enjoy it. You have become a Blue/Yellow personality. If you feel, however, that you were born a Yellow/Violet but added Blue or Logical Tan to please your parents or to be accepted by society, this extra color may be causing you to suppress who you really are. In this case, you may want to consider letting go of the characteristics of this extra color and allow yourself to explore the qualities of your true Love Colors.

Throughout the book, when I describe a person with a certain color as being "in power," I mean the person is living the positive qualities and behaviors of that Love Color. The person is living at her or his full strength and potential and in alignment with her or his life purpose. Conversely, being "out of power" means the person is living the negative qualities and behaviors of that color. The person is not living at his or her full potential and is living out of alignment with his or her life purpose.

The following pages give brief descriptions of the different Love Colors. For more information on each color, please refer to the book *Life Colors*.

Reds

Reds are strong-willed, powerful, practical, down-to-earth people who, first and foremost, love to express themselves through their physical bodies. They thoroughly enjoy the basic pleasures of life — food, drink, sex, and other physical gratifications. Reds rebel against anyone who attempts to limit their indulgences. They tend to love all the creature comforts or toys money can buy. They may have the latest electronic gadgets, plasma screen televisions, and expensive tools in the garage, or they may have whirlpool bathtubs, expensive designer clothing, and luxurious bedroom decor.

Some Reds are hard workers, while others love to be pampered. Those who are hard workers can be tenacious in their drive to accomplish a task, especially a task that requires physical strength, courage, and endurance. They can be either refreshingly honest or brutally blunt in their interactions with others. They tend to have quick tempers but can get over their anger just as quickly.

The Reds whose lives revolve around enjoying life's physical pleasures tend to want others to cater to their every whim, and they can become highly indignant if their needs are not met. These Reds are not shy about expressing their displeasure.

Relationships can be challenging for most Reds, because they tend to be loners. They enjoy the camaraderie of others, often overindulging and partying too much, but eventually they withdraw to spend time alone.

Out of power, Reds can easily become angry, frustrated, physically explosive, and potentially dangerous. They are quick to start fights. Reds have a tendency to react like threatened animals — withdrawing emotionally and striking out physically. They can be incredibly stubborn and argumentative too, and when they are, it can be almost impossible to penetrate the Reds' armor.

Oranges

Oranges are physical daredevils. Venturing into dangerous locations and putting their lives on the line to feel alive excites them. They enjoy testing their mental and physical skills by challenging nature, competing against an adversary, or performing other dangerous feats. They love the thrill and adrenaline rush that accompany daring adventures. Relationships do not fascinate them as much as the excitement of living life on the edge.

When in power, they are highly intelligent and adept at strategizing. They can inspire awe in spectators. They are often willing to risk their own lives to save others.

Out of power, they can be cold, aloof, and self-centered. They care only about their next exploit and can become so obsessed with living dangerously that they put themselves and others in jeopardy. Their needs and desires come first. They can even become reckless and develop self-destructive behavior. Typically, these Oranges are not emotionally available, affectionate, or compassionate.

Oranges are realists. To these risk takers, life is physical and tangible. They prefer to challenge and conquer material reality rather than to theorize about life and abstract philosophies. Spirituality has little or no meaning to them. They perceive discussing such concepts as a waste of valuable time.

Oranges' life purpose is to experience physical existence to its fullest, to reach the apparent limitations of their physical capabilities and dare to push past them.

Magentas

Magentas are bizarre, eccentric nonconformists. They love to shock people and challenge the status quo. They insist on living life to the beat of their own drummer and usually do not care whom they please or offend.

In power, Magentas are bright, innovative, and entertaining. They love attention and amusing people. Wild, outgoing, outspoken, and stubborn, Magentas like to explore the new and to experiment outside normal, everyday boundaries. They like to play with physical reality, to take physical substance and twist it into strange, uncommon forms. For example, exploring outrageous ideas and turning them into unique pieces of art appeals to them.

Magentas are typically loners, because most people have trouble being around their outrageous behavior. Their unusual way of thinking originates from a sense of the absurd, not from anger or rebellion.

Out of power, Magentas become withdrawn, dark, sullen, and often depressed. They retreat into their own world, where their weird and antisocial behavior becomes even stranger. They can become unreachable outcasts.

(Many Yellow/Violet aura combinations think they are Magentas because they have so many similar qualities and experiences. They both can be creative, stubborn troublemakers. Both Magentas and Violets can feel like strangers in a strange land — like they are different from others. However, Magentas tend to focus on and enjoy the strangeness of the physical world. They are not concerned about spirituality or about humanitarian or environmental causes the way Yellow/Violets are.)

Yellows

Some Yellows are incredibly shy and sensitive, while others are outgoing, playful, energetic, and funny — often the life of the party. Despite these opposite behaviors, Yellows have many traits that make them easily identifiable.

In-power Yellows are delightful to be around. They are happy, healthy, caring, and generous, not to mention optimistic, fun loving, sensitive, and free-spirited. They love to laugh. They are often creative — they are artists, musicians, dancers, designers, and so on. Their purposes for being on the planet are to enjoy life, to bring joy to people, or to help others heal. They are often found healing people, animals, or the earth. They love to exercise and eat healthy foods, and they rarely look, feel, or act their age. Yellows tend to live the longest, which is great if you want a long-lasting relationship.

Out of power, the childlike Yellows often struggle to mature. They can have a lot of insecurities, do not know what they want to be when they "grow up," and frequently have serious addictions. Out-of-power Yellows often have issues with money, motivation, and drive. They can be lazy and irresponsible. For Yellows, money is not a major priority. They would rather focus on fun, friends, and freedom. Yellows can also have a fear of commitment. They love to flirt, are usually affectionate, and love to please others, but when the issue of long-term commitment is broached, they are quick to back away or flee. They offer numerous convincing reasons why they are not available for commitment — just yet. The pleasing Yellows are also among the most stubborn of the Love Colors, so using guilt, force, or ultimatums usually will not work on them.

Tans

There are many different Tans: Logical Tan, Sensitive Tan, Environmental Tan, and Abstract Tan. Most of them have very similar qualities, so I discuss relationships with Tans as if they were all one group. For more details on each particular Tan, please refer to the book *Life Colors*.

If you are interested in having a partner who is practical, down-to-earth, reliable, stable, and a consistent provider, then a Tan is the partner for you. Tans like to figure things out in a logical and no-nonsense way. They are methodical, exploring steps one through ten in a linear fashion. The stable and predictable Tans prefer life to be rational and scientifically explained. And once they make commitments to their partners, they tend to create long-lasting and reliable relationships.

Tans, however, tend to keep their feelings to themselves. If you can get them to discuss their feelings, they will talk about what they "think" they feel. People often appreciate the calm, levelheaded, and sensible Tans. They are drawn to these partners because Tans help them feel secure and comfortable in their home environment. Most office employees are Tans. Tans bring home regular paychecks, pay the bills every month, and make conservative long-term investments.

Out of power, Tans can be very narrow-minded. They resist change and are suspicious of anything new — they can get stuck in old patterns. Unless they see the logic or proof supporting something, they tend to reject new concepts and ideas. They can become temperamental, argumentative, and domineering and may insist you do things their way.

Many people believe they are Tans because they have been raised to think and act like Tans. You may want to read the other colors' descriptions carefully to make sure you are not another Love Color trapped inside a Tan disguise.

Greens

Greens are incredibly intelligent and quick, and they are drawn to money and power. Typically, they are found in the business world and are some of the sharpest and most accomplished people on the planet. They are movers and shakers, often workaholics. They process information and ideas quickly. Projects that are too detailed bore them. They prefer instead to develop an idea, organize a plan, and then delegate the details to someone else.

In power, these shrewd thinkers are organized and efficient. They write lists of things to do and check off items as they complete them. They find solutions very quickly. When they are in power, they can accomplish anything. These powerhouses are among the wealthiest of the Love Colors. For them, there is no such thing as too much money. They always need projects or businesses to work on; without these, they become bored and restless. Being mentally stimulated and taking on tough challenges are strong priorities for them. They are highly competitive and thrive on taking risks. Gambling is common among Greens, whether in the stock market, in the casino, or in business.

When Greens are out of power, others have trouble being around them. Greens can be so aggressive and opinionated that they intimidate others. These perfectionists often become judgmental, arrogant, and controlling, and when they want something, they want it now.

Greens and Violets have many similar qualities, especially when they are out of power. You may want to read the descriptions of both Love Colors to make sure that you have identified each correctly. In particular, learn about the motives underlying each color's actions and behaviors.

Blues

Blues are the most emotional, nurturing, and supportive personalities among the Love Colors. Their highest priorities are love and spirituality. Living predominantly from their hearts, they tend to cry easily. They cry when they are happy, sad, angry, or hurt, and anytime in between.

Their purpose for being on the planet is to give love and to be of service to others. Blues are often teachers, counselors, and nurses — the caretakers on the planet. In power, Blues are unconditionally loving and accepting of others — they will give people ninety-nine second chances. People tend to turn to Blues for comfort and counsel. Blues tend to be wonderful givers, but they often lack the sense of self-worth that enables them to receive. Blues are also the most intuitive and psychic of the Love Colors. There is no apparent logic behind their inner feelings and insights. They just "know" things.

Blues are loyal to their partners, families, and friends and need to bond emotionally with their mates. They cherish being in long-term, committed, monogamous relationships but will often stay in unhealthy, unfulfilling, and even abusive relationships much longer than they should. It is easy for others to take them for granted.

The lesson that Blues most often need to learn is that they are lovable. Out of power, they usually have low self-esteem and can easily become victims, martyrs, and doormats. They suffer the most when they feel abandoned and unloved — they can feel intensely sorry for themselves and become very depressed.

Although there are exceptions, Blues tend to be females or gay men. If you meet a heterosexual male who you believe is a Blue, he is more likely a Yellow or a Yellow/Violet combination.

Violets

Violets are the visionaries and communicators on the planet. They sense they have a big purpose — to help save the planet or change it for the better, to help improve the quality of life for people, to inspire people, to spread important messages, and to educate the masses. They can be the most dramatic and intense of all the Love Colors, often choosing the toughest, most challenging paths in life.

These independent souls typically choose to work for themselves, create their own projects, or take leadership positions. They need freedom. Many become inspirational leaders and compassionate humanitarians. Violets are often drawn to careers in media, entertainment, art, music, literature, psychology, teaching, ministry, politics, and law, and to humanitarian or environmental causes. Global thinkers, they love to travel. They love music — the universal language. Violets are often famous. They are also frequently seen as being unrealistic dreamers. They need to feel passionate about life, their work, and their ambitions; otherwise, they feel something important is missing from their lives.

In power, Violets are dynamic, powerful, and inspiring. They see the big picture. They want to jump from step one to step fifty without having to deal with all the steps and details in between. People tend to be drawn to the insights and wisdom of Violets, and so they place them in positions of power and leadership. Violets are tolerant of others' differences — cultural, spiritual, and political — knowing that each has a different path to travel. Often intuitive or psychic themselves, they tend to be able to clearly perceive other people, seeing past the outer masks into their hearts and motivating them to live their truth and true potential.

When Violets are focused, they are unstoppable in their ability to influence people and events. They tend to multitask. And they want money for the freedom it gives them — so they can fulfill their great visions.

Out of power, Violets can be arrogant, impatient, critical, and self-absorbed. They can become frustrated with shortsighted, narrow-minded people. Some lose faith in their dreams and their visions, which causes them to feel scattered and to be confused about which path to take next. They then feel unfulfilled, lost, and often depressed. Violets are so intense and feel such deep emotions that, when they lose their way, they can become despondent and unreachable. Often unconsciously, they empathetically take on the pain of people around the planet. It is common for Violets to feel that they will never live their dreams, and that they are outcasts who do not belong on the planet.

Indigos

Indigos are unusual souls who seem to be born with their spiritual memories intact. Most of them remember who they are and where they came from. In power, they are usually highly aware, intuitive, psychic, independent, honest, fearless, strong-willed, and sensitive, and many can recount vivid details of their other lives or have conversations with ethereal beings. Some can read minds, and some seem to have other amazing psychic abilities. The boy depicted in the movie *The Sixth Sense* portrays an Indigo.

Indigos are usually incredibly beautiful. Some appear to be androgynous — it is often difficult to tell if they are male or female, homosexual, heterosexual, bisexual, or asexual. They seem to have both the yin and yang, male and female, qualities within them. Their sexuality is not their primary concern, however; their spirituality is. They connect with individuals soul-to-soul, and it does not matter to them if their partners are male or female, or of a different race or nationality.

Out of power, Indigos can become frightened, lost, and confused or dark, depressed, wildly uncontrollable, and self-destructive. They will not listen to anyone or be controlled by any form of punishment or any attempt to use guilt. They feel tortured inside, struggling in a world they perceive to be off-balance and lacking in integrity. Some may even turn to drugs or alcohol to escape their unhappy feelings.

Many other Love Colors, especially Violets, may think they are Indigos because the Indigos' beliefs and characteristics resonate with their own. However, while more and more Indigos are showing up on the planet, most at this point are still children. While Violets feel driven to help save the planet, educate the masses, and improve the quality of life for others, Indigos are here to live as examples of a new, more spiritual consciousness — to show us our potential to live as new cosmic and universal beings.

Lavenders

These childlike creatures are sensitive and simple. Lavenders tend to daydream or live in fantasy worlds and are often spacey and forgetful. Whimsical beings, they prefer to spend time drifting out of their bodies, exploring other dimensions and realities where life is pretty and enchanting. They enjoy escaping the three-dimensional world with all its demands and serious responsibilities. Looking into the eyes of a Lavender, it is often hard to tell if anyone is "at home."

In power, they are delightful, creative beings. They can be wonderful writers, artists, or musicians who bring to life the magical, imaginative worlds they experience in their daydreams. They do best while living quiet, easy lives surrounded by beautiful flower gardens, rather than encircled by rushing traffic, noise, and concrete.

Out of power, they can be traumatized by the world. Physical reality seems cold and harsh to them. Extremely sensitive at times, they can be easily hurt and offended. They have difficulty holding responsible jobs and earning money, which can frustrate their friends and families. Because Lavenders are not really interested in facing the down-to-earth realities of life, they can easily become dependent on others to provide for them, or they can end up living in deplorable, impoverished conditions.

Usually physically fragile and delicate, they can appear weak and frail. Many have pale or even alabaster skin. Their wide variety of illnesses can become persistent and chronic because they don't spend much time staying focused in, or giving energy to, their bodies. Many competent healers are bewildered by these hypersensitive, pallid souls who seem to defy all attempts to cure them.

Crystals

These are the "aura chameleons." The Crystal Love Color is clear and, like the mutable little chameleon, Crystals' auras change colors to match those of the people around them. Crystals take on the personalities, qualities, and emotions of those colors as well. Consequently, when in power they can get along well with almost anyone.

Crystals are rare — although it is hard to know for sure how many Crystals actually exist. It can be challenging to identify them, since they change their traits and behaviors to fit the people around them. They can one day seem like a Blue, the next day come across as a Green. Consequently there may be many more Crystals than can be easily recognized.

In power, Crystals are quick thinkers and learners. One of their gifts is to be a clear channel for pure healing energy. Keeping their thoughts and emotions out of the way, they enable the client's own natural healing abilities to be stimulated.

Because they are so fragile, Crystals tend to heal only one person at a time. Being around too many people can short-circuit their systems. After healing someone, they need to go to a serene place to rebalance and cleanse their auras. These quiet souls need to connect with a Higher Power or their spiritual Source in order to function in the world at all.

Out of power, they can be physically and emotionally fragile — often pale and chronically ill. They can also feel lost, confused, and depressed. Their healing abilities can sometimes frighten or overwhelm them, because they don't comprehend how their abilities work. They do not always understand what to do in life, so they often turn to others for guidance. Because Crystals tend to absorb the colors, emotions, feelings, and behaviors of others, people sometimes feel energetically drained when they are in the presence of an out-of-power Crystal.

Chapter 4

Your Most Compatible Love Colors

Now that you know the personalities of each of the different Love Colors, how can this help you with your relationships? Will you be happier with certain Love Colors? Are you more compatible with some colors, and are there personalities you should avoid? Any two people with enough love and commitment can create a long-lasting, harmonious relationship; however, certain Love Colors are naturally more compatible with each other, so less work will be required to maintain their partnership. There are also some color combinations with such opposite personalities that serious work and attention are needed for them to build a life together. Couples with these more challenging color combinations often decide it's just not worth the struggle.

Compatibility between any of the different Love Colors is the strongest when both partners are in power, using their positive strengths and living up to their greatest potential. When one partner is out of power and is living the negative side of her or his personality, this partner's issues will have to be resolved before the relationship can become truly harmonious.

Love Colors Compatibility Quick Reference Chart

This chapter presents each of the Love Color combinations in detail. The chart below allows you to quickly turn to the pages where different Love Color combinations are explored. To use it, find your Love Color in the list on the left. Then find the color of a partner or potential partner at the top. Where the two colors meet you'll find the page number on which the combination is discussed.

	Reds	Oranges	Magentas	Yellows	Tans	Greens	Blues	Violets	Indigos	Lavenders	Crystals
Reds	54	54	55	54	55	52	56	53	56	56	57
Oranges	54	57	58	59	59	58	60	60	60	61	61
Magentas	55	58	62	62	64	63	64	63	64	65	65
Yellows	54	59	62	66	67	68	66	67	67	68	68
Tans	55	59	64	67	69	69	70	72	73	71	72
Greens	52	58	63	68	69	73	76	74	75	76	77
Blues	56	60	64	66	70	76	77	78	78	79	79
Violets	53	60	63	67	72	74	78	80	81	82	82
Indigos	56	60	64	67	73	75	78	81	83	85	84
Lavenders	56	61	65	68	71	76	79	82	85	86	86
Crystals	57	61	65	68	72	77	79	82	84	86	88

Levels of Compatibility

The following are lists of the most compatible, moderately compatible, and least compatible Love Color relationships. Once you know your own Love Colors, you can find which other colors are the most compatible partners for your type and temperament. You may also discover which colors you have been drawn to in the past and finally understand why those relationships may have been so challenging.

Find your own colors first, and then see which Love Colors are the most compatible or moderately compatible with yours. There are also explanations of why certain colors are compatible or incompatible. Remember that you and your partner — or future partner — probably each have two Love Colors, or combination colors, so notice how each of your Love Colors matches up with your partner's combination colors. For example, if you are a Lavender/Crystal combination, and your potential partner is a Violet/Green combination, read how the Lavender part of you will get along with both Violets and Greens; then read how the Crystal side of your personality may relate to both Violets and Greens. This will give you a better understanding of your overall compatibility with a Violet/Green partner.

Most Harmonious Love Color Combinations

Reds: with Greens and Violets
Oranges: with Oranges and Greens
Magentas: with Yellows
Yellows: with Magentas, Yellows, and Blues
Tans: with Tans and Greens
Greens: with Reds, Oranges, Tans, Greens, and Violets
Blues: with Yellows, Blues, Violets, Indigos, and Crystals
Violets: with Reds, Greens, Blues, Violets, Indigos, and Lavenders
Indigos: with Blues, Violets, Indigos, and Crystals
Lavenders: with Violets
Crystals: with Blues and Indigos

Moderately Compatible Love Color Combinations

Reds: with Reds, Oranges, Yellows, and Tans

Oranges: with Reds, Magentas, Yellows, and Tans

Magentas: with Oranges, Magentas, Greens, and Violets

Yellows: with Reds, Oranges, Tans, Violets, Indigos, Lavenders, and
    Crystals

Tans: with Reds, Oranges, Yellows, Blues, Lavenders, and Crystals

Greens: with Magentas and Indigos

Blues: with Tans and Lavenders

Violets: with Magentas, Yellows, and Crystals

Indigos: with Yellows, Greens, and Lavenders

Lavenders: with Yellows, Tans, Blues, Indigos, Lavenders, and Crystals

Crystals: with Yellows, Tans, Violets, Lavenders, and Crystals

Least Complementary Love Color Combinations

Reds: with Magentas, Blues, Indigos, Lavenders, and Crystals

Oranges: with Blues, Violets, Indigos, Lavenders, and Crystals

Magentas: with Reds, Tans, Blues, Indigos, Lavenders, and Crystals

Yellows: with Greens

Tans: with Magentas, Violets, and Indigos

Greens: with Yellows, Blues, Lavenders, and Crystals

Blues: with Reds, Oranges, Magentas, and Greens

Violets: with Oranges and Tans

Indigos: with Reds, Oranges, Magentas, and Tans

Lavenders: with Reds, Oranges, Magentas, and Greens

Crystals: with Reds, Oranges, Magentas, and Greens

Reds

Most Harmonious Colors for Reds: Greens and Violets

REDS WITH GREENS. These two can be a dynamic pair. The Reds'
fiery personality fascinates and challenges the powerful Greens. Greens

admire and appreciate the Reds' strength and determination. While the highly intelligent Greens can intimidate most of the other colors, they do not typically overwhelm the forceful Reds. In fact, the Greens' mental agility intrigues the Reds. With the Greens' mental abilities and the Reds' robust energy, these two can accomplish extraordinary projects together.

One problem, though, is that often both have quick tempers. Because both are strong-willed and independent, they can live in constant conflict — a battle of wills, with each determined to win. Reds can become physically violent; Greens can provoke their partners with their sharp tongues, leading to intense shouting matches. However, this same passionate energy can make them a very potent couple.

REDS WITH VIOLETS. The Violets' charisma fascinates and attracts the robust Reds. Not only are Violets drawn to the Reds' dynamic energy and stamina, but they are among the few colors not intimidated by the Reds' intensity. Both personalities tend to be powerful and have a healthy sexual appetite. Violets are sexual, but for them sex tends to be a cosmic, spiritual experience. For Reds, sex tends to be a physical, lustful experience. Even though the two have different experiences while making love, sex between them can be passionate.

Violets have great emotional depth and tend to be verbally expressive; Reds tend to keep their thoughts to themselves until they have emotional outbursts. The diplomatic Violets, if they keep their wits about them, can eventually calm down the explosive Reds. But the relationship can hold other challenges. Reds like to see and touch physical reality. Violets are visionaries and dreamers who have strong spiritual beliefs. They must prove that their ideas are realistic for the Reds to respect them. If both partners stay in power, Reds have the physical energy necessary to carry out the Violets' visions. Violets dream up ideas; Reds take action. The power and sexual chemistry of this couple can be compatible if they do not argue over spiritual beliefs or their different ideas about reality.

Moderately Compatible Colors for Reds:
Reds, Oranges, Yellows, and Tans

REDS WITH REDS. For this couple, physical indulgences can be wonderful, passionate experiences. Reds love lustful sex and all other types of life's pleasures, and they have the ability to understand each other's needs. Out of power, however, they can experience serious challenges. Reds can be stubborn and potentially volatile, but if they allow each other the individual space and time that each one needs, and if they work together with the same goal in mind, they can make a powerful team. Both partners must watch their tempers, however, and their strong need to be right.

REDS WITH ORANGES. In some ways, these two are compatible. They share a common belief that reality is physical and tangible, and that life is to be met with courage and zest. With an Orange's ability to strategize and a Red's ability to carry out plans, this pair can pull off interesting projects together. However, both are incredibly independent and strong-willed. Because both tend to be loners as well, they must learn to find projects to do together in order to sustain a relationship; otherwise, each will go off and do his or her own thing.

REDS WITH YELLOWS. Both Reds and Yellows appreciate their physical bodies. Both love sex, being outdoors, connecting with nature, and working with their hands. They frequently choose the same environments and occupations, so they have no trouble finding each other. The Reds' passion and lustful appetites joined with the Yellows' sexual playfulness often lead to a great physical relationship.

The strong work ethic of the Reds can produce financial stability for the carefree Yellows. However, if out of power, the lazy and irresponsible Yellows can eventually frustrate the Reds. Yellows can bring lighthearted fun to the serious Reds, but the Reds must have patience and self-control not to intimidate their Yellow partners. And Yellows must remain grounded and responsible to earn the respect of their Red partners. If either slips out of power, the Red's intensity and volatile temper will overwhelm the sensitive Yellow partner, who will then typically run away.

REDS WITH TANS. Even though both colors tend to be down-to-earth, and they can bring balance into each other's life, there are inherent challenges in this relationship. Both tend to keep their thoughts to themselves, so emotional intimacy may not develop between them. More often than not, Reds have a volatile temper that can upset the logical and sensible Tans.

These two typically do not enjoy the same hobbies and activities. Reds express themselves sexually and physically; Tans usually choose to sit behind their computers and explore mental challenges. For these two to create a compatible relationship, Tans can help the Reds learn to stay calm and not overreact. The Reds can inspire more passion in the mentally calculating Tans. Reds can also find ways to bring Tans' meticulously analyzed ideas into physical reality.

Least Complementary Colors for Reds:
Magentas, Blues, Indigos, Lavenders, and Crystals

REDS WITH MAGENTAS. The bizarre Magentas like to shock people, which most Reds find unnecessary and ridiculous. The down-to-earth, hardworking Reds may occasionally want to cut loose, to express the wild and rowdy aspects of their personalities, so they may attend a party or two with the Magentas. But when Reds become outrageous, it is usually because they have gotten drunk, lost their temper and started a fight, or gotten sexually out of control. These reckless or destructive behaviors intimidate the harmless, fun-loving Magentas, who usually shake up people only to make a statement about nonconformity.

When Reds do not overindulge, their down-to-earth, practical behavior completely bores the Magentas. Reds are usually unwilling to change, so their Magenta partners, who love to try wild and crazy antics, feel stifled. The creative Magentas do not share the Reds' interest in sex and physical endurance. Eventually these two find they have little in common.

REDS WITH BLUES. Reds are too explosive for the sensitive Blues. The Reds' hostile outbursts would move the Blues to tears most of the time. Reds have a strong appetite for physical passion and are reluctant to open up emotionally. Blues are more sentimental and need an emotional connection; they want to be lovingly held. Blues love to discuss feelings and want partners who are loyal and committed. Although Reds are capable of loyalty and commitment, they are also highly independent and uncomfortable discussing feelings. Blues tend to perceive the Reds' aloof behavior as emotional abandonment.

REDS WITH INDIGOS. Indigos are much too sensitive and spiritual to deal with the Reds' physical energy and frequently explosive behavior. Indigos tend to challenge humanity's limited concepts of physical reality, while Reds prefer to see reality as physical and logical. Sexuality to Indigos is a soul-to-soul experience in which two souls connect on a higher spiritual level, whereas for Reds sex is a lustful, tangible experience. Reds usually do not understand or appreciate the Indigos' language, ideals, and spiritual beliefs, and Indigos are much too ethereal for Reds' physical, grounded personality. The two do not have much to say to each other.

REDS WITH LAVENDERS. Lavenders are too vulnerable and childlike for the volatile and lustful Reds. Reds relate to power, vitality, and courage, and they love engaging with the physical world, such as working with the earth and expressing their sensuality. Lavenders love fantasy, spirituality, and creativity and do not typically spend time in their physical bodies. These two Love Colors have no interests or beliefs in common and, as a result, have a difficult time relating to each other. Neither will instigate a conversation with the other. In fact, the strong-willed, robust Reds have a hard time being around the usually frail Lavenders. A relationship between the two would be like a union between a bull and a lamb, or an eagle and a butterfly.

REDS WITH CRYSTALS. Crystals, who need simplicity, calmness, and quiet, are usually too sensitive to be around the intense energy of the Reds. Reds are rambunctious; Crystals treasure spirituality and quiet meditation. The strong, often explosive Reds intimidate the Crystals. They love physical tasks that Crystals have a hard time tolerating, such as getting their hands dirty while changing the oil in the truck or butchering meat — things that repulse Crystals. Sex with robust, lustful Reds would also be too intense for Crystals.

Oranges

Most Harmonious Colors for Oranges: Oranges and Greens

ORANGES WITH ORANGES. Few people are willing to take the physical risks that Oranges take or travel to the places Oranges dare to go, so other Oranges may be their best companions. Oranges enjoy strategizing, and working on projects together could be exciting. But since Oranges are used to being independent and alone, to be in partnership they have to learn to cooperate with another person. Because they crave personal freedom and space and are not interested in discussing feelings, Orange partners will not be needy or emotionally demanding of one another. There won't be a push for marriage, because typically neither needs such commitment. They can have fun going on adventures together: skydiving, hang gliding, mountain climbing, racing, extreme skiing, or other feats that allow them to live on the edge.

Because Oranges are typically not interested in working out relationship difficulties, if they encounter problems they will find it easy to
part ways. This doesn't usually bother the independent Oranges, who
are used to going through life alone. In the meantime, their similarities
can bring them a lot of pleasure — they can be great companions.

ORANGES WITH GREENS. These two can be a dynamic and prosperous team. Both tend to be highly independent and self-sufficient, and usually neither is threatened by a partner's autonomy. Oranges are among
the few colors not intimidated by the Greens' power and sharp mental
abilities. In fact, both can actually thrive in this relationship as each is
mentally stimulated by the other. They can create a great business partnership as well, since both are adept at strategizing and at planning events.
The Greens' organizing skills and money-oriented ideas mesh well with
the Oranges' daring physical abilities. These two can fascinate and stim-
ulate each other as they pull off interesting and original projects.

The only obstacle this couple could face is the fact that both prefer
to be in control. Power struggles could quickly develop if each partner
is not respectful of the other's need for space and desire to pursue individual projects.

Moderately Compatible Colors for Oranges:
Reds, Magentas, Yellows, and Tans

ORANGES WITH REDS. See Reds with Oranges, page 54.

ORANGES WITH MAGENTAS. The Oranges' daredevil behavior excites and fascinates the Magentas. Magentas also appreciate Oranges'
independence and the fact that they don't smother the Magentas, which
allows the latter the freedom to go out and have a good time. Magentas'
wild antics could disrupt the lifestyle that Oranges prefer, however. For
example, if an Orange wanted to get a good night's sleep before going
off to climb a mountain, and the Magenta partner wanted to stay up

late and entertain friends, it could cause bad feelings between them. Moreover, the solitary Oranges can't relate to the Magentas' bizarre behavior and need to attract attention. Oranges are usually too serious for the fun-loving Magentas.

However, Magentas and Oranges are seldom in the same environment, and their meeting is unlikely. In the rare instances when they do meet, they are fascinated by each other's independent and unique lifestyle. In time, though, they find that their differences are too extreme and eventually go their own ways. Neither is really interested in a long-term, committed relationship, anyway.

ORANGES WITH YELLOWS. These two are possible companions because both are physical and adventurous. Both colors relish activities like skiing, climbing, surfing, diving, flying, and racing, although the fearless Oranges tend to venture into extreme and dangerous situations that are not comfortable for Yellows, who usually prefer to avoid pain. Oranges also tend to be loners, and although Yellows need their space at times too, they can become lonely and unhappy if they have no one to play with when they are ready to play.

ORANGES WITH TANS. These colors do not understand each other, and they are rarely, if ever, found in the same locations. The thrill-seeking Oranges usually find the Tans to be too safe and complacent, and Tans do not usually respect the Oranges' risk-taking actions, judging them to be self-indulgent, dangerous, and illogical. Tans enjoy calm, rational tasks; Oranges need physical challenges. Tans prefer to settle down in the suburbs, have a stable nine-to-five job, and commit to their families. Oranges do not want the encumbrance of a relationship, the responsibility of a family, or the tedium of a nine-to-five job.

What these individuals do have in common is their mental skills. Tans can be impressed by Oranges' cunning minds and organizational skills, and Oranges can use detail-oriented Tans to help them figure out the logistics involved in a feat they want to take on.

Least Complementary Colors for Oranges:
Blues, Violets, Indigos, Lavenders, and Crystals

ORANGES WITH BLUES. These two have little in common, and an attempted relationship between them would drive the Blue crazy and suffocate the Orange. Oranges tend to be independent and adventurous and to keep their emotions to themselves. Blues want their mates at home, and for them to be loving and emotionally available. Oranges need physical activity; Blues prefer spirituality. The daring, life-risking behavior of Oranges would keep the motherly Blues in a constant state of worry.

Because Blues and Oranges do not have the same interests in life and do not associate with the same kinds of people or share the same life purpose, this relationship usually is not compatible.

ORANGES WITH VIOLETS. Although Oranges and Violets respect each other's independence and intelligence, they have different views about what is important in life. Orange love to challenge the world; Violets are trying to save it. The visionary Violets believe there is a higher purpose for living on the planet — inspiring and saving humanity. They see Oranges' daring actions as an unproductive use of time. Oranges may admire the Violets' leadership ability but would resent Violets' attempts to tell them what to do.

These two have little in common. Both love to travel, but for different reasons. Both are powerful, independent, and courageous, but they disagree on the purpose of life.

ORANGES WITH INDIGOS. These two have little, if anything, in common. Indigos may admire Oranges' daring and might respect their ability to exceed accepted limitations, but Oranges would be too brash, independent, and egocentric to be good companions for them. Indigos prefer to focus on spirituality, love, consciousness, and meditation.

Oranges, however, see life as filled with physical thrills and challenges, and they live to experience one risky adventure after another.

Indigos believe that life has deep spiritual meaning. They would love to be at the top of a mountain pondering the beauty of life. This is not why Oranges go to the top of a mountain. Oranges prefer to conquer life, not to contemplate it. Indigos' concepts about the universe are too strange for Oranges, who like physical reality, excitement, and adventure.

ORANGES WITH LAVENDERS. Lavenders and Oranges have absolutely nothing in common. These colors are rarely in the same environment, so there is little chance of their meeting. If they did meet, they wouldn't understand or appreciate each other.

Lavenders are sensitive, vulnerable, and mild and are much too ethereal and unrealistic for the grounded, physical Oranges. They live primarily in fantasy worlds and are not willing to spend much time in a harsh physical environment, whereas the daring Oranges relish living and adventuring in the physical environment.

It's possible that an Orange could be temporarily fascinated with a childlike Lavender, but this fascination would quickly pass. The Orange would end up ridiculing the impractical Lavender. Ungrounded Lavenders often need their partners to take care of them, and Oranges prefer to be free from relationship responsibilities.

ORANGES WITH CRYSTALS. These two colors have absolutely nothing in common. Crystals are too sensitive and fragile for the rugged, adventurous Oranges. Oranges want to be outdoors taking on the challenges of the physical world. The quiet Crystals prefer the gentle solitude of nature. Oranges are too brash for these soft-spoken personalities and would overwhelm their delicate systems. Oranges are also too independent for Crystals, who would end up feeling lonely and abandoned. Oranges crave excitement and would not feel stimulated by the Crystals' constant need for spiritual meditation.

Magentas

Most Harmonious Color for Magentas: Yellows

MAGENTAS WITH YELLOWS. Magentas tend to be outrageous, creative, and even rebellious. Yellows tend not to take life too seriously, and they appreciate good rebellious behavior, since they lean that way themselves. Yellows also enjoy the wild creative or artistic abilities of the odd Magentas, who can be interesting playmates for them. Usually Yellows are the only ones who can keep a sense of humor around the strange Magentas. Even a fun-loving Yellow, however, can be embarrassed and appalled if the Magenta goes overboard and becomes offensive.

Moderately Compatible Colors for Magentas:
Oranges, Magentas, Greens, and Violets

MAGENTAS WITH ORANGES. See Oranges with Magentas, pages 58–59.

MAGENTAS WITH MAGENTAS. This relationship can be interesting and fun for both partners for a short time. They can have a great time together as they compete to see which can be more bizarre. They can enjoy shocking people by walking down the street wildly dressed and by sporting bizarre, colorful hairstyles. They may also enjoy attending parties and decorating their home together. But two outrageous Magentas together would probably be too intense for their friends. The more Magentas are around one another, the more bizarre and outrageous their behavior becomes as they feed off each other.

This combination is not very practical, because neither has the desire to be responsible. Neither wants to pay bills, take care of details, or make a living. Because neither is a stabilizing influence on the other, and because Magentas tend to move playfully from partner to partner, the relationship is likely to eventually fall apart.

MAGENTAS WITH GREENS. These two are an interesting couple. Magentas are creative, artistic, and imaginative, which can spark the quick minds of the entrepreneurial Greens. The Magentas' unique ideas fascinate them. Greens have the intelligence, persistence, and organizational skills to bring these ideas into form, which impresses Magentas and allows them to continue dreaming up new projects.

Problems can arise when Magentas become disrespectful — Greens need to be respected — or they behave so outrageously that they embarrass the Greens. Both are stubborn and independent, so if Greens try to manipulate or control Magentas, they will most likely encounter strong resistance.

MAGENTAS WITH VIOLETS. Violets and Magentas usually fascinate each other. Violets' futuristic visions inspire and captivate Magentas' quick and creative minds. Although Violets focus on the world from a spiritual and emotional perspective, and Magentas experience the world on a unique physical and tangible level, Violets usually tolerate the Magentas' outrageous behavior and attitudes better than most others do. Violets often find the Magentas' behavior bizarre. However, since many people perceive Violets' ideas and visions as unrealistic, Violets can relate to the Magentas.

Both colors enjoy being the center of attention, so they may compete with one another at social gatherings. They may also experience power struggles within the relationship when each partner wants to go in a different direction. Neither wants to be dominated by the other or give up her or his dreams. This pairing, oddly enough, has greater potential to succeed than many others. As long as the two colors do not compete for attention all the time, and as long as each allows the other the freedom to live the way he or she chooses, this pair can be compatible. In addition, this couple often enjoys an exciting sexual relationship.

Least Complementary Colors for Magentas:
Reds, Tans, Blues, Indigos, Lavenders, and Crystals

MAGENTAS WITH REDS. See Reds with Magentas, pages 55–56.

MAGENTAS WITH TANS. This is an unlikely pair. The Magentas' behavior is too outrageous for Tans. Tans like stability, reliability, and respectability and would become embarrassed by the Magentas' antisocial and shocking behavior. Magentas would feel suffocated living with the Tans' rules and expectations. Although the free-spirited Magentas could add spice to the Tans' predictable lives, and Tans could stabilize and ground the irresponsible, spontaneous Magentas, ultimately they would drive each other crazy. Everything Tans believe in, Magentas disrupt and challenge. They would exhaust each other with their opposite behaviors.

MAGENTAS WITH BLUES. Magentas are usually too bizarre for the emotional Blues, who have deep, emotional needs and spiritual beliefs. Both colors enjoy being around people, so they could attend social functions together. But the Magentas' deviant behavior at such functions would ultimately embarrass and humiliate the sensitive Blues and make them fearful of losing their less tolerant friends. The unconditionally loving Blues would stand by the Magentas despite their offensive behavior, but it would be challenging and exhausting for them to do so.

Blues enjoy cuddling and being close. Such behavior does not interest Magentas. Because Magentas prefer to be independent and uncommitted, the loyal and monogamous Blues would feel hurt and abandoned — they are better off with loyal, supportive, and committed partners. Magentas are happier exploring many relationships and maintaining their freedom.

MAGENTAS WITH INDIGOS. These two have little to talk about or share. Indigos are spiritual, intuitive, and sensitive, and Magentas are typically too outrageous for them. Both are seen as strange or at least unusual, so both can feel like outcasts. In fact, on the surface, these two may appear to have a lot in common, but they are really on different wavelengths. Magentas end up being loners because most people cannot relate to their shocking behavior. Indigos love people but find few they can relate to or trust. Both are stubborn, and both challenge traditional belief systems, but for different reasons. Magentas challenge rules because they want the freedom to express themselves — and their means of self-expression are usually bizarre or controversial. Indigos reject standard beliefs because they see them as limiting to their souls and their spirituality.

MAGENTAS WITH LAVENDERS. Magentas and Lavenders both tend to live in their own worlds. Magentas are outgoing, adventurous, and bizarre; Lavenders live in a fantasy world and are soft-spoken, intuitive, and sensitive. Each is the most unusual personality in their Love Color family. Magentas tend to be the most eccentric personality of the Physical Colors. Lavenders tend to be the most peculiar personality of the Emotional Colors. People have a hard time relating to either one, and Magentas and Lavenders have a hard time relating to each other. Lavenders want loving and gentle partners; Magentas are too brash, independent, and outspoken for them.

Because these two live so much in their own worlds, they rarely cross paths. Those who do meet up find they have little in common and that they have very different views of the world. Even though they would be fascinated by these differences for a while, each ultimately would not be comfortable around the other.

MAGENTAS WITH CRYSTALS. These two are rarely in the same places and rarely have friends in common. Sensitive Crystals require gentle behavior from their mates. Magentas' behavior is much too offensive and bizarre for them.

Excitement, crowds, and parties are what thrill Magentas. Crystals prefer a peaceful home environment, a healing atmosphere. Crystals want to connect with their spirituality; Magentas want to play and explore physical reality. Magentas would eventually become bored with the Crystals' introspective lifestyle, so partnership is unlikely between them.

Yellows

Most Harmonious Colors for Yellows:
Magentas, Yellows, and Blues

YELLOWS WITH MAGENTAS. See Magentas with Yellows, page 62.

YELLOWS WITH YELLOWS. Yellows want playmates, so other Yellows are perfect companions. Who better to play and laugh with than another Yellow? They can enjoy physical activities together or design creative projects as a team. They both love sex and affection, so their physical needs will most likely be met.

When either partner is out of power, however, they must both watch out for any addictive behaviors, especially when they are having fun together. Too much fun and not enough discipline can get them into trouble. In this scenario, the two Yellows can also get into financial difficulty.

YELLOWS WITH BLUES. Blues can be great partners for Yellows because both are usually nice people — both are giving, loving, and helpful. The loyal Blues tend to tolerate or even find endearing the childlike behavior of a Yellow. Blues like to nurture — they are typical moms — while Yellows are like little kids. A Blue can become frustrated, however, when the out-of-power Yellow's "inner kid" will not grow up.

A lot of Yellows fear commitment, and the loyal Blues need commitment. Even in a monogamous relationship, Blues can perceive the Yellows' need for solitude as an insult and feel that their Yellow partner is not as dedicated to the relationship. Blues tend to feel insecure if their Yellows want to spend more time with friends than with them.

Moderately Compatible Colors for Yellows: Reds, Oranges, Tans, Violets, Indigos, Lavenders, and Crystals

YELLOWS WITH REDS. See Reds with Yellows, pages 54–55.

YELLOWS WITH ORANGES. See Oranges with Yellows, page 59.

YELLOWS WITH TANS. Tans are responsible, practical, and reliable. They earn steady incomes, which can enable the youthful Yellows to spend more time playing. Trouble can arise when Tans resent having to take on the responsible parental role all the time. Yellows prefer partners who can be playful, spontaneous, and adventurous. They may either rebel against the Tans' authoritative expectations or shrink away in fear of disapproval or rejection.

If these two can understand and accept each other's qualities, they can create a balanced relationship. The Tan partner can provide a secure and stable environment in which the Yellow partner can feel free to create. The Yellow partner can help the Tan lighten up and learn to enjoy life a little more.

YELLOWS WITH VIOLETS. Violets and Yellows are both caring and compassionate and enjoy helping people. They are also creative and can develop inspirational projects together. Out of power, however, Yellows can be major procrastinators. They can be lazy and unmotivated; they lack the Violets' vision and ambition. If they fail to get their lives together, accomplish something, and move forward, then eventually Violets get frustrated and lose respect for them.

YELLOWS WITH INDIGOS. Indigos can be a good match for Yellows because both are sensitive and caring and will allow the other to do his or her own thing. Neither likes to be told what to do, and most likely neither will tell the other what to do. Indigos are independent and honest, as well as compassionate and comforting. This works well with the Yellows' need for both companionship and time alone.

When out of power, however, Indigos can become frightened and disoriented and, as a result, despondent. In their bewildered state, they may turn to addictive substances. The easily swayed Yellows may join them, thinking this is one way to comfort and support the unhappy Indigos. Because despondent Indigos can go so deep within themselves during these tough times, even the sensitive Yellows may have trouble getting through to them. However, if anyone can reach an Indigo, it is the optimistic Yellow. Occasionally the Yellows' humor and lightheartedness can actually bring Indigos out of despair.

YELLOWS WITH LAVENDERS. Lavenders are possible matches for Yellows because both are creative and childlike. Yellows and the whimsical Lavenders can be fun playmates. Stubborn and independent Yellows, however, can hurt the feelings of the insecure and sensitive Lavenders. This pair could develop problems with their finances, since neither makes earning money a priority.

YELLOWS WITH CRYSTALS. Crystals can be compatible with Yellows who are sensitive and quiet, especially if both are healers. However, the more energetic and rambunctious Yellows can give the fragile Crystals a headache. Even though both enjoy being out in nature, Crystals use time in nature for meditation, while Yellows prefer to play and be adventurous. Most Yellows are fun loving and humorous, while Crystals tend to be more introverted and quiet.

Least Complementary Color for Yellows: Greens

YELLOWS WITH GREENS. This is possibly the least compatible of all the Love Color unions. Greens are driven, goal-oriented workaholics who focus on making as much money as possible. Yellows are playful children who would prefer not to work at all. Greens are very bright. They value intellectual stimulation over physical prowess, and they love to be the boss. Yellows hate being told what to do. Since both can be fiercely stubborn, resentment can easily build between these two. Yellows do not always feel safe around the impatient Greens, and Greens typically do not respect the easygoing Yellows.

Tans

Most Harmonious Colors for Tans: Tans and Greens

TANS WITH TANS. This relationship has great potential for compatibility, since Tans are grounded, reliable, and responsible. Both partners, of course, share the same priorities, have secure jobs, and enjoy discussing intellectual topics. They stand by their commitments to each other and appreciate each other's dependability.

What could be lacking, however, is emotional passion, since Tans tend to keep their feelings under control. Nonetheless, having a partner who doesn't create emotional drama can be comforting to Tans. Ultimately, predictability could be an asset or a problem in the relationship. Tans frequently work at the same job, live in the same home, and follow the same patterns for their entire lives, which means there is very little adventure. The couple could end up doing the same thing over and over again, but if both partners are content with this safe lifestyle, they can be compatible for life.

TANS WITH GREENS. These two personalities are potentially compatible because both are intellectual and they share many of the same interests. They enjoy discussing ideas rationally and logically — although Tans typically process information more slowly than Greens, and this can cause Greens to become frustrated and impatient.

These two frequently experience conflict over money. Greens want to make a lot of money quickly; they are gamblers and risk takers. Tans believe they have to work a long time for money, and they want to build a stable foundation. Greens tend to dominate in this relationship. When Tans feel overpowered, they often withdraw in self-defense. This cuts off communication between the partners and further irritates the Greens, who want to be heard and respected.

If these two can perceive their differences as assets, then they can work well together. Tans can take care of each detail, so the Greens are free to create, organize, and strategize. Greens may appreciate the Tans' stability, or they may become impatient with them. Tans may be frustrated by the Greens' rash and impetuous behavior, or they may respect the Greens' willingness to act on their ideas.

Moderately Compatible Colors for Tans:
Reds, Oranges, Yellows, Blues, Lavenders, and Crystals

TANS WITH REDS. See Reds with Tans, page 55.

TANS WITH ORANGES. See Oranges with Tans, page 59.

TANS WITH YELLOWS. See Yellows with Tans, page 67.

TANS WITH BLUES. This is a common union. Because Blues desire a monogamous, committed relationship, they are often drawn to the Tans' stability and reliability. If both are looking for a traditional marriage, in which the Blues love and nurture their Tan providers, then this relationship can work.

With Tans, the Blues have the comfort and satisfaction of knowing they have stable, reliable, and committed mates. Tans know they have loyal, loving, and devoted partners who will take care of them. Commitment and security are the rewards for this couple. Since the two fill different roles in the relationship, both must realize that each sees the world differently, processes feelings differently, and has different priorities.

Unfortunately, what typically develops in this relationship is a communication problem. Blues communicate from the heart — they want to bond emotionally with their mates. Tans, on the other hand, process intellectually; they prefer to analyze a situation and come up with a rational solution while keeping their emotions and thoughts to themselves in the process. This can frustrate Blues, who feel isolated from the deepest part of their mates. Tans do not intellectually understand the Blues' emotional unpredictability and constant need to discuss the relationship. Tans can eventually become too emotionally unfulfilling for a Blue. If the Blue partner can become more emotionally secure, and the Tan partner can become more emotionally available and communicative, then these two can have a long, fulfilling relationship.

TANS WITH LAVENDERS. This is an interesting relationship, one that can either provide balance for the couple or cause them constant frustration. Tans want life to be rational and practical. Lavenders' lives are anything but practical: they live in a world of dreams, visions, and fantasies. Tans view Lavenders as unrealistic and irresponsible.

Tans can provide a stable environment, while the gentle Lavenders can provide creativity in the relationship. In power, a Tan can appreciate the sensitivity and gentleness that the Lavender adds to their life together. Out of power, the Tan can become frustrated with the Lavender's inability to function in the world. The fragile Lavender can become hurt by the Tan's inability to relate emotionally. Distressed, a Lavender may withdraw into her or his own world. Communication between the two then becomes difficult and sometimes impossible.

Usually this couple discovers they have no interests in common and that their styles of communication differ dramatically. The success of this relationship depends on their willingness to allow each to make a unique contribution to the relationship. One provides the secure and stable foundation; the other cultivates the emotional, creative, and spiritual aspects of the union.

TANS WITH CRYSTALS. Tans are usually much too analytical and logical to relate to the spiritual Crystals. Crystals are usually too fragile for Tans, whose rigid rules, standards, and beliefs are too limiting for them. Tans have difficulty understanding the Crystals' spiritual personality and their need to be introspective and to commune with God.

Because both Crystals and Tans tend to keep their thoughts and feelings to themselves, they often have trouble communicating with each other, which could eventually cause them to live in two separate worlds. If these two marry, they could spend most of their time in separate rooms at opposite ends of the house. Although this can make them compatible roommates, it does not create a very intimate or loving marriage. If this couple can stay in power, however, they can provide an interesting balance for each other. Tans can provide a stable environment and financial security for Crystals. Crystals can bring gentleness and beauty into the Tans' often logical and mechanical world.

Least Complementary Colors for Tans:
Magentas, Violets, and Indigos

TANS WITH MAGENTAS. See Magentas with Tans, page 64.

TANS WITH VIOLETS. Because the beliefs and behaviors of Tans and Violets are at opposite ends of the spectrum, relationships between them are challenging and only occasionally successful. Because the Tans methodically and analytically process every step between one and ten, they are upset by the Violets' habit of trying to jump from one to fifty. Tans consider Violets to be unrealistic dreamers, which can create conflict between them. When Violets do accomplish their visions, however, the Tans are impressed by the Violets' power and insight.

Violets are passionate, sexual, and creative; the reserved Tans tend to withhold in these areas. These two have a difficult time communicating on the same level. Although Tans and Violets have completely different needs, they can benefit from each other if they stay centered and in power. The skeptical and cautious Tans ground the Violets and slow them down. Tans can also provide a stable and secure foundation for the relationship by adding common sense and practical steps to the Violets' ideas. Violets can keep Tans' lives from becoming predictable. While Tans can help Violets keep their feet on the ground, Violets can help Tans keep from focusing only on the ground. Although they can provide a good balance for each other, it is more common for the Tans and Violets to frustrate and annoy each other.

TANS WITH INDIGOS. These personalities have great difficulty understanding each other. Indigos believe there's more to reality than physical appearances. Tans want the Indigos to be more realistic and practical, to not question reality in the face of obvious facts. The Indigos' inability or unwillingness to do so eventually upsets Tans.

This pair is likely to be in constant conflict, questioning and refuting each other's beliefs. Moreover, Indigos need to relate to others emotionally, but emotional bonding is not a priority for Tans. They tend to keep their feelings to themselves.

Greens

Most Harmonious Colors for Greens:
Reds, Oranges, Tans, Greens, and Violets

GREENS WITH REDS. See Reds with Greens, pages 52–53.

GREENS WITH ORANGES. See Oranges with Greens, page 58.

GREENS WITH TANS. See Tans with Greens, pages 69–70.

GREENS WITH GREENS. Fortunately, a Green is one Love Color that another Green cannot run over, so mutual respect is a good possibility here — as is money, an elaborate home, and quality possessions.

(Greens have lavish tastes.) Greens are typically ambitious, successful, and wealthy. Working together, each can encourage the other to
learn, accomplish, and advance. Most likely, life will not be boring for
these two.

This union can be a powerful combination, but it can also be one in
which the partners experience power struggles. Greens are usually
strong-willed and tenacious. Two Greens may respect each other, but
they may also butt heads. Because they like to be right, they may have
frequent and volatile arguments. They can also be competitive, with
one always trying to make more money or be more successful than
the other.

If there is mutual respect and admiration, sex between them can be
powerful. However, if there is a disagreement, each could withhold sex
until the argument is satisfactorily resolved. Despite the problems two
Greens together may have, they are likely to be intellectual equals, so
their psychological battles can be exciting for them. Greens need to
admire and respect their partners. Since Greens love to win, for harmony and balance to exist in this relationship these partners need to
create ways for *both* to win. Because they are intelligent individuals,
finding a plan that allows both partners to win should be easy for them.

GREENS WITH VIOLETS. A relationship between a Green and a
Violet has excellent potential. Greens cannot run over Violets, provided
the Violets stay in power. Their partnership can be dynamic, harmonious, and productive as long as the Violets maintain their focus and the
Greens set about accomplishing their goals and feeling good about
themselves. Even though Greens are authoritative and bright and can
quickly process steps one through ten, Violets can jump from step one
to step fifty and, in doing so, can inspire and challenge the Greens.

Violets have dreams they want to accomplish. The quick and organized Greens can either help them do so or thwart them by criticizing

their visions. Greens often accuse Violets of being unrealistic dreamers. If Violets can stay in power and remain committed to their dreams, they will inspire the Greens and motivate them to work on a plan to accomplish those dreams. If these two go out of power, however, they can experience intense power struggles because both want to be in charge.

If they can accept their differences or learn from each other, this pair has the potential to create enough money to make both partners happy. The Greens can have their quality possessions; the Violets can afford to travel and be philanthropic.

Moderately Compatible Colors for Greens: Magentas and Indigos

GREENS WITH MAGENTAS. See Magentas with Greens, page 63.

GREENS WITH INDIGOS. These personalities are usually fascinated by each other, and they can effectively facilitate each other's growth. An in-power Indigo is among the few colors who can stand up to a Green. Although Greens can be frustrated by the Indigos' stubbornness, they also respect the Indigos' refusal to be dominated. The inquisitive Indigos can learn a lot from the intelligent and well-informed Greens. Greens, who love to be quicker and smarter than everyone else, are fascinated by the Indigos' quick minds, advanced ideas, and unusual concepts.

Although the information that each brings to the relationship can enhance and inspire the other, Greens sometimes have a tendency to be too powerful, too brash, for Indigos. An out-of-power, overly sensitive, and insecure Indigo who has been crushed and intimidated may retreat inside and find it difficult to trust the domineering Green. The Indigos' emotions run deep, and they need to be able to trust the people around them. Usually Greens and Indigos do not have the same spiritual goals or understandings, so they typically go in different directions.

Least Complementary Colors for Greens:
Yellows, Blues, Lavenders, and Crystals

GREENS WITH YELLOWS. See Yellows with Greens, pages 68–69.

GREENS WITH BLUES. A Blue and a Green are not usually compatible. They have strong, conflicting priorities and methods of processing life. The workaholic Greens tend to put career before relationships, which Blues interpret as personal rejection. The loving Blues feel that people, family, and relationships are much more important than money, possessions, and reaching the top of the corporate ladder. Blues enter relationships supporting the Greens' ambitions and goals but eventually become hurt and resentful when their emotional needs are not fulfilled.

If Greens can become more available emotionally, they will find that Blues are loving and devoted partners. If Blues can fill more of their own emotional needs, they can grow intellectually with the Greens as well as be financially supported in style.

Although any relationship can work with enough love, commitment, and determination, this relationship requires a lot of effort to be successful. If these two stay in power and grow, they each have the capability to learn and mature in this relationship. If they prefer not to work quite so hard, other partners are more compatible and can better fulfill their emotional and intellectual needs.

GREENS WITH LAVENDERS. Generally, these two are not the most compatible partners. Greens are usually frustrated by the Lavenders' lack of ambition and concentration and their unreliability. Lavenders are usually intimidated and overwhelmed by the Greens' intense intelligence, power, and drive. The sensitive Lavenders' emotional needs would probably not be met by Greens, who are typically not free with their feelings. Greens prefer to stay busy and in control, so Lavenders usually end up feeling alone and unfulfilled.

In power, this pair could add balance to each other's lives. The Green partner could take the Lavender's creative ideas and put them to practical use and could add a logical aspect to the Lavender's ungrounded fantasy world. The Lavender partner could add a fun and creative aspect to the Green's work-oriented and often stressful life. However, the intensity of an angry or frustrated Green would be too threatening for the sensitive Lavender, who would retreat into a fantasy world to escape the fury.

GREENS WITH CRYSTALS. A relationship between a Crystal and a Green can be too harsh for the Crystal and too frustrating for the Green. Crystals are introspective, quiet, calm, and peaceful and are not motivated to accomplish business projects. Greens are ambitious, outgoing, and driven to succeed. A Green's energy can be too powerful and intimidating for the Crystal.

Greens need partners who can match their power. Frustrated and impatient Greens can devastate the sensitive and fragile Crystals. Only if the Crystals take on the Greens' powerful energy and then step out into the world more forcefully can they be compatible.

Blues

Most Harmonious Colors for Blues:
Yellows, Blues, Violets, Indigos, and Crystals

BLUES WITH YELLOWS. See Yellows with Blues, pages 66–67.

BLUES WITH BLUES. A Blue can emotionally bond very well with another Blue. In fact, because they tend to think and feel the same way, two Blues often experience an instant connection. Blues can be best friends within their relationship. They understand each other's emotional needs, trust each other's intuitive thoughts, and share each other's spiritual beliefs. They can cry together over the same romantic movies.

Blues are moral, monogamous, and loyal, so extramarital affairs would probably never happen in this relationship. Blues tend to put a lot of energy into their relationships and to stay in them for a long time. Besides, neither partner wants to hurt the other by leaving.

Out of power, Blues can be moody and tend to take things personally. They can be emotionally vulnerable and needy and so require constant emotional reinforcement. Fortunately, Blues are typically emotionally available to each other, so loving support and affection usually flow freely between them. Because Blues intuitively understand each other and are willing to give love, they tend to create harmonious relationships together.

BLUES WITH VIOLETS. A relationship between a Violet and a Blue has great potential. Blues have so much love to give that they can overwhelm most other colors, but Violets love being the center of attention and are capable of great emotional depth, so this relationship can be highly compatible.

These two can be a powerful team if the Blue supports and nurtures the Violet's dreams, and the Violet remains kind and satisfies the Blues emotional needs. Both Blues and Violets are intuitive. Spiritual growth and understanding are priorities for both, and both desire to help people.

One potential problem is that out-of-power Violets can become self-centered, egocentric, and arrogant and may take advantage of the giving Blues. Another potential problem is in their sexual relationship. Out of power, Violets have the highest potential for being unfaithful in their relationships. Blues, always loyal, monogamous, and committed, can be devastated by these Violets.

BLUES WITH INDIGOS. This can be a warm, loving, highly committed, and nurturing relationship. Blues are one color that can understand the Indigos' spirituality. Blues, too, want peace, love, and harmony on the planet, just as Indigos do. Blues are able to accept the Indigos' need to live with higher ideals, while Indigos treasure the spiritual understanding and unconditional love of the Blues.

Because Blues and Indigos are both intuitive, they appreciate each other's inner awareness. The Blues also appreciate the depth to which the Indigos bond emotionally, soul-to-soul, with their mates. Communication and connection can falter if the Indigos lose faith in themselves and withdraw inside, or the Blues become needy martyrs and try to use guilt on the Indigos. Both Blues and Indigos need to stay fully in power for this relationship to reach its greatest potential.

BLUES WITH CRYSTALS. This relationship has the potential to be harmonious. Blues are sensitive enough to support and protect the Crystals' emotionally fragile nature. Both have an appreciation for the esthetic and spiritual things in life, so they can create a beautiful, gentle, and loving environment together.

Blues love having an abundance of friends around them. They also love to spend time emotionally connecting with their mates. Crystals tend to shy away from people and social activities. Blues need to be understanding and not take it personally when Crystals withdraw. And Crystals need to learn to emerge from their hibernation frequently to be with the Blues. If Crystals can learn to express appreciation to the Blues, and Blues can to learn when to gently give love and when to be still, these two can create a wonderfully compatible relationship.

Moderately Compatible Colors for Blues: Tans and Lavenders

BLUES WITH TANS. See Tans with Blues, pages 70–71.

BLUES WITH LAVENDERS. Blues tend to nurture, love, and support the Lavenders. Blues are among the few Love Colors who are usually accepting and forgiving enough to let Lavenders do what makes them happy. Because both colors are sensitive, loving, considerate, and compassionate, they tend to be kind to one another. Blues, however, usually end up feeling more like parents than partners.

The Blues' needs are not always met in this relationship. Blues want stability and a deep emotional connection. Lavenders usually escape into a fantasy world, leaving the Blues feeling alone and abandoned. Lavenders do not generally relate to, and can be intimidated by, the Blues' intense needs and emotions.

In a relationship, Blues cannot usually depend on the Lavenders for emotional security and commitment. Lavenders can eventually feel trapped or smothered by Blues. These two personalities are sometimes more emotionally compatible as friends than as mates.

Least Complementary Colors for Blues:
Reds, Oranges, Magentas, and Greens

BLUES WITH REDS. See Reds with Blues, page 56.

BLUES WITH ORANGES. See Oranges with Blues, page 60.

BLUES WITH MAGENTAS. See Magentas with Blues, page 64.

BLUES WITH GREENS. See Greens with Blues, page 76.

Violets

Most Harmonious Colors for Violets:
Reds, Greens, Blues, Violets, Indigos, and Lavenders

VIOLETS WITH REDS. See Reds with Violets, page 53.

VIOLETS WITH GREENS. See Greens with Violets, pages 74–75.

VIOLETS WITH BLUES. See Blues with Violets, page 78.

VIOLETS WITH VIOLETS. A partnership between two Violets can be extremely powerful and dynamic. Together they can inspire and empower each other's visions. With their strong energy, they can accomplish almost anything. Violets are also highly compatible sexually — the chemistry between them can be electrifying.

There are a few potentially negative aspects of this relationship, however. Because Violets enjoy being the center of attention, two Violet partners can become competitive. They may each want to live a different vision, which means they may go in separate directions. They can also become scattered as they try to accomplish too many projects at the same time, creating little opportunity for them to devote time to each other. Violets are also prone to extramarital affairs.

For the most part, a Violet/Violet relationship is dynamic, charismatic, and powerful. The two will have many interests in common and are often passionate about music, sex, traveling, and inspiring humanity. They must make sure they spend time together, however.

VIOLETS WITH INDIGOS. Violets are able to relate to the Indigos' beliefs and higher principles. They can see the future that Indigos intuitively feel is coming. These two are highly compatible provided the Violets do not become so overpowering and dictatorial that this causes power struggles and strains their relationship. Indigos will not be dominated, controlled, or manipulated by anyone.

Problems can also arise if the Indigos prefer to quietly connect with a few intimate friends, bonding soul-to-soul with each, while the Violets, who love to perform and be the center of attention, are constantly surrounded by crowds of people.

Because both Violets and Indigos search for truth and higher consciousness, and both want peace, compassion, and spiritual enlightenment on the planet, they can work together toward their common goals. If both stay centered and accept and support each other, they can create a highly spiritual and visionary team. Both are curious about other cultures, enjoy traveling, and have great compassion for people everywhere. What they sense, and see as higher truth, can broaden the horizons of many people.

VIOLETS WITH LAVENDERS. Relationships between Lavenders and Violets can be highly compatible. The Violet is the powerful, independent force who goes into the world to take care of business; the Lavender is free to stay at home and create a wonderful environment for the pair.

Violets have great emotional depth and can be very accepting of others. When they are in power, the Lavender and the Violet can complement each other. The Lavender adds fantasy, lightness, and fun to the Violet's intensity and power. The Violet adds power, depth, and progressive movement to the sometimes ungrounded and scattered Lavender. There is no competition between these two. The Violet wants to be the leader and the center of attention; the Lavender shies away from attention and responsibility. The Lavender appreciates the fact that the Violet takes charge.

These colors are emotionally and spiritually compatible as long as the Lavenders spend enough time in their bodies to be companions to the Violets. Violets need communication and emotional depth from their partners at times. Both of these partners allow the other the space needed to explore their feelings, fantasies, and visions.

Moderately Compatible Colors for Violets:
Magentas, Yellows, and Crystals

VIOLETS WITH MAGENTAS. See Magentas with Violets, page 63.

VIOLETS WITH YELLOWS. See Yellows with Violets, page 67.

VIOLETS WITH CRYSTALS. These two can provide a good balance for each other, or they can feel they do not meet each other's needs. Crystals tend to withdraw from the world, whereas Violets are out saving the world. Violets have a desire to be the center of attention, and Crystals withdraw from attention. Though both are highly spiritual, they live in two separate worlds. Crystals live in an inner world, and Violets live very much in the outer world and want to improve it.

Violets love music and traveling. Crystals prefer quiet solitude at home. Violets can help educate the introspective Crystals by bringing home information concerning the outside world.

If the Violet can tone down his or her powerful energy and keep from intimidating the fragile Crystal, the Crystal can show appreciation by creating a loving home for them both. And if the Crystal can absorb some of the Violet's energy, the Crystal will become more powerful and less fragile. This couple can be highly compatible if they fulfill these needs for each other.

Least Complementary Colors for Violets: Oranges and Tans

VIOLETS WITH ORANGES. See Oranges with Violets, page 60.

VIOLETS WITH TANS. See Tans with Violets, pages 72–73.

Indigos

Most Harmonious Colors for Indigos:
Blues, Violets, Indigos, and Crystals

INDIGOS WITH BLUES. See Blues with Indigos, pages 78–79.

INDIGOS WITH VIOLETS. See Violets with Indigos, page 81.

INDIGOS WITH INDIGOS. Two Indigos together are emotionally and spiritually compatible. In power, they expect and provide honesty and high integrity in their relationship. Indigos are highly psychic and intuitive, so their communication and mutual understanding in this partnership would be strong.

Emotionally and spiritually, Indigos make highly compatible friends, mates, confidants, and lovers for each other. Neither partner will try to run the other's life, because each respects the other's experience of life. They are able to bond soul-to-soul.

The two need to stay balanced and in touch with their inner knowing; otherwise, the confusion that can ensue may upset them both. When Indigos lose touch with their inner sense of truth and higher principles, they can become self-destructive or hyperactive. Indigos are too sensitive to have this kind of disruptive energy in their environment. However, one partner remaining aware and centered would most likely be able to help the other become centered again. Emotionally, Indigos are more compatible with each other than they are with any of the colors in the mental or physical color families. They understand each other and can provide great comfort and appreciation for each other.

INDIGOS WITH CRYSTALS. Indigos and Crystals have similar needs and beliefs. The highest priority in life for each is to connect with spiritual sources and gain spiritual knowledge. Both share the need to spend quiet, reflective time in meditation. They understand the importance of going within to find answers. They also understand the need to feel emotionally secure, and they prefer spending time with sensitive and trustworthy people. In power, Indigos and Crystals feel they can trust each other.

Both understand they are unusual individuals, and they allow and accept each other's uniqueness. Usually, these two are sensitive and patient with each other. They can help each other stay secure and balanced, and consequently the Crystal can stay more open to the Indigo. Because both operate so much from their intuition, each one typically knows what the other needs in order to feel safe.

Out of power, both can tend to become lost, frightened, and confused. If either withdraws too often, these partners can lose trust in each other. If, however, they maintain their spiritual understanding and their gentle communication with each other, these two are emotionally, spiritually, and physically compatible.

Moderately Compatible Colors for Indigos:
Yellows, Greens, and Lavenders

INDIGOS WITH YELLOWS. See Yellows with Indigos, pages 67–68.

INDIGOS WITH GREENS. See Greens with Indigos, page 75.

INDIGOS WITH LAVENDERS. Spiritually and emotionally, these two are similar. Both can be particularly sensitive and gentle. Both believe there is more to life than physical reality, and each allows the other the room to explore that belief. These childlike souls live by their intuition rather than by logic or intellect. Because both are highly creative, developing artistic projects together could be fulfilling and profitable for them.

Typically, other people can misunderstand them, so Indigos and Lavenders especially appreciate their ability to understand each other. On the other hand, while they are compatible in many ways if they stay balanced and in power, they don't always have much to offer each other. The Lavender is not always capable of reaching the emotional depths the Indigo requires in a mate. The Indigo wants to bond soul-to-soul with someone. Lavenders spend so much time withdrawn in their own worlds that an Indigo partner may tend to feel alone and abandoned.

Least Complementary Colors for Indigos:
Reds, Oranges, Magentas, and Tans

INDIGOS WITH REDS. See Reds with Indigos, page 56.

INDIGOS WITH ORANGES. See Oranges with Indigos, pages 60–61.

INDIGOS WITH MAGENTAS. See Magentas with Indigos, pages 64–65.

INDIGOS WITH TANS. See Tans with Indigos, page 73.

Lavenders

Most Harmonious Color for Lavenders: Violets

LAVENDERS WITH VIOLETS. See Violets with Lavenders, page 82.

Moderately Compatible Colors for Lavenders:
Yellows, Tans, Blues, Indigos, Lavenders, and Crystals

LAVENDERS WITH YELLOWS. See Yellows with Lavenders, page 68.

LAVENDERS WITH TANS. See Tans with Lavenders, page 71.

LAVENDERS WITH BLUES. See Blues with Lavenders, pages 79–80.

LAVENDERS WITH INDIGOS. See Indigos with Lavenders, page 85.

LAVENDERS WITH LAVENDERS. Two Lavenders together could enjoy sharing stories of their wonderful adventures in other dimensions. And since they're so sensitive, they would tend to treat each other with kindness and would allow each other time alone.

However, two Lavenders together can sometimes be a problem. Neither partner wants to stay focused in this reality long enough to take care of everyday responsibilities. Each looks to the other to take care of business. Each can become disappointed and even resentful if the other doesn't fulfill the role of caretaker and provider. Lavenders fare better with mates who are reliable, responsible, and action oriented. They need mates who can provide them with stability, not keep them ungrounded.

LAVENDERS WITH CRYSTALS. Lavenders and Crystals are safe with each other because neither Love Color makes strong demands on the other or is looking for an intense love affair. Neither intimidates the other. They appreciate each other's gentle nature and can be quiet and considerate roommates; in an intimate relationship, however, neither has much to offer the other. Neither can ground, or otherwise have a practical influence on, the other. Both spend too much time in their own worlds to even communicate with each other effectively.

Although both are sensitive, intuitive beings who enjoy the simple and spiritual things in life, neither is powerful or ambitious enough to deal with the outer world. Their home environment will be quiet, because both will be meditating or exploring inner worlds. However, paying the rent on their peaceful home may be a problem. Neither wants a stable job to support the home or enjoys taking care of day-to-day responsibilities.

Least Complementary Colors for Lavenders: *Reds, Oranges, Magentas, and Greens*

LAVENDERS WITH REDS. See Reds with Lavenders, pages 56–57.

LAVENDERS WITH ORANGES. See Oranges with Lavenders, page 61.

LAVENDERS WITH MAGENTAS. See Magentas with Lavenders, page 65.

LAVENDERS WITH GREENS. See Greens with Lavenders, pages 76–77.

Crystals

Most Harmonious Colors for Crystals: Blues and Indigos

CRYSTALS WITH BLUES. See Blues with Crystals, page 79.

CRYSTALS WITH INDIGOS. See Indigos with Crystals, page 84.

Moderately Compatible Colors for Crystals: *Yellows, Tans, Violets, Lavenders, and Crystals*

CRYSTALS WITH YELLOWS. See Yellows with Crystals, page 68.

CRYSTALS WITH TANS. See Tans with Crystals, page 72.

CRYSTALS WITH VIOLETS. See Violets with Crystals, pages 82–83.

CRYSTALS WITH LAVENDERS. See Lavenders with Crystals, pages 86–87.

CRYSTALS WITH CRYSTALS. There are many reasons two Crystals can get along. Both partners understand the need for meditation and quiet solitude. They comprehend each other's need to work with nature for inner balance. Both want simplicity, peace, and harmony in the home; however, neither wants the responsibility of going outside the home to work for a living.

Because Crystals tend to be withdrawn and introspective, most likely a Crystal would not instigate a relationship with another Crystal. Often shy and lacking self-confidence, they tend to stay isolated in their own worlds, hiding in their rooms. Even though two Crystals can be compatible, since they share the same needs and beliefs, they have little to learn from each other, so there is little potential for growth; neither has anything to bring back to the other from the outside world. Crystals are better off finding self-confident mates who can take charge.

Least Complementary Colors for Crystals:
Reds, Oranges, Magentas, and Greens

CRYSTALS WITH REDS. See Reds with Crystals, page 57.

CRYSTALS WITH ORANGES. See Oranges with Crystals, page 61.

CRYSTALS WITH MAGENTAS. See Magentas with Crystals, pages 65–66.

CRYSTALS WITH GREENS. See Greens with Crystals, page 77.

Part Two

Where Are They?

Chapter 5

How to Recognize
Your Favorite Love Colors

When you meet someone who catches your attention — or if you are currently in a relationship with someone — how do you discover her or his Love Color without making this person take the Love Colors test? Many different behaviors reveal a person's colors. The following are lists of easy-to-recognize signs that can guide you in identifying the various Love Color personalities. An individual trait may not be exclusive to one color, but if your love interest exhibits many of the behaviors from one particular list, it's a good indication that the person is that Love Color. In addition, if someone reminds you of a famous personality listed below, there is a good chance that both have the same Love Colors.

Read each list thoroughly to see if many of the qualities and behaviors on one particular list seem to describe your love interest. Most likely there will be two color lists that seem to describe this person, since most people have two, or combination, Love Colors. Be aware that included in each list are in-power qualities as well as out-of-power qualities. Your friend may be displaying only the in-power qualities, which means the descriptions of out-of-power qualities will not match. If most of the other behaviors on the color list seem to describe the person, there is a strong possibility that this color is indeed one of his or her Love Colors.

Reds

You will know you are playing with fire if she or he...

- has a hot temper.

- has a strong body and robust physical endurance.

- is strongly sexual or voluptuous.

- is highly self-reliant and independent.

- is intensely stubborn.

- enjoys physical activities that require strength or stamina.

- frequently works out in the gym or has a job that is physically demanding. (This can include dancing.)

- is intelligent and quick. (Some Reds are not motivated to access their intelligence, however.)

- believes that life is about enjoying all the physical pleasures life has to offer — eating, drinking, sex, and so on.

- owns or wants to own his or her own business, is independent or self-employed.

- is typically emotionally guarded and private.

- tends to be a loner.

- is strong-willed, bossy, or demanding.

- loves to participate in or watch sports.

- is not interested in spirituality or philosophy. Life is tangible for Reds. They usually do not believe in things they cannot touch, taste, hear, smell, or feel.

FAMOUS REDS: Actors Marilyn Monroe (Red/Yellow) and Russell Crowe (Red), singers Madonna (Red with Violet) and Dolly Parton (Red/Yellow), wrestler/actor Dwayne "The Rock" Johnson (Red/Violet), and boxer Mike Tyson (Red).

Oranges

You know you are having an adventure with an Orange if he or she . . .

- is in an occupation that is dangerous or life threatening.

- does not seem to fear physical pain.

- is involved in extreme sports.

- is a daredevil and loves to take physical risks.

- hangs out with other daredevils.

- is fascinated by the stunt people in the movies.

- keeps feelings to herself or himself.

- prefers to spend most of his or her time alone.

- seems to always be planning a new dangerous stunt or adventure.

- is serious.

- has never been married and does not appear to desire marriage.

- does rescue work, especially in highly dangerous areas.

- loves to race cars, bungee jump, skydive, paraglide, or participate in other high-risk sports.

- is quick and clever at formulating strategies and calculating physical outcomes.

- can become cold and abrupt.

- usually does not include you in outings or adventures.

FAMOUS ORANGES: Actor/stuntman Jackie Chan and daredevil Evil Knievel.

Magentas

You may have bumped into a Magenta if she or he . . .

- wears odd, often bizarre clothes.

- behaves eccentrically.

- keeps highly unusual hours.

- has countless tattoos, body piercings, or outrageous hairstyles.

- has a bizarre and shocking sense of humor.

- is highly creative.

- is not interested in spiritual or philosophical topics.

- lives in a big city, or wants to, so that he or she can fit in.

- has bizarre art in her or his home.

- loves to be the center of attention but often offends people.

- tends to be a loner.

- feels like an outcast.

- does not have many friends because his or her behavior is too shocking or upsetting to people.

- is interested not in helping people or the planet, just in experiencing the physical world.

FAMOUS MAGENTAS: Artist Andy Warhol and the characters Auntie Mame and Kramer (from *Seinfeld*).

Yellows

You know you are being touched by a Yellow if he or she...

- is always smiling and cheering people up — is everyone's friend.

- tries to make you laugh — a lot and all the time.

- looks much younger than her or his age. (Or he or she has aged because of years of substance abuse.)

- does not act his or her age. Many Yellows resist growing up.

- has numerous creative ideas.

- would rather not be working — ever! — unless it's going to be fun, and then she or he would not really consider it to be work anyway.

- loves being outdoors, exercising, playing sports, and being physical, or at least dances or goes for walks.

- is concerned about the environment or wildlife.

- struggles with addictions. "Sex, drugs, and rock 'n' roll" can be a Yellow's mantra. Yellows are the most addictive of the Love Colors. If you are with someone who has an issue with drugs, alcohol, cigarettes, sex, food, sweets, caffeine, or even computer games, chances are good that you're dealing with a Yellow. Some Yellows, however, are healthy enough to know to stay away from these substances.

- fidgets a lot. Yellows usually have a lot of energy and typically have a hard time sitting still.

- tends to always arrive late. Yellows live in the moment, so it is common for them to lose track of time.

- does not handle money well. For Yellows, life is not about money, so it often slips through their hands.

- enjoys fixing things around the house and working with his or her hands, or...

- is too lazy to fix anything, preferring instead to lie on the couch and watch TV or play computer games.

- avoids commitment. This friend is a nice person and seems eager to make you happy but has a lot of reasons why she or he is just not ready to be monogamous or be tied down. (Not all commitment-phobic people are Yellows, but they lead the pack.)

- drives either a fun vehicle — a sports utility vehicle, a motorcycle, a jeep — or something that is inexpensive or falling apart because he or she doesn't have the money to fix it or buy a new one.

- regards a pet dog as her or his best friend. Yellows love dogs, and dogs love Yellows. Dogs and Yellows: the perfect example of fun, energy, and happiness. (This can apply to any pet, if the Yellow treats that pet as if it were a dog.)

- would typically prefer to be drinking beer, hanging out at a bar, watching sports, or playing in a band with buddies.

FAMOUS YELLOWS: Almost any comedian — Bill Cosby (Yellow/Violet), Tim Allen (Yellow/Violet), Ellen DeGeneres (Yellow/Blue), Jim Carrey (Yellow/Violet), George Lopez (Yellow/Violet), Jay Leno (Yellow/Violet), and Richard Pryor (Yellow/Violet with a Red Overlay); many actors — Harrison Ford (Yellow/Tan), Brad Pitt (Yellow/Tan), Will Smith (Yellow/Violet), Meg Ryan (Blue/Yellow), and Goldie Hawn (Blue/Yellow); numerous athletes — Michael Jordan (Yellow/Violet) and Tiger Woods (Yellow/Violet); and many environmentalists and animal lovers — Steve "Crocodile Hunter" Irwin (Yellow/Orange with Violet), Robert Redford (Yellow/Violet), and John Denver (Yellow/Tan with Violet).

Tans

You may think you have a Tan if she or he . . .

- is stable and responsible.

- remains calm and logical in a crisis.

- is practical and conservative with money.

- prefers to earn a steady paycheck.

- wears glasses, and especially needs them at work.

- has a job that deals with details.

- slowly and methodically tells you every detail of a story.

- takes a long time to get to the point.

- does not share feelings easily.

- talks about what he or she thinks, rather than how he or she feels — *think* is a Tan's word.

- drives a sensible or inexpensive, but safe, car.

- tends to wear the same conservative clothes for years.

- is not trendy, preferring instead to be practical.

- tends to watch the news or the business reports on television.

- is steady and predictable; does not really enjoy surprises.

- needs to plan things out; is not spontaneous.

- takes a long time to make a decision, even after hearing all the facts.

- needs facts, data, and scientific evidence before believing something is true.

- usually is skeptical of anything that cannot be detected with the five senses. Most Tans do not believe in spirituality, ESP, UFOs, or mystical experiences. (This is not always the case if she or he is a Tan combination.)

- analyzes everything.

- does not like change or trying new things.

- habitually does the same thing, in the same way, every day.

- is stubborn and set in his or her ways.

FAMOUS TANS: Actors Clint Eastwood (Tan/Violet), Tommy Lee Jones (Tan/Violet), and Kevin Costner (Yellow/Tan).

Greens

You know you have encountered a Green if he or she...

- seems to always be in a hurry.

- talks very quickly.

- finishes other people's sentences for them.

- is highly intelligent.

- is driven to make a lot of money.

- is highly competitive.

- works in or is fascinated by the stock market, money-oriented businesses, real estate, and business in general.

- drives an expensive car.

- owns high-quality and expensive possessions: clothing, furniture, and jewelry.

- owns at least one expensive home — or plans to.

- always seems to be working on something. Greens have difficulty relaxing. Even when they take vacations, their minds are on business or projects.

- drinks a lot of coffee or other caffeinated substances. This helps a Green think even more quickly.

- frequently asks "How?" Greens usually want to know how something was accomplished, how someone came up with an idea, or how someone made money.

- frequently uses the words *should*, *have to*, *need to*, *hard work*, *struggle*, and *try*.

- wants to know the point or the end of the story and does not seem interested in the details.

- speaks her or his mind, no matter whom it may offend.

- gets to the point, often abruptly.

- is often critical and judgmental of others, especially people who are inefficient, slow, or unmotivated.

- tends to argue and rarely admits he or she is wrong.

- needs to be in control.

- is very stubborn and strong-willed.

- gambles.

- has more than one degree — which often includes multiple bachelor's degrees, master's degrees, or doctorates. Greens love to learn and to excel, so usually one degree is not enough.

- is, conversely, a self-made entrepreneur who never completed school.

FAMOUS GREENS: Magnates Bill Gates (Green/Violet), Donald Trump (Green/Yellow), John Rockefeller, and William Randolph Hearst; talk-show host David Letterman (Green/Yellow); and actors Bette Davis (Green), Lucille Ball (Green/Yellow), and Arnold Schwarzenegger (Green/Yellow).

Blues

You have a Blue in your heart if she or he...

- seems to always be counseling others.

- is always on the phone talking with friends.

- has a lot of friends.

- is very spiritual or religious.

- cries easily.

- has dreamed of being married most of his or her life.

- usually has cold hands and feet.

- does not like to exercise (unless she or he is a Blue/Yellow combination).

- shares his or her home with at least one cat. Most Blues love cats, although a Blue/Yellow may also have a dog.

- talks about how she or he feels more than how she or he thinks. Blues talk about feelings.

- often does too much for people — volunteers for everything. Blues tend to give and give and give.

- feels guilty saying no.

- apologizes frequently. "I'm sorry" is a Blue's theme song.

- is always putting others first and himself or herself last.

- is friends with those who are unaccepted or even rejected by others. Blues rescue the underdogs of life.

- owns a lot of stuffed animals, dolls, or animals.

- seems to always pick the wrong relationships — choosing people who need rescuing or who treat her or him poorly.

- overstays in relationships that are not healthy or are abusive.

- uses guilt to get his or her way.

- often comes across as a martyr.

- has trouble receiving compliments.

- is married or has been married — possibly many times (Blue/Yellows).

FAMOUS BLUES: Actors Jennifer Aniston (Blue/Yellow), Kate Hudson (Blue/Yellow), and Elizabeth Taylor (Blue/Violet); Princess Diana and Sarah Ferguson, the Duchess of York (both Blue/Yellow with Violet).

Violets

Most likely you are watching a Violet if he or she...

- is charismatic and often the center of attention. Violets are often strikingly attractive.

- attracts attention whenever she or he enters a room.

- is very passionate — about art, performing, sex, causes, or saving the planet.

- loves music or is involved in music.

- is a performer, writer, or artist.

- is self-employed or is in a position of leadership.

- communicates in a way that inspires and motivates people.

- has a sense of urgency, feeling as if he or she is running out of the time necessary to accomplish major dreams and goals.

- has a strong desire to travel, especially globally.

- seems to have a million ideas or visions she or he wants to accomplish in this lifetime.

- often feels overwhelmed and scattered. Violets tend to multitask.

- talks a lot. Violets need to communicate, and often words of wisdom pour forth as if they were teachers or philosophers.

- talks about what he or she "sees," "dreams," or "envisions."

- discusses global, political, humanitarian, or social concerns often.

- is involved or wants to be involved in humanitarian causes or charities.

- cares about animals, especially exotic or global animals.

- seems older or wiser than her or his years. Violets often appear physically older or more mature.

- tends to be a serious and deep thinker.

- feels very deeply and has strong emotions.

- believes that accomplishing his or her dreams is ultimately more important than, or at least equally important as, relationships.

- has little desire to be a stay-at-home parent. Violets sense that, in time, they will need to be out in the world making a difference.

- becomes easily bored at parties if there is meaningless chatter and gossip rather than intelligent discussions about world events, travel, philosophy, spirituality, politics, or other significant topics.

- has a powerful personality that often intimidates people.

- can be highly self-absorbed.

- is dramatic or has a lot of dramatic situations in her or his life.

- is easily bored in relationships, outgrows them quickly, or has had affairs.

- can become easily depressed or sullen, often feeling that he or she is not like other people.

FAMOUS VIOLETS: Movers and shakers Oprah Winfrey, Nelson Mandela, John F. Kennedy, Robert Kennedy, Martin Luther King Jr., Maya Angelou, Mikhail Gorbachev, and Abraham Lincoln (all Violet/Yellows); singers and musicians Elvis Presley, the Beatles, Sting, Bono (of U2), Kenny Loggins, Beyoncé, and Barbra Streisand (all Violet/Yellows); actors George Clooney, Tom Hanks, Mel Gibson, Michael J. Fox, Julia Roberts, and Sandra Bullock (all Violet/Yellows); and film directors Steven Spielberg and George Lucas (both Violet/Yellows).

Indigos

You may have discovered an Indigo if she or he...

- is highly intuitive or psychic.

- communicates with spiritual beings, nature, animals, or deceased people.

- remembers clear details of other lives.

- has the ability to read minds, or did when she or he was young.

- has an unusual look in his or her eyes — like he or she knows things beyond what ordinary humans know. Indigos often seem like they are from a distant place or a future time.

- knows spiritually advanced information.

- words of wisdom pour from her or him as from a spiritual teacher or highly advanced philosopher.

- is more unusual than anyone you have ever met. He or she does not seem like an ordinary human.

- has special gifts and talents that seem to be advanced well beyond her or his age — artistic, musical, poetic, healing, mathematical, technological, philosophical, and so on.

- is unusually beautiful. It may be difficult to tell at times whether he or she is male or female.

- does not seem to have a strong interest in sex. It may be hard to distinguish if she or he is heterosexual, homosexual, or asexual.

- has strong empathy and compassion for nature, animals, and humanity.

- does not feel like he or she fits in on the planet.

- quickly understands and easily uses technology and has had that ability from an early age.

- is not influenced by guilt or threats of punishment.

FAMOUS INDIGO: Michael Jackson (Indigo/Violet); most Indigos are young and still emerging.

Lavenders

You know you are dreaming of a Lavender if he or she...

- is fragile and very sensitive.

- has pale or even alabaster skin.

- is quiet, gentle, and spiritual.

- is creative or dreams of being creative.

- has wonderful artistic ideas but has difficulty following through on them.

- surrounds herself or himself with crystals, chimes, soft music, fantasy pictures, or mythological creatures like unicorns, elves, fairies, and so on.

- often wears soft and flowing clothes.

- has a gentle and sweet smile, and childlike behavior.

- is often spacey and forgetful.

- daydreams or fantasizes a lot and seems to have trouble dealing with reality.

- often has a blank stare.

- often seems frightened, nervous, or anxious.

- is often weak and ill and has many chronic health problems.

- has trouble dealing with money — cannot seem to grasp how to make it and keep it.

- would prefer not to work. Has difficulty keeping a job.

- does not seem to have the strength or energy to be responsible for everyday tasks.

- has difficulty concentrating.

- does not seem to listen well to others.

- is typically disorganized.

FAMOUS LAVENDERS: Writers Lewis Carroll (*Alice in Wonderland*) and C.S. Lewis (*The Chronicles of Narnia*) — both Lavender/Violets.

Crystals

You may have found a Crystal if she or he...

- tends to quietly spend a lot of time alone.

- is an introvert, typically withdrawn and subdued.

- seems to be extremely sensitive.

- spends most of his or her time reflecting and connecting with God or Source.

- is very loving, patient, and caring with others.

- changes personalities often, seemingly to fit in with those around her or him.

- seems very different from other people, as if from a more ethereal realm.

- works in or would like to work in a calm, peaceful environment.

- works or desires to work in the health and healing fields. Many Crystals sense that they have healing abilities.

- enjoys creative self-expression.

- is extremely uncomfortable in crowds.

- does not seem to relate to others well.

- is awkward and unsure of himself or herself in social situations and often watches others to see how to act.

- seems lost, frightened, and unsure of a life direction and purpose.

- often lets other people make decisions for her or him.

- is more interested in other people's lives than his or her own. Crystals out of power can be busybodies.

- energetically and emotionally drains people. People often feel worn out after being with this person.

Although they possibly exist, I know of no famous Crystals.

Chapter 6

Your Love Color's Special Places

Once you realize which of the Love Colors you find most appealing, where can you go to meet them? Or if you want to plan activities that could pleasantly surprise your current partner, what types of places and activities are best to consider? This chapter looks at the occupations, hobbies, and favorite hangouts of each Love Color. Since most people have two Love Colors (combination colors), you will want to determine which two colors you find most appealing and go to the places that each of these Love Colors frequents. Of course, you'll find a wide variety of Love Colors in almost every type of occupation, activity, and place of leisure. And since many people are in the wrong jobs or in unfulfilling careers, approaching people according to their occupation is not a foolproof way to locate the partner you're seeking. Still, it's a good way to start.

As you speak to people in different occupations, find out if they are happy with their jobs or simply staying in them just to make money. If their work brings them joy and they look forward to it, then they are in places aligned with their Love Colors. If people tell you they don't like their jobs, make sure it is the *type of work* that they dislike, not just their bosses or the work environments.

If you like the description of the personality and qualities of a particular Love Color and would like to meet one, you're likely to find this color in the places listed below. Or if you sense that a certain color may not be right for you, then these are places you'll want to avoid. Again, since most people have two different Love Colors, reading the career and location lists for both of their colors could be helpful.

The most important thing to keep in mind when you try out any of these suggested locations is to have fun. Stay light and playful so you don't frighten or traumatize yourself. Let love be fun and easy. You'll experience more joy on your journey, and it will be easier for people to approach you. People are usually more attracted to those who are enjoying life.

Reds

Occupations That Reds Are Likely to Choose

Most Reds prefer to be self-employed or at least to be the person in charge. They want to be in a position that allows them control over their time and energy. They especially love physical work and are likely to be aerobic instructors, lifeguards, construction workers, physical therapists, gardeners, truck drivers, farmers, ranchers, butchers, furniture movers, laborers, delivery people, factory workers, repair people, mechanics, forest rangers, fishermen, bartenders, waitresses, and waiters.

They sometimes enjoy the challenge of being courageous in dangerous situations and can be firefighters, police officers, rescue workers, bodyguards, mountain climbers, race car drivers, and military personnel.

Reds can be involved in many different sports, especially those that require brawn, and you may find them among football players, boxers, wrestlers, coaches, jockeys, surfers, and hockey players. Or they may choose other jobs that allow them to use their physical talents, becoming dancers, models, actors, singers, or surgeons.

Where Can I Find Reds?

If you are one of those daring and self-confident people attracted to the strong, independent Reds, or if you are drawn to their powerful sexual energy, then here are some places you can go to meet them. One of the most likely places to find Reds is in the gym. Most Reds love strengthening their bodies and staying physically fit, so they will be pumping iron or working hard in their aerobics or Pilates classes. Usually fitness centers have social events so their members can get to know each other. Are you a member yet? Better join now: it's probably a good idea to get your own body into shape if you're going to keep up with a powerful, robust Red.

You will also find them running marathons and competing in triathlons, so watch your newspaper for announcements about these competitions. If you don't plan on joining the race, they usually need volunteers to hand out water and snacks to the participants as they rush by. You can also look for Reds in bodybuilding contests.

Any rugged or physically challenging sport will attract Reds. Choose which types of players appeal to you and attend their games or matches — rugby, soccer, football, hockey, polo, wrestling, and boxing are just a few of the Reds' favorites. Many of these events draw fans who are Reds, so make sure you also scan the spectators.

Reds have great respect for the power and magnificence of nature, so they often appreciate working outdoors. If you do not have Red forest rangers working nearby, maybe you'll find Reds taking care of your local parks. Wilderness-loving Reds who live in the mountains are often ski instructors and rescue workers, own ski rental shops, run the ski lifts, or operate the snowblowers. Learning to snowboard or ski could be fun. If you don't enjoy these particular activities or cannot keep up with the Reds on the slopes, cozy up to the fire at the lodge and wait for some of them to come indoors.

There are also Reds on ranches and farms. Maybe go trail riding at your favorite horse ranch or see who is buying cattle feed and farm tools at the local feed store. You can always find a Red or two at the rodeo.

In your own hometown, it is not difficult to pass by a construction site to see if any of the workers catch your eye. There may be a few Reds building a house, paving a road, or laying utility cables. Notice the repair person climbing up the telephone pole. Or observe your neighbor's landscaper, gardener, or tree trimmer. They might appreciate you offering them a cool, refreshing drink of water or lemonade. Or you can always wander through the hardware store to see who is buying building supplies.

Visiting the farmers markets', you can see Reds carrying in the produce, driving the trucks, and setting up the stands. Your auto mechanic, plumber, or electrician could also be a Red. It certainly is easy to spot the physical Reds, since most of them prefer to work outdoors rather than sitting obscured behind a desk in some office.

If you want one of the really robust Reds, take a fishing trip to Alaska or Canada. You'll find them with their own cabins and boats, living hearty, independent lives.

If this type of Red is a little too rugged for you, there are Reds working in hospitals and clinics as surgeons, physicians, and anesthesiologists. By becoming a volunteer, you could perform a valuable community service while also increasing your chances of meeting one of these Reds. Courageous Reds are also known to travel to disaster areas. You will see them in the middle of the action, their sleeves rolled up as they move debris or carry the survivors to safety. They like to solve problems by taking action, not just theorizing or talking about the problem. They like immediate and tangible results.

If you want to find a Red at your school or church, look for the person setting up the bleachers, painting the pews, or constructing the booths for the fund-raiser. They prefer to contribute by physically working on these types of projects.

Many Reds love expressing passion through dancing or acting, so attending stage performances may uncover a few of them. Try taking dance classes, especially hot-blooded Latin, fast-paced swing, or vigorous African dance — any dance that is wild, fiery, and full of life. You may just find your dance partner for life. You can also find Reds performing on Broadway, in Las Vegas, or at strip clubs anywhere in the world. Naked bodies, sensuality, and sexual exhibitions do not usually embarrass Reds.

Some Reds join the military. If you want to locate one of these Reds, you can volunteer with an organization like the USO. You can even observe nonmilitary Reds out in the fields practicing target shooting.

You may encounter the classic strong, dominant Red males who prefer the subservient, helpless females. You can sometimes find them driving alone in their trucks, a gun and hunting dog by their sides. Or you may encounter one of the strong, robust Red females who are not afraid to drive an eighteen-wheeler and chop their own wood. Truck stops are a good place to meet these Reds.

You can also find the rowdier Reds at your local bars, pubs, and restaurants. Reds like to hang out where people are having a good time. Some are content to sit alone at the bar, while others are wild and boisterous as they celebrate with their buddies. When you meet the bartender, server, or bouncer, see if they fit the Red's description. Yellows are also found in these jobs, so you will have to determine which color you've encountered. Reds tend to be stronger, down-to-earth, and more intense. Yellows are usually funny, playful, and easygoing. Overall, Reds tend to be more responsible with their finances; however, some Yellows have learned how to manage their money.

Reds have a tendency to overindulge, so they are occasionally found at recovery meetings for drug, alcohol, sex, or food abuse. But most Reds are too stubborn and willful to admit they have a problem or to share their thoughts and feelings with others. Typically, they are not drawn to therapy.

Oranges

Occupations That Oranges Are Likely to Choose

Oranges are daredevils and can be race car drivers, skydivers, hang gliders, stunt doubles, deep-sea divers, and bungee jumpers. They love other types of physical adventures as well and can be mountain climbers, wilderness guides, river rafters, wild safari hunters, explorers, extreme skiers and snowboarders, extreme surfers, and participants in other extreme sports.

They thrive in dangerous situations and can be firefighters, police officers, rescue workers, paramedics, detectives, private investigators, guards, bounty hunters, lion tamers, and trapeze artists.

Oranges often prefer to freelance, getting paid for what they love to do and then spending that money on their next outrageous adventure. You will rarely find an Orange sitting behind a desk — not a happy Orange, anyway. Paperwork is too boring for them.

Where Can I Find Oranges?

The main challenge one might face in meeting any of these daring people is that they tend to go to places others fear to tread. They also tend to be solo acts. Usually only Reds, Yellows, and other Oranges encounter these wild spirits. If you are drawn to thrills and excitement, if you really want to be with one of these risk takers, make sure you are willing to share their hazardous interests, or that you don't mind when they go off on their adventures without you.

Since Oranges love to face physical danger and challenges, you can find them in places where they can participate in many different extreme sports. If you love to ski or snowboard but prefer to stay on the marked slopes, you may have to wait until the end of the day for the thrill-seeking Oranges to show up at the lodge. Oranges tend to take great risks, sometimes being dropped off by helicopters in remote and dangerous locations.

The rescue workers at ski resorts and the lifeguards at beaches are sometimes Oranges. If you cannot catch their attention while they are saving someone's life, find out where they work out or where they go to relax after hours. If the Orange you find is aloof, which is common, you may have to initiate the conversation.

Car racing is becoming more and more popular, and at the racetrack you will probably encounter a number of Oranges. They could even be among the spectators. Oranges love the excitement, the thrill of speeding cars flying around the track, burning rubber in the curves, and narrowly avoiding deadly collisions. If you can find your way onto the track, into the pit, or better yet into the winner's circle, you will dramatically increase your chances of meeting an Orange.

If you ever wished that the love of your life could just fall out of the sky and drop into your arms, locate your nearest skydiving school so you can watch the parachutes come down to earth. Or find hang gliding and paragliding locations in your area. Watch the skies for the colorful chutes or wings, then just follow them to see where they land. How much easier could it be to spot your potential future mate than to find one suspended in the heavens right above you? More than likely there will be an Orange or a Yellow attached to each parachute. Offering to drive them back up the mountain so they can jump again might be an exciting way to share in the adventure.

Pick up travel brochures or go online to find out about the available wilderness adventures and river-rafting trips. It's easy to sign up for one of these adventures. Your tour guide or river-rafting expert will most likely be an Orange. Think of the fun you could have rushing down a torrential river in a raft, clinging desperately to your sleek and daring Orange. Can you imagine spending a romantic evening camping out under the stars after your harrowing day on the river? Realize, however, that most Oranges like their freedom and are not usually in any hurry to make a commitment. Of course, if you, like your tour guide, are excited by a challenge, an Orange may be just the person for you. If you are really adventurous, you could even book yourself on an African safari. The safari guides and even some of the other explorers could be Oranges.

If mountain climbing or rock climbing appeals to you, there are many groups that take people on these particular adventures. Some of these treks are weekend outings, and some are day trips. Other groups travel to remote areas and climb for days. You may prefer to find an Orange on your own, possibly while you are out hiking. If you see someone scaling to the top of the steepest and most treacherous cliff, there is a good possibility that the climber is an Orange.

Although it is not usually a good idea to hang around a blazing, out-of-control fire or a dangerous situation in which the police have been summoned, these are good places to spot Oranges. Their mental skills also make them excellent detectives, so keep an eye out for them when they show up after the incident. It may be easier, however, to meet one of these courageous souls at one of their events. The fire and police departments typically sponsor charity events. By attending and contributing to some of these fund-raisers, you may meet firefighters, police officers, or detectives. You can always find out how to become a volunteer at their events, which will enable you to spend even more time with these Oranges. If there are no such events in your area, bringing freshly baked cookies to your local fire or police station to show your support and appreciation might bring a smile to their faces.

If you volunteer or work at a hospital, you may discover that many of the paramedics who rush in and out are Oranges. Sometimes these rescue workers stand around outside and socialize with one another after they drop off their patients. Watch the emergency entrance to see if any of them appeals to you. Oranges take their work seriously, however, so don't loiter or get in the way.

If you have connections and can somehow get permission to be on a Hollywood set, pay close attention to the stunt doubles. Most of them are Oranges. Also, keep in mind that filmmakers do not shoot their movies only in Hollywood. Get your hands on movie and television trade publications, which sometimes list the remote locations where studios will be filming. Check online, too, to see if any movies will be shot in your area — or any area that could be easy for you to visit when you take a vacation. You may even be cast as an extra in the film. Just watch carefully to see which people are stunt doubles and stunt drivers and introduce yourself. If you are too shy to take such bold action, then you probably do not belong with a brash Orange.

You could also find out where stunt people train and where they frequently hang out near these schools. Surprisingly, stunt-driving schools exist all over the world — find them on the Internet or in the library. Or watch the credits at the end of a movie to see the list of stunt doubles, trainers, and coordinators. Many of them can be found through the Internet. Are you bold enough to contact one of them by either email or regular mail? At the very least, you will flatter them. Most people don't notice them or acknowledge their work. Just don't come across as a stalker; be a sincere, supportive admirer.

If these training centers are too far away, you can always go to the circus the next time one comes to your area. Keep an eye on the fire-eaters, trapeze artists, and wildcat trainers. People who put their lives on the line for entertainment are often Oranges.

If you are in a relationship with a police officer, firefighter, lifeguard, or any other similar type of person, and these descriptions do not seem to fit your partner, understand that not everyone in these occupations is an Orange. There are many Reds and Yellows and occasionally Violets in these jobs as well. If your partner seems to relish taking risky and dangerous chances and does not seem to fear pain, you probably are involved with an Orange. Otherwise, read the chapters on Reds and Yellows. Most Oranges prefer a solitary, single life with no family constraints or responsibilities.

Magentas

Occupations That Magentas Are Likely to Choose

Magentas are drawn to occupations that give them the freedom to express themselves, and they may be actors, clowns, and comedians. Magentas love to be creative in other ways as well. For example, they like to take ideas or physical substances and twist them into bizarre works of art, and so they may be writers, artists, photographers, costume designers, set designers, sculptors, and landscape and topiary designers. (Writing a script for a Monty Python movie would appeal to them.)

They love developing new ideas or products and may be inventors or producers of avant-garde publications. They enjoy jobs that are flexible and innovative and prefer to avoid the traditional nine-to-five schedule; thus, being an entrepreneur or an art dealer or collector may appeal to a Magenta. Magentas have short attention spans, so they prefer to work on individual projects rather than jobs in which there is no end in sight. Otherwise, they become bored and quickly lose interest.

Where Can I Find Magentas?

If they are wild Magentas and are in power, they can be easy to spot: they will be the individuals attracting the most attention. You will probably witness a number of curious stares, nervous whispers, and fingers all pointing in the same direction — toward them. It's hard to ignore people who have bright pink hair, body piercings, and tattoos covering every inch of their skin. (Even though Magentas started this trend, other Love Colors have followed their example.)

The majority of Magentas live in large cities, especially cities known for their creativity and willingness to embrace people labeled as misfits: San Francisco, New York, Los Angeles, and similar cities around the world.

One of your biggest challenges will be to stay up late enough to find

Magentas at their favorite hangouts. If you know of any little, tucked-away restaurants or trendy cafes that are open all night, and if you are willing to do something spontaneous and out of the ordinary, you may be able to find a Magenta or two eating dinner at three o'clock in the morning. Sit yourself down and scan the room. If you really want one of these rare and intriguing individuals, this will be a good opportunity to meet one. Magentas are typically solitary diners. Who else is crazy enough to eat at this hour? If you find yourself attracted to what you think is a Magenta, you will be able to tell if this particular one wants company or prefers to be left alone. If Magentas want company, you will be able to make eye contact. Watch for their quirky smiles.

Since Magentas appreciate unusual art, consider exploring a variety of galleries, especially those that feature avant-garde painters and sculptors. For example, find showings of artists who are as quirky as Salvador Dali or Andy Warhol, artists who tend to create far outside of the box. You could meet your perfect Magenta match wandering around at a gallery opening.

When you consider attending galleries, include those exhibiting photography. Magentas are not only painters and sculptors; they are also photographers and filmmakers. You could meet a Magenta or two by going to any location where you can see one of their strange works.

Similarly, these curious beings also love to attend the theater, especially experimental shows and offbeat plays. Stand in the lobby before or after the performance to see if you can pick one out. Watch for the obvious signs of a Magenta — unusual clothes, outrageous hairstyle, or flamboyant, over-the-top jewelry. During intermission, watch to see who is at the center of attention, who is laughing the loudest. In power, Magentas are not typically shy, so you can easily walk right up to them and introduce yourself. They appreciate boldness and fearlessness. If you are hoping to have a Magenta companion, this is a perfect time to get over any fear of embarrassment. Magentas appreciate companions who can share their attitudes.

If you are attracted to stage plays or musicals, maybe you could get a job or volunteer your services backstage at a theater. Because Magentas like the entertainment business, you may find them involved in almost any creative pursuits, as writers, actors, musicians, backstage help, designers, or anything else, just to be around that special creative energy. Take a glance at the costume designer or the set designer. Some flamboyant Magentas can be temperamental and high-strung, so keep an eye out for some of these divas frantically rushing around backstage.

Most Magentas prefer independent films — those that the common person rarely understands or appreciates — over the more traditional and commercial movies. And subtitles make a film even more intriguing and exciting to them. Magentas are among the few who treasure absurd and dark comedies, and in fact they are often the writers and producers of such films.

If you have any comedy clubs in your neighborhood, it may be fun to go to one. Watch the steady stream of comedians as they try their luck onstage. Magentas love shocking people, so they are typically the comedians who push the limits of morality and taste in their acts. They may also be sitting in the audience, since they love to laugh and be around people who are having a good time. (Be aware, however, that comedy clubs are usually the domain of Yellows.)

Since Magentas like to keep unusual and late hours, you may find them at an after-hours nightclub. If their wild clothes don't give them away, their behavior will. Given that they love being the center of attention, there is a good possibility they will be showing off in the center of the dance floor. You can also see them zipping around, entertaining and gregariously chatting with every person in the club. They don't want to miss out on anything or anyone.

Occasionally you can meet Magentas at private parties; however, it will probably be a rather large party — one that allows invited guests to bring their friends. Most hosts shy away from intentionally inviting the outrageous Magentas, because they can create quite a spectacle at times. But you do have a great possibility of meeting Magentas at one of these social events. They love parties.

While some Magentas are loud and outspoken and easy to spot, others may be quietly standing off to the side, alone and unnoticed. Remember, Magentas are often loners. They usually feel like outcasts and oddballs, so their behavior can appear strange and antisocial. You may be just what they are waiting for — someone who will accept them for who they are, some-one willing to befriend them and engage them in an interesting and intelli-gent conversation. Act quickly, however, and have fun. If you hesitate, your Magenta could become bored and move on to the next party.

If you find a book or article that intrigues you, one that seems to take a unique approach, makes radical and outrageous statements, or, especially, reveals the author's twisted sense of humor, consider seeking out the writer. Remember, Magentas love to shake people up. They love to look at life differently, and they usually take the path least traveled. Many writers enjoy hearing from fans, so don't be shy. Contact them. There is always author contact information in books and magazines. You may be happily surprised — it could be the beginning of a wonder-ful friendship with one of these rare souls.

You can encounter Magentas at your local florist's shop. Keep in mind they love unusual, creative environments, so wandering into your local flower shop could bring you exciting results. Or attend a flower show. There may be some avid Magenta gardeners and flower enthusi-asts gathered there. The Magentas will most likely be the ones showing rare and peculiar hybrid flowers.

Taking art classes could be fun and fruitful. It can be challenging for Magentas to meet like-minded people, so they sometimes venture into one of these classes seeking connection with other experimental artists. Attending writers' conferences, authors' book lectures, or other events where creative fiction writers gather, you may encounter at least one Magenta. Again, don't be shy. Strike up a conversation with any of the writers you find interesting.

Wouldn't you love to entertain your friends someday with a funny story about how you met your Magenta partner at the circus? Pay special attention to the clowns, mimes, jugglers, trapeze artists, and acrobats. While Yellows are also drawn to these playful forms of entertainment, there could be quite a few Magentas involved. As strange as it may sound, if you are really enamored of Magentas, you could possibly find one in clown school. There may be a number of the budding performers attending those classes. Consider hiring a clown or mime for your own birthday party. If you are concerned that others will make fun of you for acting so strangely, you probably do not belong with the bizarre Magenta.

Watch your local newspaper for any outdoor events that will be featuring clowns, jugglers, mimes, or wandering minstrels. Although it is not advisable to look like you are stalking or spying on someone's private party, there are quite a few public events held in parks that you could attend.

If your city has outdoor cultural festivals — Greek, Italian, French, any festivals that feature live music, dancers, and ethnic performers — consider participating. Magentas enjoy these types of cultural events. They love the crowds and jovial atmosphere. The Magentas will most likely be the ones wildly dancing by themselves to polka music — oblivious or not caring that all eyes are on them. Nothing really embarrasses Magentas. Also check to see if there is a one-man band — one disorderly character smacking cymbals together with his knees while he blows on a tuba and strums a banjo. Those Magentas can get pretty zany, but they are also very talented.

At your local bookstore, mosey around the sections that feature art, travel, weird inventions, design, interior decorating, exotic cookbooks, and other creative and unusual subjects. Use your imagination. Go to the aisles that have odd books — not the standard romantic, psychological, or self-help topics. Hint: Most Magentas do not think there is anything wrong with them, so they are not interested in getting "help." If you want to play with Magentas, it's best not hang out in the psychology section, near the people who will one day try to diagnose the Magentas as lunatics.

Not all Magentas are wild partiers. Some are very serious inventors and artists. These Magentas are usually solitary. Although they can sometimes feel lonely, ultimately they have no problem being alone. They accept it as part of their lives. They are intelligent but odd thinkers and accept that most people will never understand their quirky, unorthodox way of living and perceiving life. They can blend into society, moving quietly among the masses undetected and unnoticed. These particular Magentas are hard to connect with emotionally. They tend to remain aloof. They are content to work on their own innovations rather than becoming involved in other people's lives.

One place you can find some of these intriguing Magentas is at the library researching information for their inventions. Realize, however, they will most likely be so focused on their projects that they will not be aware of your presence. It will take a very bold action to get them to notice you. And if it is their habit to be unaware of others, be prepared to have to get their attention over and over again in your relationship.

Most likely you will not meet the Magentas who are out of power and depressed. They will be quietly hiding in their homes, curtains closed, surrounded by chaos and litter. You may see the rare one late at night slowly shuffling through the aisles at the all-night market. But these despondent, solitary souls will not lift their heads or make eye contact. You could brighten their lives by smiling and acknowledging them, but it is best that you not try to be their late-night therapist. They usually prefer to be left alone.

Yellows

Occupations That Yellows Are Likely to Choose

Yellows are highly creative and may be musicians, writers, artists, actors, comedians, designers, or party planners. Architects are usually

Yellow/Tan combinations. Yellows are natural healers too: physicians, chiropractors, massage therapists, energy workers, veterinarians, acupuncturists, and physical therapists. By the way, Yellows usually give the best healing hugs.

Some Yellows like to help people by being schoolteachers, therapists, or social workers. Usually Yellows prefer to fix things, rather than people's emotional problems, and they can be auto mechanics, construction workers, electricians, plumbers, and other contractors. They also love to be physically active, so they may be athletes, coaches, exercise instructors, firefighters, pilots, landscapers, gardeners, postal workers, grocery store checkers, or delivery people.

Where Can I Find Yellows?

I'll assume you are looking for an in-power, healthy Yellow, so keep in mind the fact that healthy Yellows like to be active and they love the outdoors. Think yellow, think sun, think fun. If you want to play with a Yellow, a great place to start looking is at the beach, lake, or mountains. Yellows are lifeguards, surfers, and volleyball players. They can also be found boating, skiing, hiking, or fishing. You will find Yellows running the track or on the baseball field. You can actually find them doing any and all sports, so attending bike races, swim meets, tennis matches, or basketball games could be a good way to meet a Yellow. You can also join the Sierra Club or go to the gym. Exercising next to your Yellow day after day is a good way to develop a relationship.

Yellows love working in and with nature. They are likely to take care of parks. Forest rangers are often Yellows, so try a guided nature walk. You can also encounter them selling produce at grocery stores or farmers' markets or selling flowers at your corner stand.

It is easy to meet Yellows at the dog park. If you have a dog yourself, you already have an advantage. Yellows love dogs. Once you spot a Yellow you find intriguing, ask your dog to go to work. If you don't own a dog, fawning over the Yellow's dog will be your best approach.

The dog will probably adore you — but if it doesn't, you're in trouble. If you cannot convince the dog to love you, you probably won't have a chance with the dog's companion. Best to move on to another dog owner.

Volunteering at an animal shelter or veterinarian's office is a sure way to meet a Yellow. In addition to the veterinarians, there will certainly be more than one dog owner showing up at these establishments. Or check out who is buying dog food at your local pet store.

Volunteering at a hospital will potentially lead you to numerous Yellow healers: doctors, nurses, physical therapists, medics, ambulance drivers, orderlies, or even other volunteers. Helping others is good for the soul, and it may end up being good for your relationship status.

Consider bringing a plate of cookies to your local fire station to show them your appreciation for all the hard, harrowing work they do. Most firefighters are Yellows, Reds, or Oranges. Yellows love to eat, and they especially love sweets. There are days at a time where firefighters are not rushing out to quell fires, so you can find them at the station a lot of the time.

Scores of writers are Yellows, so attending events like writers' conferences could be educational and illuminating and an easy way to meet a creative Yellow. Artists are usually Yellows, so going to art exhibits and gallery openings to meet artists and art lovers may bring a pleasant surprise.

Comedy clubs may be one of the best places to meet Yellows after dark. Yellows rule comedy. They live for laughter. If you don't find a comedic performer who rocks your world, most of the audience members will have yellow in their aura. Getting to know someone by laughing alongside her or him may be one of the most fun methods of befriending someone ever.

Most musicians, actors, dancers, and other performers are Yellows, Violets, or Yellow/Violet combinations, so attending theater and dance performances, circuses, concerts, parties, and dance clubs will uncover a lot of Yellows. Be aware, however, that you may also encounter a few out-of-power Yellows in the clubs who are there to get high and party. Remember that out-of-power Yellows often have issues with commitment as well as with substance abuse. Keep your eyes open and your antenna up. Be cautious around this type of Yellow if you are looking for a healthy, long-term, committed relationship. If, on the other hand, you just want to have a good time, then clubs are perfect places to find the fun-loving Yellows.

The majority of party planners are Yellows. Interviewing a variety of these creative people, you may find one with whom you feel a special connection. You usually plan your parties by yourself? This may be part of the problem. If you don't want to continue planning everything alone — for the rest of your life — it may be worth it to spend a little extra money on a planner for your next event. You may just locate the person who will plan your entire future with you.

There are many, many Yellows working in construction. They own the market for these jobs. Are there any homes being built in your area? It would be easy to stand on the street and observe Yellows work. If you find any who catch your attention, it doesn't take much to strike up a friendly conversation with these workers. Yellows love to flirt. Bring them some water or natural fruit drinks.

If you get involved with organizations such as Habitat for Humanity, you will encounter a flurry of Yellows. Building homes for those in need is one way these generous souls can contribute.

Notice your road repair and utility repair people. The majority of them are Yellows. Also pay attention to your delivery people, the ones who bring you parcels, bottled water, furniture, flowers, and even pizza. They are Yellows, Yellows, and Yellows. If they come to your home or office frequently, starting a simple dialog with one of them might give them the message you are interested. Some Yellows can be shy, embarrassed, or cautious. But other, flirtatious Yellows will love to entertain you and make you laugh.

Almost every worker at the post office is a combination Yellow. If your postal carrier is too busy to chat with you, make regular visits to the post office. You may even bump into an interesting patron who's there to pick up mail. There are a lot of Yellows working on cruise ships. And there are a lot of Yellow passengers on those ships hoping to have a good time. This can be a fun and easy way to meet Yellows, and at least for a short time, you will be in a location where the commitment-shy Yellows cannot run away. They will have to be on that ship somewhere.

One of the most common places to find Yellows is at beauty salons and spas. They love to color and cut hair as a creative outlet. Experimenting with different salons around town to see if you can find your Yellow partner could be a fun way to spend time. Yellows are really very friendly people. They also give great massages. These natural healers love to help people feel better. Do you have the time and money to treat yourself? What if it meant you might find your beloved?

You will have to be creative to meet these next Yellows, but if you have a strong intention to meet one, you can find a creative way. Almost every pilot and flight attendant is a Yellow combination: Yellow/Violet, Yellow/Tan, Yellow/Green, Yellow/Blue. Next time you fly, see if you are attracted to your pilots or any of the other flight crew. Consider arriving at the airport much earlier than your flight is scheduled to depart (well, do you want to meet your life partner or not?), so you have time to sit and watch the pilots and flight attendants walking through the terminals. Without looking like you are stalking any of them, you could always catch up to them and ask for directions. Most Yellows are friendly people, so they shouldn't be offended by your approach. Just don't choose one who obviously is rushing to catch a flight. There are lounges specifically set up for the flight crew. Notice who enters and exits these lounges.

There are also hotels near airports that specialize in hosting flight crews. Many of the crew members eat in the hotel restaurants or relax in the lounges until they fly out the next day or the day after. Have you eaten in any of these restaurants lately? Flying from city to city so often can be lonely for some of these people. Many of them would love to have a nice conversation with a friendly person.

Most waiters, waitresses, chefs, and other food-service people are Yellows, which makes it easy to meet a Yellow at your neighborhood restaurant, bar, fast-food drive-thru, or café. The majority of bartenders are Yellows. Most Yellows struggle to make money, so if you want to get a particular Yellow's attention, leave a great tip. Yellows typically do not enjoy school, so jobs that enable them to make money without getting an education and that also allow them to play during daylight hours are ideal for the free-spirited Yellows. Some of these Yellows may also be working in restaurants while they attempt to get their acting or art careers together.

Notice the Yellows checking you out at your local grocer's. They will literally be the checkout clerk and the person bagging your food. They also will be stacking the cans and boxes on the shelves and unloading the produce. If you hang out in the aisles long enough, you will most likely have the chance to flirt with one of these Yellows.

The majority of people at Alcoholics Anonymous and other recovery meetings are Yellows. If you attend one of these meetings, observe which Yellows are sincere about healing their addictions, or you could find yourself in an unhealthy, codependent relationship. (This is especially important advice for Blues to heed, since they tend to want to rescue emotionally scarred people.)

Special hint: You do not typically find Yellows sitting behind office desks unless they are doing creative work (as architects, designers, illustrators, and so on) or are also fulfilling their natural need to be active by exercising in the evenings and on weekends. Yellows usually want freedom to move around, and doing paperwork is not their favorite task. If a Yellow is working behind a desk, you can be almost certain it was not their first choice, unless they are a Yellow/Green or Yellow/Tan combination. Most likely they took the job just to make money.

You also do not go to a bank to meet a Yellow — unless you are looking for a Yellow/Green combination. If you think you've found a Yellow working at a bank, this is probably not a happy or fulfilled Yellow. Bankers, stockbrokers, financial advisors, and other people who work with money or investments are usually Greens.

Tans

Occupations That Tans Are Likely to Choose

Tans prefer safe, stable, long-term jobs that offer good health and retirement benefits. They like having regular paychecks and working for reliable, well-established companies. In general, they like dealing with facts and data, so they may be accountants, bookkeepers, scientists, mathematicians, and researchers.

Logical Tans enjoy working with details, and they may have jobs as engineers, architects, surveyors, technicians, computer analysts and programmers, factory assembly workers, electricians, appliance repair people, and computer repair people.

Sensitive Tans patiently help people, so they may choose jobs as librarians, office clerks, therapists, dental hygienists, court reporters, secretaries, child-care workers, teachers, and nutritionists.

Environmental Tans enjoy working with the environment as archaeologists, explorers, mapmakers, forest rangers, city planners, shipping and receiving clerks, developers, telephone repair workers, pilots, farmers, environmental researchers, and military personnel.

Abstract Tans enjoy detailed planning and designing, and they may be city planners and developers, landscapers, and building design consultants.

Where Can I Find Tans?

The best place to find Tans is at the office or other workplaces. Tans are actually everywhere — although many of them do not get out often to socialize. Typically you will find a Tan at an office, standing behind a counter, sitting at a desk, or intently concentrating on a computer screen. They are behind the desk or counter at the architect's office, your attorney's office, your accountant's, the dentist's office, the city planning desk, and most other places of business. (Working behind a counter or desk does not necessarily mean a person is a Tan. Some people take these jobs just because they need an income. This especially applies to students who take jobs before they enter their career field — unless they are in an office training for that particular career.)

Most Tans are the employees in a business rather than the owners or managers. Tan business owners and managers do exist, but Tans do not typically take the risk of starting their own business unless it is a small business with low, manageable overhead.

If you are in school, the Tans you encounter are most likely studying business, accounting, engineering, mathematics, electronics, computers, or science. Watch to see who enters these classrooms or who is reading books on these subjects at the library. (The librarians are also typically Tans.) If you are going to approach any of these Tans, learn as much about their chosen field as you can, so you can have intelligent discussions with them.

The people teaching these courses are likely to be Tans too. They slowly and methodically explain every point in each book. (Unfortunately, many of the Tans often bore their students by droning on and discussing too many details. This comment is not meant to insult the Tans. It's just a helpful way to identify them.) If you have decided you want the stability and reliability of a Tan, find a teacher you are attracted to, and you will have a winning combination. Most Tan teachers are Tan/Violet, Tan/Blue, or Tan/Yellow combinations. Tans are usually slow and deliberate when it comes to making decisions and taking action; it may be up to you to make the first move.

Many Tans attend computer classes or congregate at computer camps. It will not hurt to brush up on your computer skills and attend one of these courses if you want to meet a Tan. Also, it could be interesting to visit your local bookstore to see who is browsing the books on finances or investments. Or see who is deeply absorbed in books about architecture. Attending a financial seminar, especially one that deals with retirement planning, could be beneficial in so many ways. Tans are most interested in safe, long-term investment strategies; they are rarely found at get-rich-quick seminars.

Usually you will not find Tans in places like casinos and racetracks either. They do not enjoy taking risks, gambling, or betting against the odds. If you do venture to Las Vegas or Atlantic City, observe the people at the less risky, less expensive minimum-bet tables, not the high-stakes tables. If you find Tans in these places, they will not be throwing their money around. Some Tans will be content to sit for hours in front of the slot machines playing with nickels, dimes, or quarters. However, most Tans feel that any type of gambling is a scam and a waste of time. They know the odds are always in the house's favor.

If you attend a party or any other social gathering, typically the Tan guests will be standing inconspicuously off to the side or quietly listening to people nearby. They are not pushy people or avid conversationalists. They tend to respect people's space and privacy. Do you have any interesting ways to instigate a conversation? Tans at any events are often the workers quietly going about their business, taking care of the details.

Occasionally cruise ships have Tan workers, but they are most likely Tan/Yellow combinations. Tans prefer stable jobs, and since cruise ships are typically seasonal, it is the Yellow aspect that will have gotten the Tan/Yellow on this particular adventure.

Many Tans join the military, so if you can find any events that honor the armed forces, you will probably see Tans. Or find where Navy ships are docking to allow the sailors to come ashore for a few days of rest and relaxation. Many of these people are Tan/Yellow combinations.

Repair and delivery people can be Tan combinations. They love the challenge of working with technical details, tiny electrical wiring, or the mechanics of heating systems. There are many Tan computer repair people. It may be worthwhile to hire someone to repair something for you, rather than fixing it on your own. You could end up with a partner who will always take care of your home repairs.

Since there are many Tan combinations, it might be helpful to read the other colors' sections to see where Tan/Yellows, Tan/Violets, and so on could be hanging out. If someone is a Tan/Yellow combination, the Tan part of their personality may be at the office during the week, and their Yellow aspect could be exercising on the weekends. Even though, in general, Tans tend to be sedentary, they are logical enough to know they should exercise to maintain their health, so you may find some Tans at the gym. Tans do not usually get involved with high-risk or physically dangerous activities, so attend or participate in some of the tamer sports such as golf if you want to meet a Tan.

Greens

Occupations That Greens Are Likely to Choose

Greens prefer occupations that are mentally stimulating rather than physically demanding. Typically, they are found in white-collar careers. They love money, so they become bankers, stockbrokers, financial advisors, loan officers, and fund-raisers. They are good at sales, so they may be real estate agents, automobile salespersons, jewelers, and insurance agents.

They prefer to be mentally challenged, in charge, and in control, so they may be corporate executives, managers, administrators, directors, producers, judges, detectives, investors, developers, marketing and advertising executives, event coordinators, business owners, and entrepreneurs.

Because they enjoy competition, they can be professional golfers, gamblers, and casino owners.

Where Can I Find Greens?

One of the best places to find Greens is at a corporate office. Unless you work for a corporation yourself, however, getting inside one of these places could be a challenge. Most corporations have high security and will not let just anyone wander into their buildings. Take heart, though, because even Greens need to eat. Discover which restaurants these corporate Greens prefer to have lunch at. It will be a restaurant nearby so that they can be efficient with their time, or — if they are trying to impress a client — it will be a high-quality restaurant in the nicest area of town.

Because most Greens like to dress well and tend to spend money on quality meals, it should be easy to pick out which of the customers are Greens. Most Greens want to look good, so they take extra care with their appearance. Realize, therefore, that you will not find huge amounts of food on their plates. Look for the manicured businesspeople wearing expensive clothing and designer watches and sitting at the best tables in the restaurant. At least one of them will have the business-account credit card to pay for lunch. If one of them draws your attention, try to single that one out from the herd as they leave the table. Make sure you have a business card, with your name and number, readily available in your hand. This is how Greens do business.

Chances are, the restaurant owner and manager will also be Greens. If you catch the attention of these dignified Greens, they may, in an attempt to impress you, give you a complimentary meal. Greens love to appear affluent and important.

You may work at one of the corporate offices yourself, in which case you have the opportunity to meet many Greens at the weekly planning meetings. Or you may be chosen to travel to another city to attend a strategy meeting at corporate headquarters. There may also be training programs that the sales department is required to attend. Unfortunately, if you are a delivery person entering one of these corporate inner sanctums, you probably will not be approached for a date. Greens require mates who make at least as much money as they do. They want to respect their partners as equals or admire them as superiors.

If corporate Greens are not your style, you can also find these driven workers at your bank. One of them could be your loan officer, your bank teller, or the bank president. Greens do not like their time wasted — they are busy people — but if you have questions about your account, this can be a valid way to meet a Green. Visiting your local stockbroker's office will reveal a bevy of Greens too. Or walk into any real estate office and scan the room. Most likely every real estate agent, office worker, and manager is a Green.

If you attend a seminar on financial investing, you will be surrounded by a roomful of Greens. Because these bright, motivated people like to be in positions of authority, you can also encounter them managing hotels and running restaurants. Your best bet is to focus on the management of the establishment, however, not on the workers. Many Greens are business owners, so pay attention to the owner or the manager of any place of business that you enter. You might also spend the day shopping for cars. Most of the salespeople will be Greens.

Sometimes the Chamber of Commerce in a city will sponsor a singles' mixer as a networking event. Because this is a good opportunity for Greens to make business connections or to meet potential intelligent partners, they attend these functions. Also, most of the fund-raising events for charities are attended by Greens. Greens and Violets are usually the people with money that charities depend on for support.

It can be challenging to find Greens at play, other than on the golf course, because it is hard to get them away from the office. The golf course seems to be a great place for Greens to conduct business, and they consider golf more civilized than some of the other sports. Unless you are a member, you may not be able to gain entrance to the more exclusive clubs, but maybe you can have lunch at a club that is open to the public.

You will find a vast reservoir of Greens at casinos. They will probably be playing cards or rolling dice at the high-stakes tables. Making quick and easy money is fun for them, but they have a more important reason for gambling. Most Greens already have enough money. They love the thrill of winning. You can also find them gambling at horse races, boxing matches, and other sporting events. Realize that Greens prefer to sit in the more expensive seats; do not be fooled into thinking everyone at a sporting event is a Green. (Yellows also like to play in the casinos and at sporting events, but most do not make the kind of money Greens do.)

Many doctors are Yellow/Green combinations, so occasionally you can meet a Green at the hospital. It is more common, however, to find a Green's name on the hospital as a major benefactor.

Blues

Occupations That Blues Are Likely to Choose

Blues are usually found in careers that enable them to help people. They especially want to offer personal emotional guidance and support, and so they may be found serving as counselors, therapists, psychics, teachers, nurses, physicians, physical therapists, social workers, child-care workers, secretaries, and volunteers.

They are highly spiritual and may be ministers, clergy, missionaries, nuns, supportive office workers, and volunteers at their chosen place of worship. They are also found working as volunteers everywhere they may be needed — nonprofit organizations, disaster areas, schools, and fund-raising events. They cherish home and families, so they are often mothers, nannies, and housekeepers.

Where Can I Find Blues?

The biggest challenge in finding Blues is that they love to be at home. Blues enjoy nesting, so they typically are found cozily snuggled in their homes, reading a book, preparing a meal, or warming up their environment. And yet Blues are the Love Colors who have the strongest desire to be in love and share their lives with devoted partners. They live for love.

Special note to Blues: Come out into the world so people can meet you! We know you have been praying to meet the love of your life. We also know it's awkward and uncomfortable for you to wander around different places hoping someone will eventually find you and choose to love you. Of course, it would easier if your beloved would just show up at your door. We know you prefer to be home. But your future partner is having a difficult time finding your house. Show yourself out here in the world so the person who has been searching for you this entire lifetime can finally discover you. We know you may feel embarrassed, but just make eye contact and smile. You don't need to marry everyone who asks you out, so don't be concerned about hurting anyone's feelings by saying no. And don't be afraid that no one will love you. It's time you realize that you are perfectly lovable. Just be your compassionate and considerate self. Have faith your life mate does exist.

Fortunately, Blues eventually do leave their homes. They need to buy food. And they want to help others, so look for them in places where people need help. Attend a fund-raising event for the charity of your choice. Blues will be the tireless workforce behind the event — you can arrive early to help them hang the decorations. They will also be bringing in the home-baked goods to sell at the raffle, and later they will be at the registration table or taking tickets at the door.

If you are participating in the charity walkathon, notice who is passing out water and treats to the walkers: it will most likely be the supportive Blues. It is possible that a Blue/Yellow will be one of the walkers. Or see who is answering the phones at the telethon.

If you yourself are a humanitarian, volunteering at any nonprofit organization, hospital, help center, or disaster area can be a great idea, because Blues will be found as volunteers at all these locations. And since Blues typically have a hard time saying no, you have a good chance of getting a date with one of these helpers — unless the Blue you pick is already married. Blues are monogamous and rarely stray — unless they are Blue/Yellow or Blue/Violet combinations.

Hospitals are especially good places to volunteer, because not only will you meet Blue volunteers but also most of the nurses and office workers will be Blues. Some Blues are doctors, but most doctors are Yellows, Blue/Yellows, or other Yellow combinations.

Spiritual growth is a strong priority for Blues. Many spiritual re-treats are offered around the world, and if you find one that interests you, you may meet a very loving, openhearted Blue there. Or attend a church, synagogue, or any other religious center that fits in with your own beliefs. These places often hold special events for singles. Lectures or workshops that feature a spiritual teacher or leader will have many Blues in the audience eagerly learning new information and lending their moral support to these cherished or idolized teachers.

Typically Blues have many Blue friends, since they tend to be psy-chically drawn to one another. Since Blues love getting married, you are more than likely to meet at least one of the unmarried Blue friends at a wedding. See if you can find a clever way to separate the Blue you are attracted to from the rest of their friends so you can talk with them alone.

Blues do not usually like to go places by themselves, because they tend to be self-conscious. Most of them prefer to attend parties, dinners, or other events with their friends, and most of these sensitive souls will not break free from their crowd. If you are courageous enough to approach a Blue who is surrounded by a well-meaning but protective circle of companions, keep in mind that most of them will know by then that their Blue friend does not always choose the right dates, and they will be scrutinizing you on their friend's behalf.

If you are in school, you'll find that Blues are often studying psy-chology, sociology, nursing, child care, or teaching. Casually standing outside the doors of these classrooms, you may find Blues who catch your eye as they walk by. Blues are also the teachers of these classes, so notice who is speaking to the class.

Attend PTA meetings or other school events where concerned Blue teachers and mothers are discussing the welfare of the children. Or perhaps look for single parents sitting on the sidelines at any school's sporting event — they will be enthusiastically cheering on their children. Blues are dedicated to their children.

They also usually love cats, so if there are any events involving cats — cat shows, for example — it might be fun and educational to attend. Strike up a conversation with cat owners as well as with the people strolling around. Or see who is volunteering to take care of the cats at your local animal shelter. Maybe volunteer yourself on different days to see if there are different Blues taking different shifts. Or you could simply hang out in the cat food aisle at the pet store to see who picks up cat food. Just make sure you check prospective Blues for any wedding rings. A lot of Blues marry young, but there are many, many single ones still waiting for their fairy-tale romance.

Another good place to spot Blues is at sentimental movies. These are their favorite films — romantic comedies, period romances, and even dramatic love stories. Or go to the bookstore to see who is browsing through the romantic novels, books about finding love, or magazines giving advice on relationships. You may actually be lucky enough to find a Blue standing alone at a bookstore. They prefer being with friends, but they will shop alone sometimes. You usually won't see them dining alone, though. That's embarrassing for them.

Since Blues are such loyal and dedicated workers, it can be challenging to find them outside playing. They don't always take time to attend to their own needs. Generally, they don't even make time to exercise or take care of their bodies, because they feel they have more important things to do — which is usually taking care of everyone else.

If all else fails, go to the grocery stores and markets. These home-bodies do need to eat, and they usually prepare their own meals. If you see people you find attractive, talk to them. Blues are so considerate, they would never think of hurting your feelings. Just be kind and respectful of theirs. You don't want to frighten these sensitive creatures.

Remember, though, there are also Blue combinations in the world — Blue/Yellows, Blue/Violets, Blue/Greens, and so on — so you could always check the other colors' lists to see various places that those combinations might be hanging out. Since Yellows like to exercise, you may actually find Blue/Yellows jogging or walking their dogs at the park.

Violets

Occupations That Violets Are Likely to Choose

Violets are drawn to the performing arts, media, and entertainment business as actors, musicians, singers, artists, film or television producers, directors, photographers, and writers. Most Violets have a desire to inspire, educate, or help the masses, and so they may become teachers, therapists, seminar speakers and lecturers, ministers, clergy, missionaries, activists, environmentalists, politicians, mediators, police officers, detectives, or attorneys.

Violets need freedom; therefore, they tend to work for themselves, and they may become international businesspersons, developers, consultants, entrepreneurs, and world leaders. They also love to travel, so they may take jobs as pilots, travel agents, flight attendants, tour guides, or foreign language interpreters.

Where Can I Find Violets?

When Violets are in power, they are the most visible of the Love Colors. Many of them are performers of some kind or another, and you can find them onstage acting, singing, dancing, or speaking. You could volunteer backstage at your local playhouse or resident theater — work on set construction, design costumes, or anything else the company needs.

Taking singing, music, or acting lessons will put you in contact with Violets. Even if you join an amateur choir or singing group just for fun, at least you'll be in the presence of Violets. Attending concerts or other music events, you'll be able to see many Violet music lovers. Violets flock to jazz clubs, rock and roll events, operas, and any other type of musical performance.

Take dance lessons or join dance groups — swing, ballroom, salsa, it doesn't matter. Violets, especially Violet/Yellows, love to dance.

There will be a host of Violets and Yellow/Violets at writers' conferences. Strike up a conversation with one of these fascinating people. Just make sure you keep the conversation interesting — maybe by discussing current topics. And most Violets love to talk, so make sure you know how to listen attentively.

Photographers are usually Violets. You can walk into your local camera stores to see who is purchasing film or camera equipment. If you see photographs in galleries or restaurants that appeal to you, find out the photographers' names. You can go on the Internet to see if they have studios, or if they will be having exhibits of their work. Once you locate them, you can discuss photography with them. Ask them questions about getting started in this field. There are also various film schools and classes offered at colleges — maybe sit outside one of the classrooms to see who is interested in photography. Or take a class yourself. Also, notice the photographer at the next wedding you attend.

Violets can be passionate about cultural events — especially global or ethnic events. You'll find Violets attending art openings, cultural festivals, travel documentaries, and lectures or films about other countries. They love to expand their minds, so they attend lectures on everything from space exploration to philosophy to new science and consciousness.

Because Violets love to learn, they can be found at bookstores and libraries. Avid readers, they also attend book clubs where they passionately discuss the current selection's metaphors and story line. Sitting in on these groups will enable you to get to know some of the Violets there. While you're at the bookstore, wander through the travel section. Out of all the Love Colors, Violets are the biggest travelers, and if they have not traveled all over the world, they think about it.

Consider checking out the law libraries or sitting in courtrooms to watch the Violet judges and attorneys in action. Or attend city council meetings to see which Violets are involved in community programs. The public is encouraged to attend these meetings, so don't feel like you're invading something private.

Many Violets are concerned about the state of the world, so you can often find them at political rallies and demonstrations. They get involved in cause-related fund-raisers, benefits, and other awareness-raising events, so try attending concerts for peace, events that help disaster victims, or marches for charities, and you will meet many passionate humanitarian Violets. They will be speaking at or supporting events that have political, global, or environmental debates. Violets believe in using their voices — communicating and educating — rather than using physical violence to promote change.

Volunteer or work with a global, humanitarian, environmental, or animal charity — Amnesty International, Direct Relief International, the Peace Corps, Children International, the Wildlife Conservation Society, and so on. These nonprofit organizations are filled with Violets.

Violets are typically spiritual, so you will find them in all types of religious or spiritual places — churches, mosques, synagogues, temples, and simple spiritual gatherings. Exploring different spiritual events, seminars, retreats, or ceremonies is an interesting way to meet Violets. Discover which spiritual beliefs and practices you are drawn to, then attend meetings or services that support those beliefs. This could be a great way to rendezvous with a Violet.

Since Violets love to travel, you could meet a wonderful Violet sitting next to you on the plane. Don't be timid; strike up a conversation. Being natural communicators, they will most likely join in. Many pilots and flight attendants are also Violets, and your travel agent probably is too.

Sitting in any hotel lobby, you could encounter a Violet traveler. Find the hotels that especially cater to traveling businesspeople rather than those that cater to families. Violets often travel for their jobs. Or if you are younger and want to meet students who are traveling internationally, then staying in smaller, less expensive hotels, hostels, or pensions is a good way to find these adventurers. You may even come across some dining in the cafés and restaurants near such hotels and hostels. Or hang out at the train stations to see if you find foreign students coming or going. European travelers are especially familiar with traveling by train.

Joining travel clubs, taking cruises, and accompanying different groups to various worldwide locations could reward you with a permanent travel companion. Violets travel everywhere — exotic global locations, spiritual vortexes, cultural hubs, historic monuments, romantic cities, and remote island hideaways. Choose the places that appeal to you, because there will be Violets exploring those same locations. If your budget doesn't allow you to travel all the time, then attend travel lectures, movies about other countries, or museums and galleries featuring unusual artifacts from around the world. Take a foreign language class to meet those who are planning to travel.

Many Violets are interested in psychology and philosophy. Watch listings at your local bookstores to see who might be speaking on these subjects. Violets are always eager to learn new things, so they are likely to attend lectures on these topics.

School is a fine place to meet Violets interested in expanding their minds, increasing their opportunities, or learning new ways to contribute something to the world, so consider taking a continuing education course yourself. Many Violets study anthropology, world religions, sociology, spiritual psychology, mythology, and other subjects that involve humanity. They are also interested in photography, writing, music, and film studies. And many, many Violets are teachers. Attend any functions that draw these concerned beings. They truly want to make a difference, and they are passionate about the things they believe in. It shouldn't be difficult to get them to open up once you discover which subjects are their favorites.

Indigos

Occupations That Indigos Are Likely to Choose

Indigos don't always relate to the concept of work since they often believe that everything is energy and should manifest into whatever form they ask it to take. However, they are usually retrained at a young age to believe in a more traditional way of thinking, which is that people work for a living. Working for others can be restrictive if there are too many rules. Starting their own businesses and being responsible for employees, however, can be too much of a burden for Indigos. They often do well in jobs that allow them to be independent yet still provide financial security. Or they do well in their own independent creative work.

Indigos are typically intelligent but also highly sensitive. Most are too susceptible to tension to work in the fast-paced business world. They enjoy jobs that enable them to be creative, to teach, or to love and support others. They also enjoy occupations that allow them the freedom to travel or to connect with others from around the world.

Indigos have the sensitivity and patience to work with children, as teachers, educators, child-care workers, and nannies. And they have great compassion for people in general and may work as counselors, social workers, health practitioners, mediators, humanitarians, and volunteers.

They have the ability to understand and communicate with animals and nature, so they may choose to be animal caretakers, veterinarians, pet sitters, animal communicators and trainers, horticulturists, florists, environmentalists, botanists, landscape designers, and gardeners. They often exhibit creative talent and are artists, musicians, writers, actors, dancers, photographers, filmmakers, and designers.

Indigos seem to have an innate understanding of computers and technology, and they may be computer operators, programmers, analysts, and web designers.

Where Can I Find Indigos?

Usually, Indigos remain quietly in the background. They do not need the attention of the masses. Occasionally a talented Indigo/Violet such as Michael Jackson shows up in the spotlight, but this is a rarity.

These loving souls are often found helping children, so if you can attend any of the Special Olympic events or fund-raisers for children who have health challenges, you will probably meet some kind Indigos working with the kids. Volunteering your services may put you alongside them for days during preparation and practices, and you will be providing a loving service as well. You will get to see Indigos in action as they live the loving philosophies they believe in.

They can also be found working in preschools or serving as art and music teachers for children. If you don't have children of your own to bring to these Indigos, then possibly you would like to work as a teacher's aide in some of the classes? They are typically found at Montessori or other alternative schools that promote creativity and individuality.

The creative Indigos may wander into art galleries or attend art openings, so if you like to go to these yourself keep your eyes open for them. An Indigo will often arrive alone, which could make it less intimidating to start up a conversation.

You may even find these artists writing their novels or painting their masterpieces outdoors — in the park, a garden, or the woods or on the beach. Indigos love to work in nature because they feel so spiritually connected there. Many of the creative Indigos appear to be artistic savants, science fiction or spiritual writers, or musicians who play magnificently well beyond their age. There seems to be no rational explanation for their extraordinarily advanced talents. Some of these gifted persons are withdrawn and shy, choosing to focus only on their craft, whereas other Indigos are open extroverts who are happy to offer great words of wisdom while they work.

Indigos see that the world in general is not functioning well, that we are not living up to our greatest human potential. They do not understand why we still have such issues as war, famine, illnesses, and pollution. Because they are concerned for the planet's current predicament, they will attend concerts and other charitable events that raise money and awareness on behalf of humanitarian or environmental causes. But they will not typically be loud, antagonistic protestors. You will rarely see Indigos angrily protesting a war, not because they support wars, but because they do not believe in using force and aggression to eliminate violence and injustice. Indigos will participate in events that peacefully support education and tolerance but usually not attend those that encourage hostility and anger. In power, Indigos support understanding and harmony, so to meet them it's best to attend events that reflect their values — those that promote cooperation, education, love, and tolerance.

Because they love animals so deeply, and because they feel such a camaraderie and empathy with the earth's creatures, Indigos often work with animals. You may find Indigos at your local veterinarian's office. Pay attention to both the doctor and the assistants. You could take care of helpless little creatures and maybe meet a kindhearted Indigo if you volunteer at an animal shelter or animal rescue operation. Your local zoo could also reveal a few Indigo workers, since Indigos especially enjoy caring for exotic animals. Some of the younger ones may start out working at pet stores, especially those that allow them to love and comfort the animals. Indigos frequently get involved with charitable events that raise money for endangered species. If you don't want to volunteer at any of these organizations, you could always attend one of the fund-raising functions.

Since Indigos love nature, you may even find one giving nature tours — teaching people how to respect and care for wildlife and the environment. Often only a nominal donation is requested on these tours, so if you have found a particularly appealing Indigo guide, it may be worthwhile to take the tour over and over again. If you share the Indigo's concern for the welfare of the environment and the animals, this may endear you to him or her.

Because they have such an affinity for nature, you can also find Indigos caring for the environment in other ways too — planting trees, protecting wildlife, or saving the rain forest. If you can find ways to do the same, you may find yourself shoulder to shoulder with one of these amazing souls. Many communities celebrate Arbor Day by holding tree-planting ceremonies. Is this the case in your area? Or you may find Indigos creating wonderful environments as landscape or topiary designers. If you find some gently trimming the trees and bushes to look like their favorite animals, let them know you appreciate their art.

If you enjoy spending time in the wild, notice the many nature lovers who may be hiking in the same area. Most Indigos do not enjoy crowds, so you may find a solitary Indigo sitting on a rock next to a quiet stream or high on the mountaintop overlooking the scenery. Be still for a while, so you can observe whether or not you have a meditating Indigo in your sight. These spiritual souls need to have peace and quiet to reconnect with their inner voice. Once your Indigo has finished meditating, you are free to approach — and you may find you have located one who would love to have company. Indigos are curious about people and often love to be able to discuss life with someone. Most are not shy, so they will tell you honestly if they would rather be alone. In power, Indigos are usually considerate of people's feelings, so no need to fear being harshly rejected.

Indigos believe that we are all connected, that we are all in this together, and that if one person suffers, then all of humanity suffers. Because of this belief, Indigos often get involved with organizations like Habitat for Humanity and the Peace Corps. They are often found in disaster areas, lovingly helping those in need. They believe that helping one helps many. They often love to do global work, to travel to other countries to be of service to those in need. If you are also a traveler and are drawn to these same areas, you may encounter Indigos. Be open and honest if you have a chance to commune with any Indigos. You have the best chance of forming healthy relationships with them if they see you are being authentic. They need to be able to trust the people around them.

Since Indigos are here to enjoy living in a global community, they love to explore cultural and ethnic events. It might be fun to attend multicultural festivals, dances, plays, or music events where people from around the world are enjoying the international diversity. Indigos also see value in serving others and being in alignment with their spiritual beliefs, so you can find these unassuming individuals quietly working in supportive roles at their churches, synagogues, or temples. They do not insist that others believe what they do. If you are drawn to a particular faith or belief system, you may meet an Indigo at one of the spiritual services. Or attend a spiritual gathering or retreat center where one or more of these beings may be looking for others who share their interests and values.

Occasionally, the creative Indigos show up at writers' conferences. Watch for the people who are listening intently. Indigos look for speakers and teachers who are intelligent, who talk about high ideals and principles, and who impart these same ideals.

Many Indigos intuitively and instinctively know a lot, but they are also curious explorers, so you may find a few in classrooms. They seem to especially be interested in subjects like psychology, world religions, art, music, anthropology, and philosophy. If you enjoy learning and are also intrigued by these subjects, Indigos may be wonderful study partners. They will enjoy having inspired discussions with you.

And many seem to have a quick and innate ability to understand technology — even from a very young age, most are highly adept at using computers. Their skills baffle most people, especially if the Indigos have little or no previous training in these areas. So if you work in an office, watch your co-workers to see who seems to operate a computer like it is part of them.

Lavenders

Occupations That Lavenders Are Likely to Choose

The simple and friendly Lavenders work best in quiet, low-stress environments that allow them plenty of time to daydream and create. Working in office jobs that require a lot of concentration or that carry a lot of responsibility is detrimental to their health. They shrivel at the first sign of pressure and can become physically ill if exposed to too much stress. They are typically too forgetful and scattered to stay organized. They usually struggle to remember details.

Lavenders enjoy creativity and may be artists, writers, interior decorators, set designers, costume designers, hairdressers, makeup artists, cosmetologists, fashion designers, florists, and musicians. They love fantasy and creative expression, so they may become dancers, mimes, or storytellers. Lavenders also relate to children and may serve as preschool, kindergarten, or elementary school teachers; art and music teachers; and teacher's aides.

Where Can I Find Lavenders?

If Lavenders can stay focused in their bodies long enough to produce something tangible, they make excellent artists. While many of them can spend hours creating wonderful paintings, magnificent flowing sculptures, fanciful jewelry, or lovely poetry, most, unfortunately, do not believe in themselves enough to bring their work into the world. So it can be rare to find their art out in public. And even if they are willing to show their work, they typically do not have a strong enough business mentality to market it.

However, sometimes Lavenders have a chance encounter with someone who loves their work and has the ability to promote it. If you are looking for artwork by Lavenders in galleries or stores, locate the paintings or sculptures that feature mythological creatures, fairies, elves, or angels. Their art typically reflects a magical, spiritual, or otherworldly quality. The whimsical Lavenders love using their imagination, and they prefer fantasy. Usually the colors they use are light, flowing, and ethereal. Once you find this type of artwork, find the artist's name and contact information. Possibly the gallery will feature this person in a special showing. If not, you can always contact this creative soul directly to see if there is any magic between you.

Wandering into your nearest furniture store to see which interior designers are working that day may be an interesting approach. Or go to design expos to see who is featuring their latest ideas. Lavenders are drawn to this type of work, so if you can travel to locations where they have these expositions for interior decorators and designers, you may be lucky enough to fall in love with a Lavender.

Careers in the performing arts appeal to Lavenders because these give them the opportunity to explore their imagination and creativity. Professional theaters can be an excellent place to encounter these souls. You will have to find access to the backstage area, however. They are not usually organized enough to work in the box office or interested in just taking tickets at the door. Often the dancers are Lavenders, and occasionally you can find a Lavender actor, but most of them are too shy and sensitive to perform in front of large audiences. They prefer to stay safely hidden in the background.

They will usually be behind the scenes as the set designers or the makeup artists. You could have a great time playing with the people involved with the show. If you don't actually work at one of these theaters, maybe volunteer your time for a particular performance — help paint the sets or assist the performers with their costumes. Being around these creative creatures could give you a good sense of what it would be like to be involved with a Lavender, and a good indication of whether or not a Lavender is a good match for you.

Lavenders often love to work with small children, so you may find them in preschools or in alternative schools where the kids are encouraged to express their creativity and individual talents. Lavenders prefer to work in environments that are less structured and less dogmatic than most are. If you have children in any of the Montessori schools or other alternative educational systems, see if any of the gentle and patient Lavenders are working as teachers or teacher's assistants — you may find them involved with arts and crafts or music.

If you don't have children of your own, these schools often hold fund-raisers to make money to support their programs, so you could always be a volunteer or a generous donator and attend their event. Other Lavenders are also drawn to support these events. Or go to your public library and local bookstores when they present story time for children. See if any of the fun-loving storytellers catch your eye. There may be children's events in the parks, where the entertainers, the clowns, mimes, musicians, or singers are the simple Lavenders. Keep in mind that, since most Lavenders are too fearful and embarrassed to face potential rejection, they appreciate people who are willing to initiate the conversation.

If you stroll through parks, keep your eyes open for the quiet Lavenders. They love to surround themselves with flowers or rest by tranquil lily ponds. You may find them sitting quietly on benches enjoying the serenity. Even though they are usually shy and introverted, they are still friendly. If you sit quietly next to them, you may eventually share a pleasant conversation.

Occasionally Lavenders are found working in hair salons. They express their gentle, creative nature through coloring hair, painting nails, or giving facials. There are even Lavender massage therapists in some of these salons. Wouldn't it be wonderful to pamper yourself with a manicure or a massage? If you don't meet the partner of your dreams in one salon, try another. Beauty salons abound in most areas, and having a manicure once a week is not that costly.

Since Lavenders typically love flowers, wander into some of your local floral shops to see if any Lavenders are working there. If you find one who strikes your fancy, maybe you could buy that person some of the flowers. It might be fun to order the flowers and have them shipped to that very person at the shop. Or you could always take your time wandering through the store, choosing a variety of flowers, as your Lavender worker puts together the arrangement for you. This particular florist may enjoy your asking for her or his opinion on favorite flowers. Once the transaction is complete, if you felt any small spark between you and the helpful florist, go somewhere else to find an accompanying gift — a box of chocolates or a small trinket. Then return a short time later to surprise this Lavender with both the bouquet and the small gift. And perhaps, if you receive a warm smile of appreciation, you will also receive a positive response to your dinner invitation.

There are a wide variety of other places to meet the naïve Lavenders. They are often clerks in retail stores, servers in fast-food restaurants, or receptionists in small offices. The truth is that many of the childlike Lavenders, like the Yellows, do not stay focused enough or motivated long enough to follow through on their dream careers. Many end up in basic, paycheck-producing jobs where they are not happy and ultimately do not belong. An ideal situation for many of the ungrounded Lavenders would be to have a trust fund that supported them throughout their lives so they could just focus on their creative interests and simple pleasures.

Crystals

Occupations That Crystals Are Likely to Choose

Crystals tend to be found in quiet, simple, reflective, and serene environments. For the most part, they prefer the security of working for others. They arc not usually powerful or ambitious enough to start their own businesses, but they do prefer jobs where they can work quietly and alone. However, the healing fields are the areas where Crystals express their greatest and most natural talents. They are especially interested in holistic medicine. They are natural healers and energy workers and may be massage therapists, chiropractors, acupuncturists, physicians, nurses, physical therapists, dentists, dental hygienists, counselors, teachers, herbalists, or aroma or craniosacral therapists.

They love quiet, low-key offices where they can take care of the details, so you may find them working as librarians, secretaries, receptionists, office assistants, researchers, clinicians, editors, and medical technicians.

They are also naturally creative and may be interior decorators, writers, artists, florists, illustrators, designers, and musicians — especially those who play soft, melodic instruments like the harp, flute, violin, cello, or piano. Crystals appreciate the quiet beauty of nature and may work as gardeners, flower or herb growers, landscapers, and topiary designers. They love spiritual serenity and solitude, so some choose to be nuns, monks, priests, lamas, or rabbis.

Where Can I Find Crystals?

Crystals can be some of the most challenging people to find and meet. Not only are they a rare Love Color, but they tend to hide out. They also camouflage themselves by pretending to be other colors. It can be challenging to identify a real Crystal even after you have encountered one.

They typically spend a lot of time alone in their own home, office, or sanctuary. They are very private, introspective people, so chances are they will not be outgoing enough to approach you. Crystals and some of the introverted, sensitive Yellows have a lot in common and can easily be mistaken for one another. You have to pay close attention to details to notice the small differences between them; otherwise, you won't be able to distinguish one from the other.

You may find quiet Crystals working at your local libraries. If you can keep your voice down and be very polite, you may be able to engage one in a conversation. If you find yourself attracted to one of these workers, ask for help locating a certain book, or explain that you are doing research on a particularly unusual subject and that you need extra assistance.

Or spend some time in galleries and museums. Crystals appreciate fine art, so these are natural places to encounter them. They can often be found wandering around quietly by themselves. They are genuinely interested in learning about the artists and their work, so if you brush up on the artists, you could have an intelligent and interesting conversation with the Crystals you meet in such places.

These creative individuals also enjoy beautiful, soothing music, so attending classical concerts or string quartet performances may be a delightful way to spend the afternoon and an opportunity to make new friends. Watch your newspaper to see if there are any sophisticated art or music events happening in your area. Crystals do not stray out in public often, but they will brave small crowds to attend fine cultural events. Pay attention to the guests sitting quietly off to the side or in the back of the theater. One of them may be a Crystal.

If you attend an afternoon wedding or other social event, notice the unassuming harpist playing almost unnoticed in the background, or find out who provided the floral arrangements. Occasionally these will be Crystals, although they could be Crystals' sensitive and creative Yellow counterparts.

Assuming you get medical or other health checkups occasionally, see if you are attracted to your physician, nurse, dentist, hygienist, chiropractor, acupuncturist, energy worker, alternative healer, or any of the office personnel. If not, find out which hotel will be hosting medical, dental, or healing conferences. There are many of these gatherings, and they attract healers from around the country. Sit in the lobby to see if anyone catches your eye. Also, Crystals give wonderful healing massages, so if you have the time, money, and inclination, you could try out many different massage therapists to see if you fall in love with one of them.

Remember these gentle beings are usually shy and reserved. They could be reticent even about making eye contact with you, so you may have to come up with interesting but sincere opening remarks. Never come on too strong with Crystals. Doing so will frighten them away for sure. If the conference lasts for a couple of days, this will give you time to take a slow but steady approach. Sincerity is the key when talking to these souls. Crystals appreciate people who are sensitive, honest, and calm. Know that they can also be extremely bright, so do not misinterpret their quiet nature for a lack of intelligence.

For another approach, your city may have flower and orchid shows. Find out when and where, and mosey on in to see which delicate Crystals are appreciating the beauty and smelling the roses. Or attend a home and garden show. Crystals do not like crowds, so go early, before it gets too busy. Crystals love to find beautiful items to decorate their homes. Or find stores that feature crystals, chimes, and New Age books and music. Crystals often wander into these serene environments to feel the calming, peaceful energy. They may hope to have a synchronistic encounter with another rare Crystal, someone who may be from their same loving, spiritual soul family.

Now that you understand how quiet and sensitive Crystals can be, here's a twist: If they have been spending time with other colors, Crystals' personalities change radically. If the Crystals you are attracted to have been fraternizing with Greens, their behavior will be much

stronger and bolder. If they have surrounded themselves with supportive Blue friends, you will see the same Blue behavior in these Crystals.

Crystals appreciate partners who are comfortable with their sometimes confusing and changeable personality traits. If you can learn to go
with the flow, you may be excited and stimulated by their different personalities. If not, you could become one very scattered and perplexed
life partner.

Chapter 7

Intermission — Inner Mission: Simple Steps to Allow Love into Your Life

Let's take a short a break from exploring the external things you can do to meet your special someone and consider the inner work you can do to make this journey much easier. Taking care of your inner well-being — your thoughts and beliefs — is just as important as, if not more important than, any of the external steps you may take to create your perfect relationship. Balancing your inner world and making sure you are open, willing, and emotionally prepared to be in a healthy, fulfilling relationship is paramount in creating a successful, happy relationship.

You may have had a number of relationships. Possibly they all began pleasantly enough, but then they eventually eroded into something unsatisfying, disappointing, or even painful. You may have identified a familiar pattern in your relationships or a similarity in your choices of mates. If your relationships all seem to be alike, with the same issues emerging again and again, these are sure signs that you have one or more limiting beliefs that are perpetually causing the same outcomes. In order to change the outcomes, you have to change your thoughts, beliefs, and actions.

If you have beliefs that are counterproductive to having a great relationship, then ultimately none of the information in this book will help you. If you honestly believe you want love in your life, but you subconsciously fear being involved with another person, then even if you go to all the right places and meet the Love Color perfect for you, you could find a way to sabotage your relationship.

See if you hold any of the following beliefs:

- Finding the right person is hard.

- There are just not that many available single people out there — at least, not many that I find attractive.

- Even if I do find someone I like, that person probably won't be interested in me, at least not for the long term.

- I need to change some things about me before someone will find me desirable: I should lose weight; change my appearance to look younger, prettier, or more handsome; get bigger breasts or a nose job; or make more money.

- I don't know how to meet the right person.

- I have chosen the wrong people in the past, so I can't trust myself to make better choices now.

- I will eventually find a mate, sometime in the future. (How much time something takes to come into your life depends on how safe you feel having it. That which you desire will show up in your life as soon as you are truly willing to accept and receive it.)

- I may end up single my entire life, even though most of my friends find love.

- Love hurts.

- I think most people have mediocre relationships. Most of the couples I've seen seem bored or unhappy. Or they may act happy, but I think they probably fight or are secretly dissatisfied with their partners.

- It's not okay for me to be happy and fulfilled when so many other people are suffering.

- It's not possible to have everything I desire. I will have to compromise in order to be with someone.

- My standards are too high.

- I am so strong and intelligent that I intimidate most people.

- There is a good chance that I will get hurt again. The person I choose could eventually reject me and leave me.

- I may like someone more than he or she likes me.

- The next partner I choose could end up disappointing me the same way the last one did.

- Being with the same person my entire life might get boring. The excitement eventually wears off, and then people are stuck with the everyday business of life.

- After a while, couples stop having sex and feeling passion.

- I am not making enough money, or my finances are a mess, so someone could become angry or disappointed in me.

- I may have to take care of someone financially, which could drain away my money.

- I may have to give more than I receive.

- Men (or women) tend to cheat on their partners, which means they could cheat on me.

- I don't know if I can be trusted. I may get restless and want to be with another person.

- I am so frustrated that nothing has worked out for me. I just need to give up and not think about it. If I pretend it doesn't bother me, then someone will show up — maybe.

- My parents did not have a great relationship, and I certainly do not want to end up like them.

- My parents had a wonderful, loving relationship, and I want to find someone exactly like my mother or father. But so far, no one has matched them.

- I could really fall in love with someone, and then something bad could happen — like, that person could die.

- I am alone and single.

You may have some of these or many other similar beliefs. Any one of them can keep you from attracting a wonderful partner or allowing him or her into your life. These limiting and fear-based beliefs may be responsible for the delay you're experiencing in being with your best partner. Most of these beliefs reveal fear. Fear can be powerful. It has the ability to keep us from accomplishing great things in our lives, including experiencing fulfilling relationships. Some of the beliefs reveal limiting definitions we have of ourselves. These definitions can limit our experiences. If you continue to see yourself as single, you will most likely continue to live as a single person. It's possible that if you imagined and perceived yourself as part of a happy couple you would become that.

Imagine the game of tug-of-war. If one side of you desires to have a loving partner, but the other side of you fears it and wants to avoid it, then your two sides will pull the rope back and forth but not get very far. In order to move your life forward, you need to eliminate your resistance. One side or the other has to walk away with the rope.

Once you uncover some of your limiting and self-defeating beliefs, you can take action to detach them. Doing the following exercises can be a very effective method to diffuse these powerful, blocking beliefs.

If you *really* believe — no, if you really *know* you can keep thinking and behaving as you have been and your love will eventually show up, then you need not look at your beliefs and behaviors. As long as you really *know* love is already on its way, then trust that. Just relax and enjoy your life.

However, if you sense that your fears or beliefs are sabotaging your happiness, then this process is meant to assist you. No one but you is going to know if you did these exercises. No one is forcing you to change or to do anything else. These exercises are meant to help you improve your life

If you choose to continue with this process, then begin by writing a thorough list of all the thoughts and beliefs you have about relationships, past partners, and the negative things that might happen if you were to meet someone. The list of statements above may help you get started with your own list. Yes, making this list will take some time, and yes, it may be uncomfortable to look at all the fears and negative thoughts you have. But you are worth it. And what else would you prefer to do? Are you just going to continue doing what you've been doing, hoping that someday something will change? Has that worked so far? When are you going to commit to making *you* a priority and get rid of these limiting beliefs? When will you move these blocks out of your way so you can have a fulfilling relationship?

I realize you may have undertaken similar processes before, and you probably think nothing changed. But maybe something did change and you don't realize it. Is anything different in your life? Have you changed? Did you really focus your time and energy on changing your circumstances by changing your thoughts and beliefs? Well, are you willing to do it again?

The second step is important. Realize that each statement on your list is just a *belief* you hold about reality, not reality itself. Even if you have created or gathered a lot of evidence to support your belief, it is still just a belief you hold about yourself or reality.

Begin to challenge each belief by asking if it is in fact the truth. Write down questions and thoughts that can negate the fear-based belief you wrote down. Is it necessary, for example, for you to create the same dysfunctional, unfulfilling relationship that your parents created? After all, aren't they different people with personalities different from yours? Don't they have their own issues, fears, and beliefs, which you don't have? Take the time to go through and challenge each and every limiting belief, until it releases its grip on you. You may not have really challenged the veracity of these beliefs before. You may have just accepted them as fact, as unchangeable truths. Believe that you can change your circumstances.

Rather than holding on to the belief, and therefore the picture — and therefore the experience — that "I am single," change your belief to: "I am part of a loving, compatible relationship. We are perfect together. Whether or not I have met this partner, this person exists, right now, and we perfectly match each other. We are a couple." Stop seeing yourself as single and see yourself as already in a loving, fulfilling relationship.

Here is a list of potential alternative beliefs that you could incorporate into your life to change your experiences. If you like any of these new beliefs, focus on them instead of your old, limiting beliefs and use your imagination to reinforce the new beliefs and pictures.

- My partner and I are currently headed right to each other. We are finding our way easily and effortlessly.

- There are so many wonderful, single, attractive, and available people in the world. It would be easy to love any of them. As I meet and enjoy these wonderful people, I meet the perfect one for me.

- There are many people who are inspired and excited by powerful, intelligent people like me.

- My beloved finds everything about me wonderful and exciting. We are so compatible.

- My love is attracted to exactly my type: my appearance, my weight, my hair, and everything else about me.

- I know exactly where to go to meet my love. I will be light and playful and have fun going to different places and different events to show the universe I am ready and willing to meet my beloved now. And my love will show up at the perfect time. We will laugh at how synchronistic our meeting was.

- All my past loves existed to help me learn and get to this place so I could be the best person and best partner possible. I have grown and learned so much that I can now appreciate my life partner.

- I feel my partner around me now. I am getting better and better at sensing my love. We talk telepathically to each other every day, so I feel calm, happy, and comforted.

- Our love is an inspiration to others. Others feel happy and believe now that true love does exist, and that they can have love too. We show them what is possible.

- Love is so fun!

- Source/Universal Intelligence/God knew exactly what I wanted and was just waiting for me to relax and not be afraid.

- I am excited to have love!

- I focus on giving love and appreciation in my life, and good things always show up.

- I can have everything I desire. Source/Universal Intelligence/God wants me to be happy and have my heart's desires.

- People can have whatever they desire. I will be an example of this, so others can feel safe being happy too.

- What I desire is perfect for me. My soul tells me exactly what I want to create in this lifetime, and I trust and accept my soul's guidance.

- My beloved truly desires to be with me.

- We are in perfect harmony with each other. We both want the same things.

- We both love and support each other.

- Life gets more fun and exciting every day. Life is one fun and interesting adventure after another.

- It is easy to feel happy, content, and fulfilled.

- Almost everything I have wanted in life I have now.

- I am happy with my life and therefore have love and happiness to share with my partner.

- Intimacy and sex are easy with this person I love and trust.

- Creating money and abundance is easy for me.

- I trust that other people's souls know what they are doing, even if they have created challenges in their lives. I allow them to follow their higher path and I live as a loving example of my own happiness.

- Life is easy and wonderful. Life loves and supports me.

- It is easy for me to give to people, because I have everything I need and can easily create more.

- I trust myself because my intentions are kind and loving.

- Life always works out for me.

Come up with your own list of wonderful, happy, and empowered beliefs. Even if you don't think you can accept these new beliefs now, write them down and focus on them, instead of on your fear-based beliefs, and eventually these new beliefs will become stronger. And your life will begin to reflect them. Your perceptions about yourself and life will also begin to change.

Spend time each day focusing on each new belief and realizing what each one means. Reinforce each new idea by recognizing that it can be true. Imagine yourself surrounded by and immersed in a new picture that relates to each new belief. Absorb the feeling that goes with each new belief.

You have nothing to lose, unless you really are attached to your old beliefs and your old unhappy struggles. It may be easier and more comfortable to keep doing the same old things and feeling the same old emotions because they are familiar, but are you happy? Are you afraid these techniques won't work for you? I have seen many examples that show they do work.

A wonderful client of mine realized she had the belief, and therefore she had proof, that "love hurts." After all, every relationship she had ever been in ended badly. She was always sad, always miserable, when her relationships broke up. After really looking at this belief about love, she recognized that she had, in fact, had a lot of good times in love, and that she had been focusing on the bad times near the ends of these relationships, rather than recalling all the joy and warmth she had felt many times with her partners. She had had many days of exciting expectations waiting for her new beaux to call and then feeling thrilled when they finally got to be together.

As she focused on those memories and feelings, her energy shifted. She grew less afraid of love: love had actually given her wonderful times, for many months at a time, and the pain at the end was only a small percentage of the overall experience. She even admitted that she had actually outgrown and become bored with a couple of her partners, and that it was a good thing she was no longer with them. She had had pleasant times with them, but they weren't really what she wanted. She took those breakups off her list of "love hurts" incidences. She shifted her statement to: "Love hurts for a few days, but love is fun, exciting, and warm most of the time, so love is worth it." After all, doing taxes can be painful too. But if you spend every day focusing on and worrying about the few uncomfortable days out of the year that you have to do your taxes, you ruin all the great days that are tax-preparation-free.

As the intense energy and fear from that particular belief lifted, this woman found herself having more fun with each person she went out with. She had changed her perspective, had realized that she had survived many breakups and was still alive and kicking. She admitted she couldn't even dredge up the feelings of sadness she had experienced during each breakup. Do you too believe that "love hurts"? Can you look for similar realizations?

This is the third step. Once you identify the faulty beliefs and begin to challenge each one, use your imagination to see a different picture. This will help eliminate the belief. For example, rather than fearing you will be hurt or abandoned by some future partner, imagine the love of your life looking deeply in your eyes and promising you that he or she will never leave you, that you will be devoted and passionate partners forever. Then imagine having fun and feeling deeply in love. Imagine that, far from becoming bored with each other, the two of you will find that your love grows stronger and more exciting every day. Really spend time experiencing this picture. Get into it. Surround yourself with the colors, sounds, scenes, smells, and other sensations of this picture. Lose yourself in it. No one has to know you are doing this. You are creating your world. Enjoy the feelings.

The fourth important step is to focus on the essence of what you desire, rather than on the things you do not want. Most people spend their energy bemoaning their current undesirable situation. Focusing your attention on the negative — on what you do not have yet, just draws more of that to you. Rather than waking up every day unhappy that you are not in the relationship you desire, focus on and imagine the warm feelings of love. Whatever you focus on will increase. Spend a few moments every day immersing yourself and surrounding yourself with these feelings.

And bring your imagination into the present time. Imagine your wonderful, ideal beloved with you now, not sometime in the distant future. Visualize this person standing next to you, relaxing in your home, or sitting next to you in the car. Imagine this person walking, talking, and eating with you and accompanying you on all your other activities throughout the day. Even if you cannot see a face or imagine a hair color, anything you can imagine is helpful. Getting a visual picture can be helpful, as you'll see in the next example. However, steps five and six are the most important, so don't worry if you have difficulty visualizing. You might consider creating a dream board — some type of board that you can fasten pictures onto — to help you visualize your dreams. Cut out pictures of weddings, and paste your face over the bride's or groom's face in each picture. It's probably best not to choose pictures from celebrity weddings, as this could affect your belief that a marriage to this particular person would be possible.

Another client believed that love was hard to find, and that there was no one out there for him. Even in all his travels, he hadn't found anyone he felt a connection with. He was discouraged and tired. He didn't want to keep searching. Instead he started using the visualization techniques. He created a quiet, comfortable place in his home and spent time every day imagining a woman stepping from an ethereal realm into this world, like an angel taking physical form. He couldn't imagine that his life partner existed in this world; he hadn't seen her anywhere. So he imagined his loving partner coming from another place, as if she were being created in this world just for him. He imagined her walking toward him and lovingly embracing him. He felt his fear and resistance melt. The scene felt warm and real to him. He found himself enjoying the process and looked forward to imagining the scene every day. It was the first time he ever remembered feeling this level of love and connection, and he didn't seem to mind that it was all in his imagination. He commented that the feelings were just as real, just as wonderful, as if it were really happening.

One month later he met his angel. They were married two months from the day he began imagining her coming into his world. He had stopped his resistance and started focusing instead on a positive picture. He focused on the essence of what he wanted, not on the doubt and disappointment he had been experiencing. The exercise also took his focus off the belief that he would have to work hard to find someone. He just saw her easily coming to him. He felt it in present time. Then he went about his day. His energy became so light that he found it easier to smile at people and greet them sincerely, and this is how he met his partner. They smiled at each other and started talking. He wasn't guarded or anxious, so the conversation flowed easily and eventually developed into something more.

The fifth step is to use your imagination to sense how you would feel in your physical body if this wonderful person were holding you and being affectionate with you. Focus on the physical sensations as best you can. We all know the sensation of touch. We have all been hugged. Take the time to use your memory and your imagination to feel the sensation of being held. Take the time to feel safe and warm in the arms of this person. Feel yourself blending and connecting with the other, feel your two hearts beating together.

Notice if you resist this exercise or feel tension in your body when you try to imagine someone touching you. You may still have some emotional trauma from a past experience. If so, allowing another person into your life at this time could be challenging. If you can keep practicing this exercise until you no longer feel resistance or tension in your body, you may be able to work past your fears. Go through the fear. Don't avoid it.

Another woman, after doing these exercises, realized she was the one who had the fear of commitment. She was afraid of being smothered and of losing her freedom. She noticed her body tense up every time she imagined someone hugging her. She had continuously accused the men in her life of never being able to commit to a relationship and of always disappointing her. After the lightbulb came on in her mind, she continued to imagine someone holding her and loving her. But she also imagined the person allowing her to go when she wanted to do her own projects. Subconsciously, this woman had been expecting relationships to look and feel a certain way — a suffocating and limiting way. She had an old belief about what relationships were supposed to look like — a picture she didn't actually like. Once she felt a shift in her perception, she didn't feel the same resistance or mistrust toward men. She accepted that it was she who wanted freedom. Shortly after this, an amazing man came into her life who was just as independent as she was. They are now having a grand time together and, oddly enough, discovering that they both enjoy being around each other more than they thought they would. The woman stopped denying her true desires and accepted that she wanted freedom and independence, and the perfect partner, matching her own energy exactly, appeared.

The sixth step is to imagine how you would feel *emotionally* having this amazing relationship. Imagine this person holding you close, talking lovingly to you, comforting you, and reassuring you that she or he will be there for you, that you two will live as devoted, dedicated partners. Most of us fear being hurt or abandoned, so if you can clearly imagine feeling loved and treasured instead, you can reduce or eliminate this fear. Our fears block the good that would otherwise come to us.

As you do these exercises, notice if feelings of fear or unworthiness arise. If you feel unlovable, if you have trouble imagining that someone could love you deeply, then you are not going to be able to attract or accept love into your life. We are telepathic beings, and people will subconsciously pick up your fear and resistance and avoid you.

If you can use your imagination to surround yourself with visual pictures and infuse yourself with these physical and emotional feelings, you will have a much stronger possibility of creating your dreams. What you focus on will increase.

Another exercise you may want to play with is to start talking to this person in your mind. Hold the intention that your future partner will hear your thoughts. As you speak to him or her, send your communication out into the atmosphere. See it flowing out from you like a beam of light from a lighthouse. Send it out in all directions. The energy within your thoughts can act like a homing beacon, and your future partner will finally be able to find you. Trust as you talk to your beloved that your signals are reaching that person. You may want to see if you can hear your partner replying to you, telling you all about himself or herself. This may help you relax and learn to trust this person.

One client imagined sending flares up into the sky so that her beloved future partner could see where she was. She imagined him seeing the signal and walking right to her. Her husband-to-be showed up in her life four weeks later.

My clients have had great results from these exercises. Whether you are currently single or in an unfulfilling relationship, you can practice these exercises. Either your present partner will shift and become more of what you desire, or a new partner will emerge in your life.

There is a great story about a farmer whose donkey had fallen into a dry well. The well was so deep that the farmer knew there was no way to reach the donkey to pull it out. The neighbors all encouraged the farmer to kill the donkey so it wouldn't have to suffer a slow death. Everyone started throwing rocks at the donkey, trying to hit it on the head to put it out of its misery. But instead, every time people threw rocks into the well, the donkey stepped on top of them. Eventually the people had thrown so many rocks that the donkey was able to climb out of the well.

Every time you perceive life or other people throwing rocks at you, gather up your strength, believe in yourself, and climb on top of the rocks. Overcome your challenges by becoming greater and stronger. Otherwise you may just die unhappily in the well.

Before you embark on your interior housecleaning project, I want to describe for you the process we all use to create everything we currently have in our lives, whether or not we are aware of this process and are happy with our creations: Our thoughts and beliefs give rise to our imagination, which stimulates our emotions. In other words, what we think about, we imagine, and this stirs up emotions in us. Sometimes this process is subtle; sometimes our thoughts are stronger and more obvious. This is the creation trinity: thoughts and beliefs, imagination, and emotions. (A belief is merely a thought you practice until it manifests itself, thus causing you to "believe" it.) These three energies working together bring things into physical form or experience. You may not get everything you desire, but you will always get what you believe.

Let go of hoping you will someday be in a wonderful relationship, and *know* that one is already on its way to you or is already happening. Hope has fear and doubt attached to it: you hope something will happen, but you are not sure: maybe it won't. Go deeper inside and get in touch with your knowingness, the inner voice that knows who you are, what you want, and what is available to you. Your inner self knows you are lovable. Your true being knows love is already yours.

Recognize that you are in alignment with a Source, or Power, that wants you to be happy and to have everything your heart desires. Feel connected with this Source or Power, which can create things easily and effortlessly with you.

Once you meet your life partner, trust yourself and life enough to feel safe and supported. Be kind, generous, patient, and understanding. Treat your beloved as your friend. We tend to have higher expectations of our partners than we do of our friends. If we treated our mates with the same patience and courtesy that we do our friends, our relationships would be healthier and last longer.

And above all, cherish the gift you have given yourself: a healthier, more authentic you, ready to be in the fulfilling relationship that you desire and have designed.

For more ideas about how to identify and change your beliefs and your life, read my book *Make Your Dreams Come True: Simple Steps for Changing the Beliefs That Limit You.*

Part Three

Once You Have Found Your Match

Chapter 8

What to Expect in a Relationship with Your Love Colors

Whether you are currently in a relationship and you want to understand why your partner is thinking and acting a certain way, or you are still looking for your potential companion and want to know what you can expect in your relationship before you make any type of commitment, the information in this chapter can help you better comprehend the behaviors, attitudes, priorities, and perspectives of each particular Love Color. All the Love Colors have a positive side to their personalities, as well as a more challenging side. You may want to know about both of these sides if you are going to be in a relationship.

Remember that most people have two Love Colors, so you will want to read about both to understand the two different colors of their personalities. If the qualities of one color seem to match those of your partner, but not entirely, most likely your partner's second Love Color is overriding or balancing out the first color. For example, if your partner is an Orange/Yellow combination, the easygoing, playful Yellow aspect of her or his personality may mellow out that independent, thrill-seeking Orange aspect enough to make her or him willing to spend more time at home with you.

Reds

Many Reds are full of fire and passion! These exciting individuals can bring heat and flavor to any relationship. Fiery Reds love raw power and intense energy; they are quick and intelligent, sensuous and sexual. They desire and relish every animalistic pleasure life has to offer. Most are extremely physically fit — many dancers, athletes, and firefighters are Reds. The Reds' strong presence can be fascinating and captivating, as well as intimidating to most people.

Reds love their vitality and stamina. Matching their powerful and never-ending energy can be challenging. When Reds are in power, they live in the moment with zest, strength, courage, and self-confidence. They respect partners who can do the same.

Anyone who is going to spend quality time with these Reds will need to be healthy and in great physical shape. In-power Reds enjoy strenuous, robust activities, so your time together will most likely involve sports or other vigorous physical activities. You may find yourself camping, hiking, or biking across the country with them. Reds often spend long days surfing, kayaking, river rafting, cross-country skiing, or taking long motorcycle trips; or your Red may want to dance late into the night or have a raucous time at parties with friends. Regardless, you will need a great deal of endurance to keep up with the pace of one of these highly physical creatures.

Although all Reds have strength and vitality, some are traditional, hardworking, salt-of-the-earth types rather than the zesty, hot-blooded adventurers. These Reds are reliable, loyal, and straight thinkers. They are typically independent and quiet and do not require much in a relationship — respect, trust, time alone, food, and sex. This sounds basic, but so are these Reds. Most of these individuals desire simple physical comforts in their home. They want a roof over their heads, a comfortable bed, a dependable truck, and good food.

Whether a lively, passionate Red or a down-to-earth, practical Red, all of them are powerful and intense. Having a strong sense of self-worth is essential if you are going to embark on an adventure with a Red. Self-sufficient and independent, Reds will accept partners, but they do not always need them. They are among the Love Colors that don't mind being alone.

Reds are often the epitome of the strong, silent type rather than deep or sensitive communicators. Many are tough, practical, and grounded, and they tend to keep their feelings to themselves. Reds will expect you to know their thoughts, desires, and intentions by their actions. They may assume that, if they provide a living, come home at night, and stay monogamous, then you know they are committed to you. When they withdraw from you, they expect you to respect their need to be alone. Eventually, they will reemerge and share their presence with you.

Because Reds value their word, they keep their commitments. They can be trusted to follow through on any job or project they start. In power, Reds respect hard work, so they will put in an honest day of labor to earn money. Most Reds do physically active or labor-intensive jobs.

The majority of Reds provide a decent standard of living for themselves, their partners, and their families. If security is a priority for you, it should be easy to feel safe with this type of Red. They will work long, hard hours to guarantee financial stability, and if necessary they will work two or three jobs to maintain their self-respect. Most would never think of accepting charity or welfare. They will also expect you to support their decisions. They can be fierce protectors — zealously defending the rights and safety of themselves and their families.

These physical creatures relish manual work and will spend hours fixing your car, repairing a leaky kitchen sink, or mulching the lawn. Or they will prepare a gourmet meal, create a sensual bedroom environment, and share a long night of intense passion with you. Reds value physical expression and immediate gratification, so be prepared to have an active sex life. If you are at all timid about your body or your sexuality, you could encounter significant challenges in this relationship.

Reds can be demanding: if their needs are not met, they can become temperamental and aggressive, or sullen and brooding. If you are able to stand your ground and not be intimidated, your Red won't be happy but will respect you. Reds are happiest if their partners are available and accommodating.

Since these individuals are strong-willed, arguing with them is usually senseless. If you want something, the best strategy is to let them know exactly what you want, then allow them to go away to mull over your request. Typically, they will figure out ways to fulfill your desires. Realize, however, that stubborn Reds will not easily bend to pressure or give in to unwarranted demands.

Reds do not need or want much sympathy from people and prefer to be strong, competent, and in control. They expect you to perceive and treat them accordingly. While some like to be waited on, catered to, and spoiled by their mates, others are uncomfortable with pampering. They do not want to be treated like children. You will know very quickly which type of Red you have on your hands. Reds can be blunt and honest when making a point. You will never have to guess what yours means.

As parents, Reds are good financial providers, and they will teach their children to work hard and have strong values, but they will not always be emotionally available to their offspring. Reds are not always sensitive or affectionate and are uncomfortable exposing their vulnerabilities. Often their blunt, powerful, and forceful behavior can frighten and intimidate their children. You may end up teaching or encouraging your Red partner to emotionally connect with his or her children. Usually Reds think shopping together or tossing the football around with their children is sufficient.

When they are out of power, Reds can be demanding, critical, and domineering, and living with them can be challenging. Moody and sullen, out-of-power Reds prefer to be alone. Spending quality time trying to connect and build a meaningful relationship with these grizzly bears can be frustrating, if not impossible. Some prefer to sit around and watch ball games rather than actually play in them, or they may prefer to lie in bed and watch their favorite soap operas, reveling in the intense drama of these shows. Reds can sit for hours watching television and be completely unaware that you are even in the house. Or they will go to bars, drink, and play pool. Some out-of-power Reds love to start fights, especially when they have had too much to drink.

Reds can also exhibit fierce jealousies. Remember, they evaluate situations according to physical actions and appearances, not words. If your actions seem disrespectful, they will angrily let you know. They usually get over anger quickly, but when they feel betrayed they can hold serious grudges or even seek revenge. Once they lose respect or trust in their partners, it is difficult to regain that trust. They can also misinterpret actions and be too quick to judge. Even if their partners have done no wrong, Reds can stand firm. Stubborn Reds often deny responsibility for their own misperceptions and refuse to apologize for their mistakes.

Oranges

Relationships with Oranges can be extremely exciting adventures, provided you are willing to accompany them on their dangerous exploits. If you like the thrill of climbing Mount Everest or participating in extreme sports, then you will have a great time with these risk takers. If, on the other hand, you are not quite that daring, you could end up home alone every night, biting your nails and wondering if your Orange will live through the day. As dramatic as that sounds, it really is this radical with most Oranges. Being in a relationship with one will not be the easiest thing you ever attempt to do. But you will be sharing your life with one of the most exciting and daring of all the Love Colors.

Oranges are bold. They love the adrenaline rush of putting their lives on the line. Anything less bores them. These thrill seekers are not homebodies, and they despise ordinary, mundane, regular jobs. They would rather leave dull, predictable, everyday living to others. To be happy, they need to be on the cutting edge, pushing past limits to test their physical prowess and mental agility. Most Oranges would prefer to burn rubber around tight corners at the racetrack, explore deep underwater caves, scale hazardous cliffs, or raft through treacherous rapids than cuddle in front of the fireplace at home. They may spend a few nights at home with you, but then they become restless and need to adventure out into the world again. They prefer to live life with zeal and passion.

Bright and cunning, they painstakingly plan every aspect of a daring feat. They are not foolish or careless risk takers but instead calculate every detail before attempting any endeavor. They meticulously measure distances, check and recheck their parachutes, or practice stunts over and over again before removing the safety devices. Still, they are daredevils. Even though Oranges plan their ventures thoroughly, they enjoy the element of surprise. They will be as prepared as they can be to handle any unforeseen possibilities before they set off. However, seeing how quickly they can react when they come face to face with unexpected danger thrills them. Journeying into the unknown to face the elements is an Orange's true love.

You may marvel at the Oranges' willingness to rush into dangerous situations on a lifesaving mission. They are known to accomplish heroic feats, even receiving medals for bravery, but medals are not their motivation. They believe they are just doing their jobs. You may be awed by their ability to grab life by the horns and live to the fullest measure, and sharing your life with an Orange could inspire you to live more freely and deliberately. You might break through your boundaries and live a life you never imagined.

If you are independent and truly enjoy spending a great deal of time alone, then an Orange might be perfect for you, because Oranges too tend to be loners. If you prefer to be with people who are autonomous, efficient, highly intelligent, and stimulating, then these unconventional individuals will probably fit your needs. If you need a strong partner, one you can respect, one who can stand up to you even though you are strong-willed, an Orange can be a good match. They are powerful enough not to let others run over them.

They also enjoy sex, so physical, passionate encounters with Oranges can be exciting. However, sex is not their main priority: ultimately, Oranges are more interested in having unusual journeys out in the world than in lying safely by your side, being predictably affectionate with you every night, reassuring you that they care about you, and watching late-night TV with you. They would rather experience the outrageous adventures they see on television than watch someone else having all the fun.

Most Oranges are intelligent and self-reliant enough to know how to make money, so you will not find yourself stuck with an unmotivated or lazy partner. However, the methods they choose to earn that money could cause you trepidation. Whether they get jobs as stunt drivers or run into blazing fires every day as firefighters, you may question whether the money is worth it. Where they choose to spend their income could also be an issue for you. Rather than paying a mortgage, most Oranges prefer to spend their hard-earned money on gadgets or equipment for their next adventure. Arguments will likely arise if you desire to own an expensive home and live a traditional lifestyle. While Oranges don't mind owning houses, they just don't spend much time in them and, therefore, don't always want the financial responsibility that a house entails. Oranges love freedom, and while some people make security and stability their highest priorities, many Oranges perceive these as death sentences — death by boredom and limitation.

Oranges appreciate partners who are willing to consider alternatives. One option could be to buy income property that generates a passive, positive cash flow, thus allowing your Orange more independence. If it generates enough cash, you could use the money from the income property to pay the mortgage on your own residence, lessening the pressure on your Orange to earn more money. Everyone wins. You have your home, money is coming in from your investment, and your Orange has more freedom to adventure.

Too many people try to force Oranges to live regular, traditional, and responsible lifestyles. Don't be one of those people if you want this relationship to last. Most Oranges start their lives feeling misunderstood and unappreciated. While growing up, Oranges rarely encounter people who are on the same frequency, who have the same bold and audacious desires as they have — then they finally get to travel to the remote places they always dreamed of and get to experiment with the dangerous sports they always craved. Once Oranges have tasted freedom and experienced these intense thrills, rarely can they be stuffed back into the bottle.

Although this is not a rule for every Orange, most prefer being single or at least unencumbered. They may take pleasure in having a companion but typically are not interested in marriage or family. The majority of Oranges prefer spending time alone or sharing their fun and exciting lives with free-spirited buddies. (You could be one of those buddies, if you are also adventurous.) They want the freedom to pick up and travel anytime they want, to any exciting destination they choose, without having to explain themselves to some concerned spouse. They may even grow to love having a comfortable home, as long as they also have their exciting challenges and adventures.

However, if your vision is to have a cozy, secure home and raise children, this may not be the best partner for you — unless you truly prefer to be a liberated, financially self-reliant, single parent. If Oranges become frustrated because they feel trapped, they can become surly and difficult. Out-of-power Oranges may snap at you so you will leave them alone. It can be confusing to watch them comfort the small child they just rescued from a burning automobile but not display the same tenderness toward you.

Oranges are not soft and fuzzy or overly emotional, and they're not interested in having deep philosophical discussions about love or in talking about relationship problems. They won't show affection when they are not in the mood. Out of power, they can become cold, self-centered, and distant. They can also become so obsessed with living dangerously that they become reckless and develop self-destructive behavior and even put others' lives in jeopardy.

Having someone admire and respect them for their prowess is great, but Oranges usually don't need or want emotional bonding — except possibly with their buddies. Experiencing the same adrenaline rush, struggling side by side to survive the same perils, tends to bond people, and these are the relationships Oranges relish.

If you are in a relationship with someone who works in a potentially perilous job and does some of the same sports or other activities mentioned here, but the Orange description doesn't seem to fit, understand that not everyone found in these occupations is an Orange. Many Reds and Yellows and sometimes Violets enjoy these as well. If your partner seems to relish taking risks and does not seem to fear pain, you probably are involved with an Orange. Otherwise, read the chapters on Reds, Yellows, and Violets.

If you find yourself in love with an Orange, rest assured that life will never be boring. On the positive side, Oranges can teach you how to live with little or no fear. They can inspire you to go after your dreams — especially if your dreams involve exploring places few have dared to go. Anything you have the courage to imagine will probably be less dangerous than anything your Orange could think up. After spending time with one of these brave souls, you most likely will not be afraid of anything.

Just remember that, in order to have a compatible relationship with Oranges, you will have to be brave enough to accompany them on many, if not most, of their adventures. If their exploits do not interest you but you love your Orange, you could always learn to be independent and self-sufficient enough not to be bothered by your partner's excursions. Relax and allow this free spirit to go alone. It does no good to anxiously sit at home, waiting for him or her to return — which make take days. This would only create stress and unhappiness for you and cause your Orange partner to feel uncomfortable, pressured, or even guilt ridden. Whenever you do have time together, relish life, listen to the stories of the latest journey, and enjoy your partner's company.

Magentas

If you find yourself attracted to a Magenta, be prepared for a fascinating roller-coaster ride. These outlandish characters are the nonconformists and eccentric personalities of the Love Colors. They love the absurd. They love laughter, creativity, and mischief. In power, Magentas are fun loving, free-spirited, and spontaneous. They enjoy living outside of the box, exploring beyond society's traditional rules and boundaries. You won't be bored if you spend any time at all with Magentas. They look at life with a sense of humor, and they love to take physical forms and ideas and stretch or twist them into strange, bizarre, and unrecognizable shapes. They prefer to experiment and play with physical reality, not the world of spirituality, philosophy, or mysticism, unless they can take a far-out mystical idea and transform it into some outlandish physical art project.

Make sure, though, that you have found a Magenta, not a Yellow/Violet combination. They have many similar qualities. Yellow/Violets are also rebellious, stubborn, and creative, but they prefer to explore spiritual ideals, to save the planet, help the masses, or protect the environment. Magentas like to challenge the status quo, they enjoy pushing boundaries and being as wildly shocking as they can be, but they are not interested in saving the world.

It's best if you have a great sense of humor and are not concerned about what people think of you, because if you hang out with Magentas they will test your sensitivity in these areas. Most people are uncomfortable around these odd beings, whom they see as bizarre. There is a valid reason for this perception: Magentas' strange sense of humor is often warped and scandalous.

Many Magentas love being the center of attention and don't seem to care whom they upset or offend. In power, they love entertaining people, and they often act, perform, sing, juggle, or create outrageous works of art. They like all kinds of people and can be comfortable with anyone they meet. In fact, their assortment of friends can be as wild and eclectic as their taste in clothes and hairstyles. Their home decor is often a slapdash of crazy colors and unmatched, miscellaneous furniture. And it all changes frequently. They love for their homes to reflect their radical individuality.

However, there are also serious, moody, and sullen Magentas, who rarely have friends and who do not care about the color of their clothes or what kind of furniture they have. They tend to live in their own world and are simply not that interested in their surroundings. These loners often become increasingly eccentric as time goes on. If you were to meet one of these individuals, you would probably struggle if you tried to create an emotional connection, because these Magentas are adept at shutting people out. They can be fascinated or obsessed with their own inventions and creations, and not interested in much else.

Magentas are usually found in large cities, where their shocking behavior and their often wild, nonconformist appearances are better tolerated by others. Living in small towns, Magentas can quickly feel like outcasts, aliens in their own homes. If you desire to live in a rural community, a Magenta is probably not the best potential mate for you — unless you will be living in a broad-minded commune where everyone accepts everyone else just the way they are. Magentas could feel safe in such an environment; however, they could just as easily become bored. Typically they like varied cultural activity and wild nightlife.

Now that you understand the basic temperament and personality of

Magentas, are you sure you're up to the challenge? Your life will be unpredictable and often crazy, but if this excites you, then a Magenta is the right partner.

In power, Magentas are a bit like the "Energizer bunny" — they never stop. Their energy and enthusiasm are unmatchable, and keeping up with them can be exhausting. You may feel like you're at the Mad Hatter's tea party. In fact, these unusual characters can shock and confuse even other Magentas with their crazy antics. The wilder they live, the happier they are. Magentas appreciate partners who can be a little zany and impulsive — the more spontaneous you are, the better. They can become bored quickly if things become too predictable.

They also don't like relationships to get too serious or demanding. To them, being emotionally responsible for anyone is confining. Be warned: many of them do not enjoy monogamy. These individuals prefer open, explorative, and adventurous relationships. They see this not as being selfish, but just very curious about people. Life is too short to be limited, especially when there is so much in the world to experience. They enjoy finding out what makes others tick — how people think, what they do, how they spend their spare time, and what they know. Magentas like to push people's buttons to see how uptight or how loose and flexible people are. These agitators are not hostile or angry toward people — just the opposite. Magentas are fascinated by people, so they metaphorically turn them inside out and upside down to find out who they really are. They enjoy disregarding people's boundaries. They rarely suffer feelings of guilt and will not be confined to others' standards of proper and moral conduct.

In power, these outrageous souls are happy and free. They love life. They enjoy being innovative and creative. They often conceive harebrained, peculiar, or one-of-a-kind projects, because unusual inventions and preposterous ideas are not only fun but make their life worth living. They enjoy seeing if they can bring some of their strange ideas into physical form. Even though yours may enjoy working alone, they will still be thrilled to have your support and assistance as they work to give birth to their creative ideas. Seeing admiration and fascination in your eyes would bring a smile to a Magenta's face.

In power, Magentas need the freedom to explore new people, weird ideas, unusual places, and peculiar lifestyles — they find excitement in randomly changing their lives. These unique personalities are generally cheerful and optimistic, they like and accept who they are, and they allow others to be themselves too. They also tend to be strong-willed and determined to live life exactly the way they want to.

One major challenge for Magentas is keeping their relationships. Because they are so erratic, they usually end up alone. Although some people can be amused and entertained for a while by their outrageous behavior, most of them eventually become too embarrassed or fatigued to stay with the Magentas. You may want to take an honest look at your emotional stamina and tolerance levels before getting involved too deeply with a Magenta. Even though these wild cards eventually get over disappointments, their feelings can still be hurt if they are rejected and abandoned.

Once you are involved with one of these enigmas, you may find many of your friends pulling away from you. If you are a people person and love having close friends, keeping company with a Magenta could cause you trouble. But if you are independent and do not feel a need to surround yourself with a lot of people, then a Magenta may be the perfect partner for you. In fact, Magentas can actually help keep boring, unpleasant people at bay.

Sadly, the majority of Magentas are not in power. Most have felt misunderstood and suppressed their entire lives. They know society sees them as misfits, and they feel judged and shunned for their "inappropriate" or "unacceptable" behavior every day. Trying to conform is unbearable, however, so many Magentas have learned to live their lives alone and keep their unusual activities a secret.

When these individuals lose their sense of themselves, when they lose touch with their unique and creative styles, they become bored and unhappy and lose their desire to experience life. They can become despondent, isolated, and lonely. Living then seems like a burden or a punishment instead of the wild and fun experience they know it should and could be. From there, it is easy for them to become severely depressed. They close themselves off from others and slip into a world of their own where no one can reach them. If you are in a relationship with an out-of-power Magenta, realize that withdrawing and hiding is a Magenta coping mechanism. Magentas will isolate themselves from everything and everyone — including you. They may begin to exhibit antisocial behavior — acting out in hostile, self-abusive, or self-destructive ways. Many Magentas turn to drugs or other detrimental substances to numb their pain. Their world is very dark and dismal. And since Magentas cannot be manipulated by guilt or social mores, you will not be able to use these to snap them out of their self-loathing and self-destructive behavior. They won't care what others think. Even well-trained therapists can have difficulty breaching the emotional wall Magentas set up around themselves. Being around them can be frustrating and sometimes frightening.

Because it is typical for Magentas to hide out, many people do not even know these damaged individuals exist. Magentas can live in small, unkempt, darkened hovels like little moles, thinking that no one knows they are alive or that no one cares about them anyway. They often keep unusual hours, emerging only late at night when everyone else is sleeping. They can further camouflage their existence by enveloping themselves in clutter. Their hovels can be disheveled and filled floor to ceiling with stacks of newspapers, food wrappers, old clothes, magazines, bills, and all types of extraneous items they have had for years and never discarded.

If you find yourself involved with one of these lost Magentas, you could become isolated too. Even sitting with one, you could still feel alone. If you tend to be an emotional rescuer, if you have a habit of trying to save wounded souls, you will find it an extra challenge to reach this loner. Magentas typically go down the rabbit hole by themselves.

In power, Magentas are fascinating, fun, and entertaining. Out of power, they can be physically and emotionally unreachable.

Yellows

One of the most basic things you can expect in a relationship with an outgoing Yellow is that you are going to have a lot of fun. If you have an in-power Yellow, your life is going to be filled with one amusing and joyful experience after another. A healthy Yellow will be your best friend. Yellows want you to be happy. Even the shy, sensitive Yellows want to please you.

Each Yellow has a different definition of fun, so your adventures with a Yellow could include everything from camping trips and river rafting to watching funny movies together. You may go to numerous parties or spend time exercising together, or, since Yellows like variety, you may be doing all of the above. They like to be spontaneous, so anything could happen at a moment's notice. With the Yellows' natural sense of humor, you will probably be laughing through each and every activity. Yellows are the cheerleaders of life, the one Love Color who believes the purpose of life is simply to enjoy it.

These adventures may or may not involve spending money. Since Yellows do not always have money, they seem to have a knack for finding or creating fun activities even when money is scarce. It doesn't take much to make Yellows happy. They can enjoy hiking up a mountain, riding a bike, sitting at the beach, or playing ball. A simple life and simple pleasures make for a happy Yellow.

Yellows do not want to hurt anyone's feelings, especially not those of their favorite companion and playmate; however, there will be many times when they need to retreat and spend time alone. Don't worry, they will soon return just as jovial and playful as ever.

Yellows have a great ability to stay young. They are the Peter Pans of the Love Colors and tend to live long, youthful lives. At the very least, they stay young at heart, so be prepared to spend a long, happy, playful life with your Yellow partner. Most centenarians — those who live to be one hundred — are Yellows. (Both George Burns and Bob Hope were Yellow combinations.) Being physically active personalities, Yellows make their health a priority, and as natural healers, they have the ability to heal their own bodies. In power, they tend to choose natural and holistic methods, and they know how to eat right and exercise. As long as Yellows are joyful, they can stay young and healthy. When they are unhappy, however, their bodies carry the burden. Yellows prefer to avoid conflict; they don't like dealing with problems. Developing aches, pains, and illnesses, however, forces them to pay attention. Only when something goes wrong with their bodies will they admit something is wrong with their lives and finally face their issues.

Yellows like affection, but showing affection needs to be their choice — they don't like being forced to be close. They are one of the most sexual of the Love Colors and tend to be lighthearted even in bed. Sex is a physical release but also a playful experience. In power, Yellows like to please their partners. Out of power, however, they can make sex a selfish physical gratification, one they will flee from once they are satisfied.

When they are younger, Yellows can develop serious crushes, and they will playfully and eagerly talk about the future with you. Yellows are usually idealistic optimists. However, as they age, Yellows no longer enjoy having serious, drawn-out discussions about relationships, finances, commitment, or other adult responsibilities and may look for any excuse to escape dealing with these topics.

Many Yellows prefer freedom and variety over commitment, and one-night stands can be easy for some. You could have an incredible evening with one, have more fun than you ever remember having in your life, and then not hear from this person for days...or ever. You may be left scratching your head and wondering why. Yellows do not like conflict or hurting anyone's feelings, so rather than tell you honestly that they are not really interested in a committed or long-term relationship, they may just avoid you or disappear altogether.

Yellows are notorious for flirting and playing games. If you chase them or want a commitment, they will run away. If you finally decide to move on with your life, they will show up again just to make sure you still like them. And yet, even though Yellows love variety and are great flirts, once they truly fall in love they are typically faithful. If they feel they are with their very best friend and playmate, they want to stay forever — they enjoy storybook endings. They also know they are on the planet to bring joy to others and to help them heal, not to cause people's pain and suffering, so they would never want to cause others' unhappiness by abandoning them or getting caught in any indiscretions.

However, it's common for Yellows to become disheartened in relationships, because often their loving companions eventually become their "jailers" or "parents." Things change when their partners decide the Yellows need to finally grow up and become more responsible. Then these Peter Pans feel betrayed and tricked because they never wanted to grow up or grow old. It's the lucky Yellows who get to be with their playmate and best friend through their entire lives.

When Yellows are not happy or fulfilled in their relationships, if they are no longer having fun, their eyes can wander. They just want to have fun and be happy, so they are naturally attracted to anyone who laughs at their jokes or flirts with them. Yellows can attract many admirers, since most people adore their youthful enthusiasm and playful attitude. Yellows are just so cute. Many caretaker personalities are drawn to unhappy Yellows when they sense these childlike souls need rescuing from unsatisfying relationships. Also, the simple Yellows can be easily seduced. Some naïve Yellows are easy marks and can be quickly manipulated by skilled, intelligent people searching for companionship.

Yellows want to escape when life becomes burdensome, so they don't always tough it out when their relationships become difficult.

Discovering other fun and enticing options appeals to them — most people who have multiple marriages are Yellow combinations.

If you want to ensure that your relationship doesn't fall apart, find fun and easy ways to work out your difficulties. Don't come down too hard on these sensitive pleasers. Patiently train them to be responsible and more grown up the way you would a child. Give them positive feedback and reinforcement when they act in ways that please you. If you constantly condemn their displeasing behavior or give them the impression that they perpetually disappoint you, they will eventually give up trying. They'll figure they are bad and incompetent, so they will subconsciously continue to find ways to sabotage the relationship. Most of the Love Colors work to repair their own imperfections and correct their mistakes, but Yellows can eventually become so discouraged while believing they have ruined your life that their behavior worsens. With Yellows, you typically make more progress with kindness.

In-power Yellows are full of energy and creative ideas. They will earn an income as long as they enjoy what they do. However, they don't care that much about money, so they are not driven to work hard for it. Honestly, they would rather be playing. Out-of-power Yellows usually lack money and motivation. They can be irresponsible with money — spending foolishly or spontaneously — which can cause a lot of friction in a relationship.

Yellows can also be charming, which frequently enables them to get away with undesirable or immature behavior. Out of power, they can take advantage of kindhearted people who are willing to help them out financially. Since Yellows are not interested in working hard, they figure that if they can find generous souls who will support them in exchange for laughter, entertainment, or companionship, this is an equitable arrangement.

If you want to have children, make sure you have a Yellow who is in power. They are fun, kind, dedicated, and loving parents who spend time playing with their children. In-power Yellows will be their children's best friends.

If your Yellow is out of power, however, you could find yourself raising three children instead of having two children and a spouse. Out of power, Yellows run from responsibility. There are many divorced mothers who were married to irresponsible Yellow partners. Ask them about the challenge of getting child support from these Yellows.

The problems of out-of-power Yellows are compounded if they have addictions. Yellows are the most addictive of all the personalities. When they are unhappy and don't know how to solve their problems, they numb themselves with substances like drugs and alcohol, or obsessions like sex and computer games.

Tans

There are actually four different types of Tans, each with different personality styles and behaviors. However, all Tans have a common theme: they tend to be more logical and detail oriented than most of the other Love Colors, and financial stability and personal security are high priorities.

Tans usually develop long-term relationships. They are the Love Colors who stick to their commitments. This is not to say that the other Love Colors cannot have lasting relationships. It's just that many of the others can become easily bored or grow restless if their relationships are not perfect. Other personalities find it easy to flee or search for more adventurous partners when life becomes mundane or unfulfilling. Tans, on the other hand, seem to have more realistic expectations. They tend to be more practical in their assessments of their partners, and they require less excitement and passion. When the allure of the relationship fades a little, they are less apt to see it as a disaster. It is easier for Tans to be content living simple lives devoted to their partners.

An interesting and important fact about the Tan Love Color is that many, many people believe that they are Tans when in reality they are not. Many people have been raised to believe that they must be Tans in order to survive in society. These people believe they should have steady, dependable jobs in order to provide for themselves and their families, so they have learned to be Tans. They have taken on the behavior, thinking patterns, and priorities of Tans rather than living as who they truly are.

If you meet people who are content in traditional nine-to-five jobs, if they enjoy working with details and bringing home regular pay-checks, then chances are you have found genuine Tans. However, if you meet people who feel trapped in unfulfilling but safe jobs, if they are working for a paycheck solely to pay the bills, if they feel obligated to work but are in jobs where they feel no passion, you may not have found authentic Tans. If someone tells you that earlier in life he or she dreamed of becoming a famous performer or envisioned doing some-thing big and important in life, then you've probably found a Violet, not a Tan. If he or she reports feeling like an eagle trapped inside a cage, you most likely have found a Yellow/Violet combination who was taught to live and think as a Tan.

Someone who is working in an office job but would rather be help-ing people is likely a Blue. Someone who would rather be playing or making others laugh is probably a Yellow — or a Yellow/Tan combi-nation, in which case the Tan is actually a natural part of this person's personality. That person could be experiencing inner conflict between the responsible Tan side and the fun-loving Yellow side. If you have met a Yellow/Violet combination who has added many Tan qualities, you may want to read the Yellow and Violet descriptions to understand the real personality and qualities of this person.

If you truly desire to be with a down-to-earth, practical Tan, and you have hooked up with a faux Tan instead, you may encounter trouble later in your relationship, which is why I'm discussing this issue. This person's real priorities and behaviors are bound to surface at some point, and this typically will cause her or him feelings of frustration and discontent that ultimately will affect your relationship. If you know your partner's actual Love Colors, you can find ways to deal with the challenges and help this soul live up to her or his potential. But it will not help to continue encouraging a Blue, for example, to live like a Tan.

What can you expect if you are in a relationship with a real Tan? The good news is that you will probably be assured of a long-lasting, committed relationship. When Tans make promises, they usually keep them. They are the Love Colors who will stay in marriages and jobs their entire lives. They work hard to earn a reliable income so they can have a secure home environment, not to mention a healthy pension and retirement plan, which will enable you both to live comfortably for the rest of your lives.

You can count on them to work hard to make enough money to pay the bills every month. They usually plan for all possible scenarios, which includes taking out adequate insurance — unless they think the insurance costs are unreasonable, at which point they will pinch pennies. Tans do not like taking risks or doing anything illegal or immoral, but they also bristle at being overcharged. They work long hours for their money and want to keep it.

Most Tans believe it takes years of dedicated work to get ahead, so they are typically conservative with money. They'll make sure the checkbook is balanced every month and that they are keeping a close eye on all financial investments and bank accounts. They are not risk takers or gamblers; they prefer safe, sensible, long-term investments. Arguments over finances can be common if Tans' partners are lavish or irresponsible spenders. Tans see no justification in squandering money — on anything. They prefer to spend a reasonable amount of money on the basic necessities in life: furniture that is low maintenance and functional, a comfortable but moderately priced house, and plain, simple food.

They also see no need to waste money on extravagant vacations. They will figure out the most economical method of transportation and the least expensive places to stay. They want the most for their money and may drive miles out of their way to save a few cents on a gallon of gas — just on principle. A Tan will be proud of you if you find a great deal at a sale or you use coupons to purchase groceries. Just make sure you bought items you actually needed. Tans have little respect for people who buy unnecessary things on a whim. They see it as a fast track to getting into debt.

Basically, Tans are grounded, practical, down-to-earth, and reliable. The positive side of being involved with one is that you know you'll be able to count on him or her. Because Tans choose safe, stable jobs, they will most likely go to work at the same time every day and come home every night. Tans like keeping schedules and feel best when they know what to expect every day.

Tans also like the comfort of knowing they can come home to a warm dinner, watch their favorite TV programs, and have their partners beside them every night. Even though they are not especially emotional or highly sexual, they do prefer companionship. Being habitual, they like to sleep on the same side of the bed and may even keep a weekly schedule for sex. In the living room or den, they prefer to keep their favorite easy chair in the same comfortable and practical position — preferably a position that faces the television or has the best light for reading. If one day you decide to move the furniture, you will have a disoriented and unhappy mate. Your Tan will question why you made that change and probably insist you move all the furniture back.

If you are planning a family, you should know that Tans love their children and provide for them, but because they have difficulty sharing their feelings, Tans are not always good at emotionally connecting with their children. Sensitive Tans and Abstract Tans are more vulnerable and expressive. Logical Tans and Environmental Tans tend to be more guarded. Tans tend to be disciplinarians when it comes to raising children. They want to make sure their children learn to follow rules and grow up to be responsible, respectable citizens. And usually Tans will stay in unhappy marriages just to provide a stable environment for their offspring.

In power, the more flexible and easygoing Tans can be wonderful to be with. They will methodically solve problems and take care of the tedious details that others shy away from. Their calm nature comes in handy when a crisis develops. They will rationally look at all the facts and decide logically the best course of action to take. They prefer to quietly and rationally work matters out in their minds first, then discuss or implement the solution with little fanfare or drama.

There can be a downside to the Tans' tendency to live in their heads, however. They typically see no need to share their thoughts or emotions with others — including their partners. Tans are a mental Love Color, not an emotional Love Color. It can be challenging to know if they are happy, sad, or angry, since they tend to keep things buried deep inside. It may feel at times that they are taking a partner for granted because they are not demonstrative or expressive. Nor do they usually know how to a handle a partner who is overly emotional. They strongly dislike drama in their lives and definitely do not enjoy discussing relationship issues.

Your Tan will most likely be a responsible provider, but if you need a deep emotional connection or frequent discussions about your relationship, then there are more suitable life partners for you. Remember, though, that you may have a combination Love Color, so there may be another side to your Tan. You could have a Tan/Yellow combination, who is likely to be a little less conventional. Yellows can be more fun, lighthearted, and spontaneous.

Most Tans are content to sit quietly reading the paper, enjoying a ball game, or watching their favorite, trusted newscaster on the evening news. They may have strong opinions about politics, government, finances, health care, and other relevant problems. The frugal Tans especially have difficulty with government agencies that levy high taxes and spend too much money. They would prefer to discuss those subjects with you than hear about emotional dysfunction in the family. Nor are they interested in discussing spirituality, the paranormal, or other topics they usually consider to be "ridiculous hoaxes." They tend be skeptical about anything that science has not accepted or proven. However, some, especially Sensitive and Abstract Tans, are more emotional and open to spiritual ideas.

Some Tans were brought up within traditional orthodox structures, so they may follow those religious teachings. They may have been taught that a book of laws exists and that they should stick with the rules. If Tans had traditional religious training, they will most likely practice their religious traditions for the rest of their lives. They do not like to do anything that could get them into trouble. Or they may continue to honor these traditions in order to pay tribute to their parents and their parents' beliefs. Many Tans continue to accept the basics they were taught in school (even if some of those teachings have changed over the years). And if they accept certain beliefs and traditions, they will expect their partners to accept them as well.

Other Tans, even those raised in religious homes, outgrow or challenge those beliefs as they age. They question the logic behind religious concepts, seeing them as childlike fairy tales or dogma created to control the masses. These Tans see religious people as weak-minded, wishful thinkers, not as logical realists. If you, on the other hand, consider yourself spiritual, this difference could be a point of contention. In order to live in harmony, you'll both have to learn to allow each other your individual beliefs. Tempting as it may be, it is not advisable to try to convert your Tan partner. It is better to teach by example, to reveal your philosophy by living it.

There are certain issues that may arise during your time with a Tan that you should be aware of and be prepared to deal with, because they may affect your relationship. Most Tans believe that if they follow the rules, remain hardworking, loyal employees, and do a good job, they will be rewarded for their service. They expect long-term financial security, modest acknowledgment, and decent retirement benefits. When things don't turn out that way, they see life as unfair. They often blame their difficulties on outside circumstances or other people — for example, an unreasonable and ungrateful employer, a poorly run and mismanaged company, or even corrupt policies. If they lose a job because of company downsizing, they may blame this on people coming in from other countries. They may believe that foreigners or even younger employees who work for less money undermine everything they have worked hard for. They are disappointed and feel cheated when the rules change and cause their long-term plans to disintegrate. The same will apply to your relationship if you change the rules in the middle of your life with a Tan. If you decide you are going to change your lifestyle, your career, or your relationship dynamics, your partner could become upset.

These days, the traditional Tans, despite what they were taught, are discovering that there really is no such thing as guaranteed protection, there are no secure jobs, and circumstances can change quickly. The rules are changing. They can no longer depend on companies to provide for their retirement, and marriages do not necessarily last forever. Tans are learning they may need to take responsibility for their own futures. Some companies no longer offer retirement plans or pensions. Tans like a predictable, cause-and-effect world. But as much as Tans are trying to keep the old, traditional standards and values alive, the world is growing and shifting rapidly around them. It is the die-hard, traditional Tans who can feel the most threatened when the old structures fall apart. They resist and even fear change and can become mistrustful, skeptical, and even cynical.

If you are in a relationship with one of these Tans, create a plan so he or she can feel safe. Help your Tan find ways to regain a sense of control over his or her life. Otherwise, you will have a grumpy, disgruntled partner on your hands.

In power, Tans do not usually force their opinions and ideologies on others but quietly keep their thoughts to themselves. When Tans become out of power, however, trouble can develop. Their downside is that they can become stuck in their ways and may stubbornly argue with anyone who disagrees with their perspectives. Once they have decided they know the truth, Tans consider it to be the only truth and will not listen to any ideas that dispute it. It does no good to disagree with them. These Tans will not bother to search for new facts or stay open-minded enough to see the other side. They will stubbornly stay the course and make judgments based on information from the past. These Tans can also become judgmental, critical, demanding, controlling, and intolerant of others. Anyone who has ever become involved with Tans like this will tell you it is virtually impossible to reach them once they close their minds.

Tans expect their partners to behave themselves, follow their rules, and support their decisions. On the positive side, you can take comfort in knowing that your Tan will probably be there for you for the rest of your life. This may be because Tans are stable and committed, or because they just don't like change. Moving from their homes or altering their relationships is uncomfortable for them. Once they have settled in and have become familiar with a certain lifestyle, they like things to stay the same.

Greens

If you are interested in finding an intelligent, ambitious partner with a strong, commanding presence, then a Green may be the perfect match for you. Greens are among the most accomplished people on the planet. They can attain any goal they set their minds to, they are movers and shakers, and they are among the world's most respected people.

You can expect to have money, lavish possessions, and possibly more than one home if you join forces with a Green who is in power and motivated. Greens want to live a quality lifestyle and will not hesitate to spend money on items they desire. Realize, however, that these workaholic Greens may not be at home much. They prefer the challenge of working on various business deals or investments to sitting at home watching television. Actually, Greens are often the ones producing the television shows you watch. They see more value in creating a new project or figuring out ways to make more money than in joining in activities they consider frivolous. If you find Greens appealing but were hoping to have fun with your partner too, do not be dismayed. Greens also want to benefit from the fruits of their hard work, and typically they are not ashamed to enjoy or show off their wealth and success. You will probably enjoy fine dining when you go out, travel first class, and stay in expensive hotels.

Greens expect great things from their partners, but they will also deliver great things. If you are up to the challenge, life will never be boring. Greens respect partners who are strong and self-confident enough to match their own dynamic, quick-thinking personalities. They need to be with people who are not intimidated by power and who are mentally stimulating — their intellectual equals. They can quickly outgrow and become disinterested in mates who are not as ambitious and goal oriented as they are. If they do become bored, they will bury themselves in work or find outside sources of entertainment.

Greens need to know that being in a relationship will not deter them from accomplishing their goals, so it is best if you are independent and self-reliant. Their high expectations for themselves, and their workaholic behavior, may cause them to isolate themselves from you, but if you enjoy your independence and free time, a Green can be ideal for your lifestyle.

On the flip side, Greens can also become intensely jealous and possessive. They demand loyalty and propriety, so do not humiliate yours by flirting with others or displaying a lack of decorum. Greens do not appreciate such mind games. Your Green will require a high level of honor and integrity from you. If you treat Greens with respect, they will more than likely treat you with respect as well.

If you desire to have children, have a serious and honest discussion with your Green early on. Not all of these overachievers are interested in having a family — some do not want the responsibility of raising children to get in the way of their financial or professional success. Greens often agree to have children if they are making enough money to obtain domestic help. Once they do have kids, they want the best for them: the best education and opportunities money will buy. And Greens are disciplinarians; they love their children but also want them to achieve their greatest potential. They have high standards and want their offspring to act with respect and integrity. They do not want to be embarrassed by their children's behavior, which they see as a reflection on them.

Greens are risk takers and gamblers, so if you cannot tolerate having your money and financial security threatened by a Green partner who loves to constantly take on new and risky ventures, you may want to consider choosing a different Love Color. Greens do not want their authority questioned or their power undermined by their partners, and they rebel against restrictions. If you complain about their business methods or challenge their style, you will have an irritated and disgruntled partner on your hands. They require support and encouragement from their mates.

Some out-of-power and unfulfilled Greens overcompensate for any dissatisfaction they feel in their lives by overspending and getting themselves into serious debt. Greens like money, they like nice possessions, and they like to be pampered. They believe having nice things will make them feel better. If their financial circumstances do not allow for this, they will often spend money anyway. Not having money and feeling powerless frightens most Greens, and they can panic or slip into denial. Buying things they cannot afford can become a serious obsession for them. Many hide this obsession, only to be exposed later when the bills begin arriving. This out-of-control behavior usually sparks serious fights in couples. If a stubborn and tenacious Green will not admit to the problem, the relationship could eventually be in serious jeopardy.

To overcome this challenge, work with your Green partner. Most Greens have strong problem-solving skills and will try to fix the problems themselves, usually by means of determination and willpower. If you see them attempt but fail, try in an undemeaning way to help them find solutions — discover new ways to increase the income, create a budget that they can live with, or locate ways to reduce spending: for example, cut out weekly trips to the manicurist, spa, or golf course. Find a great financial consultant. Greens fear embarrassment, however, so make sure you find an understanding, discreet, and competent advisor.

Then create a nonjudgmental, supportive environment and together search for the underlying reasons behind this out-of-control behavior. The biggest question these troubled Greens must explore is why they feel disempowered. Until Greens feel strong and in control of their lives, they will continue to sabotage themselves. This sense of helplessness may have originated in childhood, or it may be a side effect of their current job or relationship. All possibilities must be considered and examined. If Greens feel disrespected or powerless in their work or their relationships, they will find ways to sabotage their lives. They may be unaware of their feelings or hidden motivations. Unfortunately, Greens can be their own worst enemies — they are harder on themselves than anyone else could be. If they have done something wrong, they may act stubborn and defensive, but inside they are tormented. Because Greens pride themselves on being disciplined and perfect, denial may be the only way they can live with themselves. Hiding shame or avoiding their fears only complicates the problem.

A good therapist may be able to help a Green uncover the source of her or his issues — but therapy can be challenging for these iron-willed personalities. They have a hard time trusting others and are adept at keeping their information bottled up tight. To be able to open up and reveal their fears, they must work with someone they respect and whose power matches their own.

One of the more frustrating behaviors you can expect from these unyielding creatures is their tendency, when they become angry and resentful, to withhold sex and affection. Greens need to be listened to, and to feel valued and respected, before they will allow themselves to become intimate with another person. If they feel their partners have disrespected them, those partners will find themselves standing on the other side of a locked door, sleeping on the couch, or staying at a hotel. When Greens are angry, they do not hold back; they speak their mind. They let others know exactly how they feel and what they think. They often attempt to control or intimidate others with their intelligence, their financial status, or their forceful, often irate, personalities. And they can hold grudges. So even if you gather up the courage to apologize, your Green may not forgive you right away. And be assured that the next time you have a disagreement, your Green will remind you of your transgressions all over again. Greens tend to keep score.

Out-of-power Greens can be very selfish, demanding, and self-absorbed. They know what they want, and they will not let anyone prevent them from acquiring it. Their needs and desires come first — always. If you will not meet their needs and bow down to their wishes, they will move on to find someone else who will. It can be frustrating to be with someone who finds you so easily replaceable. And when Greens are out of power, there is no reasoning with them, no arguing with them. If you will not see things their way, they will turn around and walk out the door. They will not look back. Their proud egos can destroy even long-term relationships. On the other hand, they may stay in problem-filled relationships if their financial status is threatened. Many Greens have remained stuck in unfulfilling relationships because they were afraid of losing their money, their possessions, and their standard of living.

Another challenge you may encounter with Greens is that, when they are out of power, unhappy, and stressed, they can have the greatest health challenges. These type A perfectionists can experience many stress-related illnesses, including ulcers or other stomach and digestive problems; heart attacks or other heart ailments; asthma, allergies, or other breathing problems; chronic fatigue; and many other ailments. Alzheimer's is also common in the highly intelligent Greens. Sadly, illness may be one of the few ways to slow down these quick-thinking powerhouses.

To make matters worse, when Greens are seriously unhappy they can become the greatest hypochondriacs in the world. You will never convince them that their ailments are psychosomatic. They will fiercely defend their belief that they have problems, blaming others and outside circumstances for their conditions. They seem determined to struggle with life. Sadly, this seems to develop in Greens who have not received the attention or accolades they desired in life. They want to feel important, and if they cannot get others' attention in one way, they will create life-threatening illnesses to get attention another way. Until Greens tire of their own illnesses and dramas, there is no arguing with them. Most doctors and healers eventually reach an impasse with them. Greens can be tenacious, even with their illnesses. Until they are ready to heal, others will struggle in vain, sincerely trying to help them.

The powerful Greens tend to thrive on challenges. Usually, by using their quick minds and superior abilities they are able to overcome these challenges, but sometimes the challenges they take on can overwhelm them. If Greens can learn not to take life so seriously, their health problems can improve. The stress they create in their lives is usually responsible for the illnesses they do develop. If they can remember how powerful they are and find ways to heal themselves, or if they can give up their need for control and find ways to relax and let others help them, their lives can dramatically improve. However, usually the stubborn Greens want to do it their own way, in their own time. Again, no one can suppress or destroy the powerful Greens; they do it to themselves.

These may seem like harsh words, but often, speaking forcefully is the only way to get Greens to listen. One needs to be direct and honest.

Even so, there will always be Greens who will argue with this information anyway.

Blues

In power, Blues are among the most loving, devoted partners you could ever wish for. One of their greatest joys and sources of fulfillment is knowing that they are in loving, committed, and monogamous relationships. When Blues fall in love, there is nothing they will not do to keep their relationship together.

While most of the Love Colors hope their unions will last, many have a realistic understanding that relationships are not perfect and will probably require work. Many of these Love Colors have other priorities as well — saving the planet, becoming wealthy, creating music, or scientifically analyzing the universe. Some people relish their independence and are not in any hurry to give up their freedom. They may never get married.

Blues, on the other hand, live for love and relationships. Besides spirituality, there is no greater priority. Blues love the Cinderella story. They optimistically believe in happily ever after. From a young age, they dream of finding their prince or princess and being married for life. If you are going to be in a relationship with a Blue, you might as well know that this person has been praying for you to come into his or her life for years. (Prayer is a Blue's most powerful and most frequently used tool.)

Most Blues will do their best to please their partners, so you can expect they will do everything in their power to make you happy. When they fall in love and dedicate themselves to a partner, they stick things out, through thick and thin, till the end. They are so devoted that they often stay in unhealthy relationships longer than they should. Blues will tolerate behavior that very few others will. (This does not always apply to Blue combinations, the Blue/Yellows, Blue/Greens, and Blue/Violets. Blue/Yellows especially tend to have multiple relationships. While

Blues love to be in love and they cherish commitment, Yellows often fear commitment and tend to run away when they are not happy.)

Blues have a difficult time dating casually, which is important information if you want to date one. They are afraid to hurt anyone's feelings. Blues fear that if they are not attracted to their dates or don't want to marry them that they will offend or hurt them. So Blues often hide from dating. If you reassure them that you will not fall apart or die if things do not work out between the two of you, they may agree to go out with you.

Because Blues have such warm hearts, they love and support people whom most others have rejected. They tend to look past the outer appearances and see the good in people. The Blues' life purpose is to teach and give love. Their greatest desire is to experience love. And their greatest life lesson is to learn they are loved.

Blues are extremely compassionate and empathetic. If one person near them cries, it usually brings them to tears. If you are in a relationship with a Blue, understand that Blues are highly emotional and can cry very easily. They cry when they are happy, sad, hurt, and angry, and even when they are just tired. As long as you have done nothing to upset them, don't be alarmed. Sometimes they just need to release pent up stress by crying.

If you aren't the cause of their tears, then simply be patient, comfort them, and quietly listen to their story. Sometimes they just need a gentle and supportive shoulder to cry on. Typically it is the Blues who provide the loving support for others, so when they are sad and upset they need the same sympathy and compassion from their loved ones. If, however, you have hurt them, holding them and sincerely apologizing to them will usually assuage them.

If you are thinking of becoming involved with a Blue, you need to know Blues take relationships seriously. The strongest need Blues have is to love and to know they are loved. The good news is that, when Blues are in power, they accept and love people unconditionally. They are willing to be the super supportive and loving partners, the super parents, the super neighbors, and the super helpers. Blues have a tough time saying no. They don't want to hurt or offend anyone, so they are the perennial volunteers. When they feel loved and appreciated, even in the midst of feeling overworked they will continue to give and to love everyone — especially their partners. As long as they feel they have devoted and appreciative partners, they will do anything for the sake of their relationship and their children. Blues will even willingly accept and raise any children their partners may bring in from previous relationships.

If you are in a relationship with an in-power Blue, this person will support your dreams, create a warm home environment, and patiently listen to all your hard-day-at-work stories. Emotional intimacy is much more important to Blues than physical intimacy. Actually, they are not very driven sexually and often have difficulties with sex if they don't feel an emotional and trusting connection with their partners.

One of the Blues' greatest joys and strongest priorities is their spirituality. They hope to be with partners who share their beliefs and who will accompany them on their spiritual path. Blues desire partners who will join them or at least support them when they attend their spiritual services and programs. If Blues have children, they prefer mates who will support their desire to raise their children in the same faith.

Blues are not usually as independent, stubborn, or argumentative as many of the other Love Colors. While some of the colors enjoy the challenge and passion of fighting once in a while, Blues dread it. They prefer harmony, peace and quiet, and a conflict-free environment. (In certain combinations, however, this may not be the case. In a Blue/Yellow, for example, the spunky, rebellious nature of the Yellow aspect can flare up. Blue/Yellows are typically more stubborn and feisty.)

When Blues are young, their friends mean everything to them. They bond, empathize, and surround themselves with a tight circle of friends — often a group of other Blues. When any of their relationships fall apart, the hurt Blues run back to the safety of their loyal friends to receive comfort and support. Blues often remain close to some of their childhood friends well into adulthood. Once the Blues become older, their immediate circle of friends may change and evolve, but their need for a supportive team of kindred souls will not.

This information is important to know if you want to keep your Blue happy and healthy. Even though your Blue partner will choose you over friends, he or she still needs time with them. Blues tend to give themselves away in relationships. They often lose their identity or become swallowed up by their home life. Help yours stay balanced by encouraging them to connect with their confidants. Otherwise, everything will fall on you. If you are not there for your Blue every time she or he needs support, your Blue will eventually become lonely and depressed.

Blues can be easily hurt and insulted. They take things very personally, which can cause them to sulk or even become depressed. While Blues can be tolerant, forgiving, and accepting, they do not easily forget cruel words thrown at them. Having an affair would be the most devastating betrayal you could commit. Any kind of infidelity cuts Blues more deeply than any type of physical abuse. Even though long-suffering Blues tend to forgive their partners and stay with them, their trust and faith in a wandering spouse is never again the same. Their friends may be amazed and dumbfounded that the Blue took back this spouse. It is typically the Blues who stand by their promises despite any pain and humiliation. It is usually Blues who stay in unfulfilling marriages for the sake of the children. Blues tend to put others' needs and happiness before their own.

When Blues are out of power and unhealthy, they can be needy and clingy. They will chase after or pine over unavailable people; they will cry in their pillows at night, sobbing and begging God to bring them someone to love. When Blues are out of power, they do not believe or cannot accept that they are lovable, so they desperately search for someone who will make them feel secure and valued.

They are often attracted to emotionally wounded partners. Blues are emotional rescuers, after all, so they tend to be drawn to people who need extra love and care. Many insecure Blues hope that these people will appreciate their love and not run away from them. In short, Blues do not always choose the best or the healthiest partners.

Blues also stay in unhappy relationships because they fear being alone, especially as they age. Or they feel guilty and concerned that their partners will be alone. Ironically, it is usually Blues who have tolerated being treated badly by their partners who ultimately end up being hurt and abandoned by those mates, because their mates lose respect and interest in the sacrificing Blues.

The Blues' deepest and greatest fear is to feel alone and unloved. Their life lesson is to learn to love themselves, to learn to value and appreciate who they are. However, most Blues are afraid that caring about themselves will make them appear selfish and then no one else will love them. Eventually, after becoming exhausted and disappointed by unappreciative individuals, Blues may finally realize that what they truly desire is a partner who is healthy, emotionally available, loyal, trustworthy, and willing to love them for eternity — not just until they die, but throughout eternity. Perhaps you are that partner.

Trying to encourage Blues to move on from a destructive past relationship is challenging. Is not even advisable to use the words *let go*, which they interpret as meaning they must stop loving someone — which is virtually impossible for them to do. Once Blues love someone, they will always love them. The best advice you can give Blues in such cases is that they are allowed to keep these people in their hearts, but that they need to expand their circle of friends and open up to love others as well.

If these Blues cannot seem to break their self-sabotaging patterns, the best treatment is therapy. Even friends with the best intentions will eventually run out of advice or become exhausted by the Blues' problems.

Violets

There are many words that could describe a relationship with a Violet: *fascinating*, *intense*, *passionate*, *overwhelming*, *busy*, *dramatic*, or *intimidating* — it all depends on what type of Violet you have. In power, Violets can be loving, devoted, caring, and exciting partners. Out of power, they can be either scattered, disorganized, ineffective, and frustrating or self-centered, domineering, and arrogant.

In power, Violets are expressive, enthusiastic, and dynamic. They frequently use their passion and vision to inspire others. Most Violets have strong charismatic personalities. They are natural visionary leaders. They often radiate a tremendous sexual chemistry that can be exciting to others. This is one reason so many Violets become famous — or have always felt from a young age that they should be famous or important. They are easily spotted in the entertainment industry or by the world at large. The grand aura of a Violet is hard to hide. When they are in power and not concealing their powerful energy, they are noticed everywhere. This same magnetism can also intimidate people. Violets often sense that people are jealous of them.

In power, Violets can have magical, synchronistic, and profound lives. They can live big, important, and prosperous lives. Violets *need* to live such remarkable lives. They feel they have a lot to accomplish in this lifetime. They are here to awe and inspire the masses, to improve the quality of life for others, to get important messages out, to promote peace and understanding, or to save the planet — although some Violets have not yet acknowledged that they feel this way. They struggle to admit to themselves that they have these grand thoughts and feelings. Many fear coming across as arrogant or self-important. They also fear that their dreams are too big, too unrealistic.

Most Violets prefer to be self-employed so they have the freedom to fulfill their own visions. If they are not self-employed, they at least need to be in positions of authority and leadership or have jobs that allow them the freedom to come and go. If you need a partner who has a safe, secure job, a partner who is certain to come home every night for dinner, this may not be the best Love Color for you. Violets need to work toward greater ideals and have more freedom than most conventional jobs offer.

Violets are one of the Love Colors who have the capacity to connect with their partners very deeply and emotionally. They can be open, communicative, and responsive. And they believe their life partners should just appear, with no effort or struggle on their part to find them. They know this is the way the universe operates. They can visualize events, which then come to pass. They can become frustrated if things don't happen quickly and easily.

Early in life, they may believe they want a sensitive, loving, and supportive spouse, someone who will cherish their every word and look up to them. Violets eventually realize, however, that to feel fulfilled they need companions who are their equals, partners who share their visions. They must maintain excitement, passion, and inspiration in their relationships, and they enjoy mates who encourage them to reach their highest potential. They love to feel stimulated as well as supported. If they marry people who are weak and uninspiring, Violets can become bored, apathetic, and unfulfilled.

When Violets are in power, they share. They are compassionate and loving partners. They want their partners to enjoy and experience all the amazing gifts that come from the Violets' achievements. They want to share with them all that life has to offer — a beautiful home, the freedom to travel, abundant wealth, devoted love, and exciting adventures — and will strive to achieve those things. Violets also tend to be romantics. Since many of them actually write romantic or adventure movies, they themselves often desire a life filled with romance and exciting voyages. They will build dreams with their partners. Their visions can soar well into the future. They often want to make enough money to someday be free from working so they and their partners can travel the world or create humanitarian, life-changing projects together.

Violets flourish with partners who are self-confident and have a strong personal identity. In power, Violets can be very independent. They are not usually content to sit quietly at home while others make their voices heard. Violets desire it all — a wonderful life partner as well as the ability to achieve their greatest life missions. So Violets tend to be active — not necessarily physically active, but socially, politically, spiritually, creatively, or culturally active. They love to be involved in projects that are powerful or creative or have an impact on the masses. Their projects can take many forms, and they need this variety to keep from becoming bored.

Whether they are involved in causes, international business, music, film, or charities that change the world, they will be on the go. Violets do best with companions who will travel with them, get involved in the projects they are passionate about, become enthralled and busy with their own ventures, or be self-reliant and comfortable spending time on their own. Violets will be devoted, faithful, and passionate mates provided you are also fascinating enough to keep their attention. Violets love to be stimulated, to be constantly growing and evolving.

One challenge Violets' relationships can encounter occurs when both partners become so involved with their own projects that they rarely spend time together. By constantly traveling in different directions, these passionate souls can become lonely. Even in the midst of being surrounded by people, Violets often feel alone. This can create a dangerous situation for couples. Violets desire companionship, and if you are not there to provide this for them, they can easily attract someone who will fill this need.

Violets are good at rationalizing behavior that can bring them into the arms of lovers other than their mates. They do not want to hurt anyone; it's just that they want their needs and desires met. Even if they feel guilt, they will still convince themselves that their behavior is justified. Violets want passion and excitement.

Out of power, Violets can be so narcissistic and self-centered that they do not care who they hurt. As long as their needs are met, they are happy. In power, however, Violets feel a sense of guilt and remorse. But even if they love their partners, they may have a tough time separating themselves from those who have stimulated their passion. Affairs are more common among Violets than among any of the other Love Colors.

Because they do not tolerate boredom well, many Violets often resist making commitments to long-term relationships. They have a fear of becoming apathetic and losing their passion if the relationship becomes uninteresting or stagnant. It is actually challenging for most Violets to find partners who are not intimidated by their power and intensity, or who can keep up with their pace and continue to excite them.

Early in life, the romantic and idealistic Violets can be impatient and anxious to fall in love. They fear they are going to always be alone, and they desire passion in their lives. They watch most of their young peers easily form intimate relationships while they struggle to figure out why they feel so different and why others shy away from them. On the flip side, other young Violets can be the center of attention, the most popular kids at school. If these Violets stay in power, they are inspirational leaders at school. If they are out of power, they can abuse their natural charisma by taking advantage of others who put them on pedestals.

And then there are those young Violets who have bigger visions and plans. Relationships do not interest them at this point, and marrying early is not on their minds. Either way, no matter which Violet you have found, most Violets are better off waiting until they are older before making long-term commitments. Otherwise, if they marry too young, it is common for them to outgrow their mates. Violets need to continuously grow and evolve. They need the same change from their partners, or they will move forward without them. If you are young, and if you have fallen in love with a Violet, allow yourselves to become great friends. Encourage each other to grow and evolve into your greatest potentials. If you can manage this type of strong and healthy relationship while you are both young, you have a better chance of creating a healthy relationship that lasts into adulthood.

If you desire to have children with a Violet, you can rest assured that typically Violets are loving, supportive, well-intentioned parents. They want the best for their children. In power, they realize that the young beings are their responsibility, and that their children deserve guidance and support. Violets are not typical stay-at-home parents, however. They prefer to be out in the world accomplishing things. So your Violet partner may not be at home as much as you would like. Violets can contribute to the lives of their children by inspiring them and being living examples of what is possible. They can encourage them to follow their dreams. Violets do need to live what they are teaching, however. Otherwise, their children will not trust them or believe their words of wisdom.

Violets do not always need to have children. Some of them fear that having children could keep them from accomplishing their bigger dreams, or it could force them into ordinary, trapped, middle-class lives. Violets love their freedom.

Other Violets relish the idea of having children. Violets are so deeply compassionate and kindhearted that being able to love and care for their own children, being able to have an impact on young souls who could one day accomplish great things, inspires and touches many of them. These Violets often dedicate their early years to their children either by working in steady jobs to provide financial security for them or by staying at home to devote all their time and energy to the children's training and education. Once their little ones are older, however, the Violets want to return to the bigger world to take on other life-changing, important tasks. It is at this point that many Violets change careers — possibly finding the careers of their dreams. Or they further their education so they can reach even higher and greater levels of achievement and contribution.

Be warned, however, that if you do have children with one of these powerful souls, your partner will want to be the center of attention or to at least feel important. Violets desire partners who will continue to give them quality time, respect, admiration, and attention. If you devote too much of your time to your children, your job, or other projects, and you ignore your Violet, you may end up losing this particular partner. Violets' egos can bruise easily. They need to feel they are just as important, if not more so, than all your other priorities and obligations.

If you honestly believe you have fallen in love with a Violet, then see if you can sense the great energy, depth, and charisma of this person. If you believe you have found a Violet, but he or she seems to be living a small, simple life, going to work every day at an ordinary job, then realize there may be a different person, a suppressed person, hiding deep inside your Violet right now. All Violets need to feel they are accomplishing something important.

Many Violets begin their lives feeling powerful and special. They sense that they are here to do something out of the ordinary, something that is more substantial and greater than the average person will accomplish. As children, however, many of these Violets were not recognized as the dynamic visionaries they truly are. They were prevented from expressing themselves. They were suppressed verbally or creatively. They were rejected or ignored when they attempted to tell others about their visions, insights, and feelings. Consequently, they were taught not to believe in their dreams, they were stuffed into traditional "boxes" and trained to act like everyone else. They may have been told their dreams were foolish, unattainable, or unrealistic, so sadly they began thinking more realistically and practically.

On the outside, these Violets can appear to be well adjusted. They can have reliable, stable jobs like their peers. But underneath that ordinary and controlled behavior, you can sense something is wrong. Suppressed Violets never seem completely happy. They sense that something is missing in their lives but usually are not sure what that is. They have learned to believe this is just the way life is. In addition, if they have learned not to express themselves, they may have also lost the ability to connect with their deepest feelings and inner guidance. They will not remember how to hear their true inner voice. These out-of-power Violets can be confused, scattered, uninspired, unmotivated, or frustrated.

If you are attracted to any of these wounded Violets, you may feel that you can never quite connect with their true soul. You can sense they feel stuck and unfulfilled, but you may feel unable to help them. You can sense their emotional depth, intelligence, and potential, but you realize that, unless they commit to reconnecting with their powerful Violet nature, they will never achieve their dynamic potential. If this is the case, you will experience limitations in your relationship.

Possibly one day, your partner's true dreams and passions will reemerge. Her or his hidden desires may finally come alive. At this point you could see a dramatic shift in your Violet's life. She or he may develop a strong pull to go into humanitarian or global work, or to sell everything and travel around the world. It is also common for Violets at this stage to suddenly let go of everything they have built or created — including their relationships. If you have remained aware, supportive, and connected to your partner, this transition period does not have to mean the end of your relationship. Instead, it could bring about a new, more authentic life together.

Perhaps your Violet's dreams will come alive. The alternative is not as pleasant. You could end up with a very sullen and unhappy partner for life. Unfulfilled Violets can become depressed or seriously ill. Often they arrive at a life-threatening crossroad that forces them to look at their life and their choices. Perhaps your Violet can make life changes without this level of intense drama. Often Violets, trying to ignore these feelings of dissatisfaction, find themselves exhibiting self-destructive behaviors. They can become obsessive shoppers or compulsive overeaters. They can hide out by becoming absorbed with television or computer games — anything that will numb their feelings of emptiness.

Violets frequently create drama in their lives to distract themselves from their fear — their fear of never achieving their dreams.

Other out-of-power Violets can become arrogant, self-important, and self-serving. They believe they are superior to others. These Violets can be difficult to live with because they believe they know better than anyone else. They also see themselves as more important and deserving than others. The self-centered Violets will justify any of their actions and selfish desires. These are the individuals who can abuse their power, important positions, wealth, or sexual magnetism by having numerous affairs or by taking advantage of their trusting, devoted admirers. Out-of-power Violets are very similar to out-of-power Greens. Both are motivated by power, greed, and a selfish desire for pleasure. Watch these Violets. They are smooth talkers. Violets have a natural ability to communicate, to inspire, and to persuade. They can captivate an audience and keep them spellbound for hours. They can convince anyone of anything. They are also great storytellers and, out of power, can lie about anything to serve their needs.

In power, Violets feel a strong sense of compassion and are motivated to make a difference. They understand their important role here. They know their mission is to inspire and educate the masses, to help change the planet, and to improve the quality of life for others.

Indigos

Your experiences in a relationship with an Indigo will differ dramatically depending on whether your Indigo is in power or out of power. When in power, Indigos are intelligent, loving, generous, sensitive, and extremely intuitive; many of them are even psychic. They are also extremely honest, aware, independent, fearless, and strong-willed. Most exhibit a wisdom that is beyond their physical years. If you develop a relationship with an in-power Indigo, you can expect to have a caring, wise, and supportive partner.

Out-of-power Indigos, on the other hand, can be lost, frightened, and confused or rebellious, angry, self-destructive, and out of control. They often close off from everyone and hide in their own worlds. You could find yourself working extra hard if you try to develop a relationship with one of these wounded souls.

If you are in a relationship with an Indigo, you may already know just how special and unusual Indigos truly are. Looking into their eyes, one often senses that Indigos are from a distant world, a different dimension, or another time, and that they know something far beyond what is known on earth. They comprehend spiritual and philosophical concepts that are beyond the understanding of most people.

Indigos don't seem to fit into any traditional descriptions we have of human beings. They frequently have abilities that are unexplainable. They are extraordinary souls who often remember who they were in the past and where they came from. Many of them can recall in vivid detail their other lives (sometimes referred to as "past lives"). Some can read minds, and others have amazing, psychic abilities. The awareness and wisdom of these advanced beings is beyond rational explanation.

While these can be fascinating qualities to have, they are not always without challenges. If you are with an Indigo who is comfortable with these talents, your life together could be inspiring and intriguing. If, however, you are with an Indigo who is frightened of these abilities, then life could be a nightmare. Because most people have not developed these same skills, Indigos have very few, if any, mentors or teachers who can guide them through this world. Instead, these sensitive souls must rely on their own inner guidance for answers. Few people are living what Indigos feel to be the truth.

Indigo is a rare and rather new Love Color on the planet. Most Indigos at this time are children and young adolescents, although a few of them arrived years ago as forerunners and are now trying to live life as adults in a pre-Indigo world. While Violets feel driven to help save the planet, educate the masses, and improve life, Indigos are here to live in the new world Violets are trying to create. Indigos are not here to save the planet, even though many of them become spiritual or philosophical teachers. Their life purpose is to live as examples of a higher, more advanced human potential — aware beings thriving in harmony with other people, animals, and the environment. Indigos are ushering in a new way of thinking, a new consciousness. They are here to live in a world of peace and harmony. They represent the universal, cosmic being. They have a deep love, respect, and compassion for all life, and they want this new type of thought and behavior reflected in their relationships as well. They are not interested in having one of the old, outdated, dysfunctional marriages that they see around them.

Indigos desire to completely and profoundly bond with their partners, to be able to trust them with their deepest secrets. They want someone to connect with soul-to-soul, to explore magnificent spiritual ideals with. It often doesn't matter to them whether this person is male or female, homosexual, heterosexual, bisexual, asexual, a different nationality, or a different color. They recognize the person's soul. They relate to people's inner essence rather than their outer form. Some out-of-power Indigos, however, those who have been taught to accommodate society, can be confused and disturbed by the fact that they are often attracted to both males and females. They know this doesn't fit into any accepted definition of the traditional relationship, but they have no alternative model to help them understand their unusual feelings and desires. Relationships can be challenging for Indigos, since they seem to approach them differently than other people around them do.

Although Indigos see the value in every person, they are highly selective when it comes to making long-term, monogamous commitments. They want to find the right person, the one who matches their spirit. Indigos desire to live with that one lifelong soul mate, or at least one of the souls who comes from their familiar soul family.

Most Indigos seek out familiar souls, those with whom they have shared a common bond and common interests in many other lifetimes.

And yes, Indigos believe they have lived other lifetimes. Some know immediately if they have found a member of their soul family. Occasionally, though, Indigos marry souls who are not familiar to them just to have a unique experience in this lifetime.

Indigos desire and expect partners who are loyal, loving, spiritual, understanding, and patient, partners who will value them and treat them with respect. They prefer their partners to be first their best friends and companions, then lovers. They need companions who have loving values and high integrity. They also enjoy mates who are open-minded, emotionally adventurous, and willing to learn new things.

Indigos desire partners who can be spiritual and philosophical but also be their playmates. They want soul mates who can be fun and enjoy this intriguing physical life with them. They also admire partners who treat other people with love and respect. Indigos believe we are all in this together — that we are all connected, and that when one being suffers it hurts us all.

Healthy Indigos are delightful, spiritually connected, and balanced partners. They are honest, respectful, and faithful. Their high spiritual integrity does not allow them to injure, harm, or disgrace another person. Indigos will take your feelings into consideration and honor your needs and desires, as long as you do not ask them to do anything that goes against their principles, their intrinsic understanding of truth, or their high standards. They will stay true to themselves. If they are not feeling a connection with you or cannot go along with your wishes and desires, they will tell you the truth.

In power, Indigos show no fear. When they sense you need love and comfort, they are not shy, embarrassed, or hesitant to show their concern and affection. They intuitively know when you need a gentle touch, and they are never afraid to give you support. While some people fear that others will drain them emotionally by demanding too much of their attention, Indigos who are in power seem to know how to draw boundaries. They typically do not allow themselves to be taken advantage of or abused.

Indigos will teach you how to understand them, because most are forthright. You will know exactly who they are, what they believe, and what they want. On the other hand, some of them can be challenging to live with because they are so stubborn, independent, and self-sufficient. Sometimes they feel no need to discuss anything, to convince anyone of anything, or to explain or defend themselves to anyone.

As children, many of these progressive souls could speak in complete, complex sentences long before their peers could form simple words. Other Indigo children refused to speak at all until they felt they had something important to say. Many parents were concerned with this behavior, fearing that something was wrong with their child. But their strong-willed Indigos just did not feel like talking. You may encounter this same behavior in your relationship. Indigos do not like to be pressured. They follow their own guidance system and act according to their own beliefs. They will do what they want when they want.

Some people feel uncomfortable with or threatened by these unconventional souls. They see Indigos as strange or out of touch with reality, at least the reality they see. You may find that the reactions your Indigo elicits from others are challenging for you to handle. Most partners want to protect their loved ones or at least explain their odd behavior, but in this case it will not be necessary. Indigos are not interested in defending their beliefs or actions. They appreciate having partners who are unaffected by others' opinions and judgments as well. In-power Indigos can take care of themselves.

There is a strange dichotomy to Indigos. Usually they do not judge or criticize others, because they understand that everyone has his or her own path to walk, lessons to learn, and beliefs to work out. However, Indigos also struggle to accept actions that go against their higher beliefs and their principles of honoring life. You will often see Indigos distressed by the conditions of the world. They will become deeply upset over people's lack of awareness and consideration. They will be disturbed by actions that dishonor or destroy life: actions that cause harm to the planet, and atrocities that debase both spirituality and humanity.

The sympathetic Indigos understand that people have fears, and while Indigos will not encourage you to live in fear, they will not criticize you or abandon you because of your fears. They will instead do everything in their power to help you move through and beyond your fears. If you do anything that is dishonest or lacking in integrity, your Indigo partner will probably become disturbed by your actions. But he or she will compassionately discuss your behavior with you, help you get to the bottom of what caused you to behave in such a fear-based manner, and then help you find healthy ways to correct your self-destructive and dishonest actions. Or your Indigo may recognize that you are merely struggling to find your way in the world, in which case she or he will send you silent prayers of love and support. Your Indigo will pray that you are able to discover inspired answers that can help you through your fears.

When it comes to their own actions, Indigos are not always as lenient. They will not tolerate any behavior in themselves that lacks integrity or is dishonest, insensitive, or cruel. They sense that they must walk their talk; they must be living examples of their higher ideals and spiritual beliefs.

In power, Indigos never cheat, lie, or steal, so others can always count on these loving souls. Their principles do not allow them to be unfaithful or deceitful. And, in a perfect world, they expect the same from their partners. With any luck, you are up to the challenge of living with such a person. Nothing will go unnoticed. They will be patient and compassionate, but they will also expect you to eventually live up to your fullest potential, your highest spiritual and moral standards.

On the positive side, one of these souls could bring out the best in you. An Indigo could inspire you to live a stellar, introspective, and fully examined life, reaching personal heights you never knew possible. Indigos can teach you how to be grateful for your very existence. They believe life is precious and worth living. On the other hand, living with these insightful beings may lead you to feel you are not allowed to live as a flawed human. Indigos know and expect more. In power, they are loving and accepting. It's just that they want the best for your soul, so they may continue to encourage you to live a higher and better life.

Indigos prefer to be with partners who desire to live at a high level of consciousness. They believe that, when we truly realize who we are, nothing is impossible. We can achieve all things and live our greatest dreams. Not that Indigos strive to be rich or famous. To them, a purposeful and meaningful life means living with integrity, at the highest spiritual level of consciousness they can achieve. Some Indigos fulfill themselves by being in service to other souls, while some desire to express themselves creatively — bringing into physical form the beauty they see in life.

If you desire a partner who is an honest, reliable provider, an Indigo will do fine. Indigos do not always relate to the concept of work, but they will be responsible and do their share, nonetheless.

If you desire to have a family with a healthy, in-power Indigo, you can feel confident in knowing your Indigo will be loving and generous with the children. He or she will graciously provide for them, protect them, and make sure they receive an education. Indigos have a sense that they are here to encourage and guide their children until they are old enough to develop a life on their own. Expecting that these young souls already have an intrinsic understanding of right and wrong, Indigos are not strict disciplinarians. They don't feel a sense of control or ownership over their children. They respect children as individual souls who are here to follow their own unique paths and experience their own distinct adventures.

Out-of-power Indigos are not helpful or effective parents. They often are extremely frightened of life and may pass their fears on to their offspring. If you fall in love with one of these fearful Indigos, it is better to wait until she or he has regained balance and rediscovered a strong spiritual connection before you embark on bringing children into the world together. Otherwise, you may find yourself raising the children alone.

Although Indigos can be powerful and self-confident, they are also highly sensitive beings. They can be hurt and abused by those who do not understand their unusual qualities and unique complexities. Over time, they learn many people cannot be trusted, so they put up emotional walls to protect themselves. When they stop trusting and they lose touch with their inner knowing, they can become frightened and disoriented. These out-of-power Indigos close off and retreat into their own worlds. If you are in a relationship with one of these damaged beings, you could end up feeling lonely and abandoned.

Out-of-power Indigos can feel betrayed by the people around them or by the world in general. People are not behaving the way Indigos believe they should. Friends and family may not understand or accept the sensitive Indigos, which can cause them to feel rejected and alone. And according to the Indigos' belief system, there should not be war, violence, poverty, or starvation on the planet. People should not be hurting or killing one another. The world feels dark and hostile to these wounded beings.

While some out-of-power Indigos become reclusive, others develop intense and irrational behavioral problems. Some become angry, frustrated, and self-destructive. They avoid any and all attempts at intimacy. They push everyone away, including their partners. Indigos' caustic behavior can become so erratic and out of control that eventually no one trusts them or feels safe around them. Many out-of-power Indigos turn to drugs or alcohol, which causes them to become even more lost, confused, depressed, or self-destructive. These Indigos have difficulty holding a job or fitting into society in any way.

Lavenders

If you can learn to appreciate the beautiful, simple, and fanciful qualities of Lavenders, then you can expect to have an enchanting and intriguing life with such a partner. A Lavender can take you to places no other personality will take you. If you require a partner who will be hardworking, responsible, and down-to-earth, then a Lavender is not your best match.

Imagine riding on the carousel at your favorite amusement park. See the beautiful, multicolored wooden horses circling around, and hear the fun, gentle music playing in the background. If you remember enjoying your time on this magical slow-moving carousel, you may enjoy being in a relationship with a Lavender.

Lavenders are lovely, sensitive, whimsical creatures. They are innocent and childlike, wonderful explorers of the imagination. Daydreaming is one of their greatest pleasures. Lavenders are gentle free spirits who are not happy following rules or being limited by anyone who tries to dictate how they should live. They would love to drift through life, going wherever their imagination leads them, and playing in any world that catches their fancy. They want to be free to move in whatever direction they desire, and their directions change as often as clouds do.

Lavenders are not here to make social statements, save the planet, or counsel others. They just want to be free to explore their imagination and to enjoy life. Their fanciful and creative talents could inspire a sense of awe and wonder in you. They have the ability to remind us of the magical qualities of life. Living with an in-power Lavender can offer you a lifetime of joy and happiness, of fascination, surprise, and wonderment.

Lavenders offer an unusual gift to the world. Very few other Love Colors have their imaginative qualities or ability to venture into other dimensions or other realms of thinking. These interesting spirits can travel into dreamlike dimensions, see the beauty and the variety there, and then return to share their amazing adventures and fantastic visions. In power, Lavenders often have the ability to transform these visions into amazing literature, paintings, or other works of art, thereby touching the lives of others. If they can stay in their bodies long enough to follow through with their ideas and be productive, these innocent children can create fanciful stories so that the rest of us can imagine sights and sounds we have never experienced.

Lavender writers such as Lewis Carroll (*Alice in Wonderland*) and C.S. Lewis (*The Chronicles of Narnia*) enrich our lives by producing unique imaginary worlds. They take people into fantasy worlds that are alive with feelings, sensations, and sounds. They help us appreciate and see life from unusual perspectives. If it were not for these strange souls, life would be boring and predictable. We would stay within known boundaries and therefore live unimaginative lives. Lavenders should be treasured for their extraordinary abilities. Perhaps the Lavender you meet will be in power and producing similarly creative projects.

If you find yourself in a relationship with a positive, in-power Lavender, your time together could be an untraditional but delightful experience. Happy Lavenders can bring fun, joy, and whimsy into your life. Being the creative creatures that they are, they can fashion marvelous environments. Your home could be filled with crystals and unicorns, or with pastel-colored art and furniture. The atmosphere will most likely be magical, spiritual, and light. Lavenders are typically disturbed by the harsher elements of the world, so they prefer their environments to be beautiful, serene, warm, and sunlit, possibly accented by chimes, butterflies, and flowers.

If you can keep in mind that Lavenders are much like fragile butterflies or delicate songbirds, you will see the importance of providing a beautiful, stress-free environment for them, rather than trying to capture them, put them in a restrictive cage, or ruthlessly insist they become anything other than the gentle souls they are. Your Lavender partner could take you into places and realities that you did not know existed; even during sex you could travel with him or her on a series of fanciful adventures.

You can expect to have some unusual challenges with Lavenders, however. The greatest difficulty these peculiar beings have is in staying in their bodies. They tend to daydream, to energetically float out of their bodies and into fantasy worlds where they do not have to face the harsh realities of physical life. They prefer mystical experiences rather than the dense confinement of three-dimensional reality. You may look into the eyes of your Lavender partner and find it difficult to see anyone home inside.

Lavenders have an unusual dilemma. While drifting away too often from the physical world can cause them to become spacey and ungrounded, being forced to stay in their bodies too long can actually cause them physical pain. It can create nervous tension or even depression. They need to escape into their dream worlds for the same reason people need to sleep. Floating in and out of their bodies helps them relax and recuperate from the stress of the physical world. At the same time, Lavenders need to occasionally focus on their bodies to take care of them.

At first, people are attracted to and fascinated by the imaginative Lavenders. Many soon discover, however, that they are living with delicate individuals who are sometimes present and sometimes not. Lavenders can be elusive. They can become mentally and emotionally unavailable because they live so much in their own inner worlds. Intense intellectual conversations are rare in a relationship with a Lavender. If you don't need consistent mental stimulation or deep philosophical discussions with your partner, then a Lavender can be a fun mate. However, if you do need thought-provoking debates, then either gently and patiently teach your Lavender how to engage at that level or find others who can fulfill that need. Moreover, expect to be the financial provider in this relationship. As you may have already surmised, these are the least rational and logical of all the Love Colors. They live by their feelings and intuition, rather than by their intellect.

If you plan on having children with this partner, realize that Lavenders will love, cherish, and play with their children, but they will not be responsible disciplinarians. Lavenders are more like juveniles themselves, so most likely you will be the one to guide the family.

When Lavenders are out of power, they have difficulty functioning well in physical reality. They leave their bodies so often they don't accomplish anything. They are frequently spacey and absentminded, and they often forget their promises. They have a hard time following through with any of their creative ideas and visions. These scattered personalities can be incredibly irresponsible, and many perceive them as selfish, unaware, and inconsiderate.

Although Lavenders are kind and good-natured, they are not always willing to be equal partners when it comes to sharing responsibilities. Because many out-of-power Lavenders cannot hold jobs, they frequently require others to support them. They are like lost little children — they just want their lives to be simple and easy. They are happiest when they have partners willing to handle all the financial matters. They would rather be playfully creating, and they resent having to labor hard at jobs they detest just to supply such boring basics as rent and car payments. Struggling and working hard to earn dirty, disgusting money is repulsive to them and makes life less fun. Lavenders just want the money to materialize so they can buy fun items — pretty clothes, sparkling jewelry, spa treatments, or other fanciful items.

Most partners quickly become frustrated with the Lavenders' inability or unwillingness to make a living. Because Lavenders resist dealing with such mundane topics as budgets, investments, or financial planning, they can easily get themselves and their mates into financial trouble. You could have many arguments trying to teach them to save money, be reliable, keep their word, or follow through with commitments. Discussing money problems is so undesirable to Lavenders that they will look for any means possible to escape. They will get sick, become distracted, change the subject, or avoid coming home altogether.

Many Lavenders can become adept at dodging their responsibilities. Running away, avoiding, and hiding, they can become lost in a twisted world of pretense. They are usually naïve individuals, so they are not deceitful to be mean or vindictive. Fearing rejection or reproach, they may fabricate their own version of reality. They are great storytellers.

They just lose their way and then have a difficult time telling fact from fiction, truth from lies, and reality from fantasy. Lavenders often lose their self-identity too and then feel like misfits. If they feel unloved, if they sense people judge them as being lazy, irresponsible, ineffective, or weird, they shrink inside, disappear, or escape into another reality to avoid facing people's ire and disapproval. These Lavenders can become depressed and withdrawn or feel invisible.

Being in relationship with one of these wounded souls can be sad and challenging. Many Lavenders have lost their sense of purpose and feel that their unique personalities are detrimental to their happiness and possibly their survival. Some Lavenders fear life. These Lavenders are difficult to reach or to help. Some will retreat into the world of drugs or medication — especially drugs that make them feel euphoric — to escape a bitter and cold world.

When Lavenders feel apprehensive living in the physical world, they can develop serious illnesses or become hypochondriacs. They always seem to be ill. Many face serious, chronic health issues because they feel so unsafe in life, so criticized and misunderstood, that they don't send energy to their bodies.

One of the best places for Lavenders to go to reconnect with their true selves is out in nature or some other quiet place, so they can meditate or drift into another realm where they don't feel threatened or trapped. Drifting outside and beyond normal physical boundaries, Lavenders can once again find answers to many of their questions — mostly their spiritual questions.

If Lavenders shift their awareness to these other dimensions to gain insights and answers, and then return to physical reality to implement these answers, then all can be well and they can regain their health. If they leave their bodies just to escape life, however, and refuse to deal with their issues or change their habit of eluding reality, then their lives and their bodies will continue to be dysfunctional and problematic.

Lavenders can also learn to feel safe in their physical bodies if they can find a way to receive nurturing touch — whether from loved ones or from healing practitioners. These gentle souls need to be patiently coaxed back into their bodies by people who can make them feel safe and nourished. Finding enjoyable forms of exercise can also reconnect them to the physical plane. They need to retrain themselves to believe there is pleasure being in a physical body.

To stay in power, Lavenders need to be courageous and adventurous enough to face the real world, to stay in their bodies long enough to be a useful and functioning part of society. Once they understand that the world contains not just buildings, dirt, concrete, and "normal" people but also rainbows, waterfalls, beautiful songbirds, and sensitive Lavenders — and once they realize and accept that even though they are wildly different from most people, they still play a special role here, as unique, creative souls — they may again connect with the amazing, playful imagination that is within them.

As unusual as Lavenders are, without these sensitive loving beings, life would be dull and mundane. In a world that has majestic redwoods, magnificent mountains, and powerful oceans, Lavenders are the rainbows and clouds — ethereal, illusive, and lovely. Each Love Color has a place and purpose; each brings a different aspect of beauty and wonder to life.

Most Lavenders are combinations — for example, Violet/Lavenders, Blue/Lavenders, and Yellow/Lavenders. When these gentle souls are combination colors, they can either experience incredible inner conflict or get help from the more powerful side of their personality. If the person's Violet aspect feels driven to be in the world accomplishing something meaningful and important, but the Lavender aspect is too frightened of the outside world, this person may have a challenging time accomplishing anything. On the other hand, while the Lavender aspect of the person may drift away into a fantasyland, the dominant Violet aspect could use the creative visions to produce something valuable — and make a living.

Crystals

The first thing to know about Crystals is that they are rare and elusive. It is challenging to know whether or not you have met a Crystal, because these individuals are chameleons. They change their aura colors as often as they are around different people. Crystals have clear auras and tend to take on the Love Colors, personalities, and temperaments of those around them. They will behave like driven Greens in the presence of Greens or become playful, energetic Yellows whenever they interact with Yellows. On the positive side, this gives them the ability to get along with almost anyone. On the downside, it can confuse you if you are trying to create a relationship with them. You may never quite know which personality they will take on from day to day.

On the off chance that you have actually encountered a true Crystal, here is what you can expect. Crystals are usually quiet and introspective beings and require a tremendous amount of time alone. They love to be at home, quietly sitting in meditation or puttering around in their garden. Healthy, in-power Crystals can be happy, well-adjusted, respectful, and considerate partners. They tend to be loving, kind, and serene. But they do require a lot of time alone.

Crystals are clear conduits for healing energy, which they allow to flow naturally through them and into the people around them. If they do healing work for a living, they usually need to work on just one person at a time, then retreat to cleanse their energy and reconnect with their Source. If they are in power, you can feel energetically well fed and healthy around them.

Crystals are sensitive, delicate beings, much like fragile crystal vases. They can be shattered easily by being around too many people or by being overwhelmed by too much responsibility. They treasure spending time in their sanctuaries. Reconnecting with their souls, finding their quiet spiritual center, is a must if they are to function at all in the world.

It can be challenging for Crystals to be in relationships, because they absorb the emotions, feelings, and struggles of their partners. It is especially important for them, therefore, to be with people who are in power and exhibiting positive behavior. Crystals can become energetically drained and depressed if they are with partners who are unhappy, angry, or in any other way dysfunctional. If their partners have addiction problems, Crystals often feel affected by the substances just by being in proximity to their partners.

By taking on their partners' qualities, Crystals can lose themselves. It can be challenging for Crystals to maintain their own identity, their own goals, and their own dreams when they are in the presence of someone who has a stronger personality. It can take them years to discover who they really are, as opposed to who they thought they were as they were growing up. As children, many Crystals take on the qualities and behaviors of their different family members, all the while believing this is their own personality as well. It can be disturbing to Crystals to watch themselves struggle to separate themselves from their parents' identities, only to find themselves reforming to match their partners'.

Crystals need to spend quality time alone so they can get in touch with their own true nature, to learn about their own beliefs, feelings, needs, and priorities. If they don't discover their own center and their own truths, they will find themselves lost in a maze of confusing personality changes throughout their entire lives.

Crystals need to either remain single, only connecting with close friends who are loving and supportive, or choose partners who are in power and expressing their best qualities. When Crystals are with healthy partners, those who also understand and accept their sensitive and unusual qualities, they flourish. Once they connect with mates who support them and send them energy rather than draining them, Crystals feel alive.

Crystals can be intelligent, but they are not usually overly expressive. They can feel quite deeply but often keep their feelings and emotions hidden. They are not interested in saving the planet or conquering the world. They are not driven to create a vast reservoir of wealth. They do not need to surround themselves with a lot of possessions — it only clutters and complicates their existence. They like their environment to be clean, organized, and simple. Their homes will be simply decorated but comfortable. There may be subtle spiritual touches to their decor — crystals, quiet music, and gentle chimes — or an understated, natural touch, such as flowers, fountains, plants, and a gentle breeze. Having peaceful surroundings that reflect their quiet nature is important to them. Out of power, however, Crystals can sometimes create sterile environments. Their overly sensitive nature can cause them to develop phobias about germs, mold, and dirt. Living in an overly sanitary environment could eventually become challenging for their partners.

If you crave serenity, if you would love to create a beautiful haven with a deeply reflective and spiritual partner, then an in-power Crystal can be a perfect partner for you. The challenge is locating one and, even more, finding one that is healthy, in power, and willing to share a life with you. The majority of these elusive beings would rather hide out than interact with the fast-paced world.

Once you do find a Crystal, you may have to be the one who instigates the encounter. If you treat the shy and withdrawn Crystals gingerly, with courtesy and respect, they may feel safe enough to commune with you. Usually kind, they will take your feelings into consideration when they respond to your invitation to join you for dinner. If you take them to a small, quiet restaurant, they will immediately appreciate your discriminating taste and sensitivity.

If you want to take them somewhere else, maybe to a concert, know that the environment, as well as other people's energy, can easily affect them. Most Crystals are happier listening to a pleasant string quartet than a rambunctious rock and roll extravaganza. Being surrounded by crowds or engulfed by too much loud noise and chaotic energy can actually damage these sensitive beings. Most Crystals do not relish wild, drunken festivities. And they typically honor their bodies enough not to put drugs, alcohol, or other toxins into them.

It's not as if they don't enjoy going out occasionally; it's just that Crystals do not require wild adventures, raucous parties, and daring exploits. They are not comfortable with loud, outspoken, and brash personalities, and they can become easily overwhelmed and fatigued by too much activity.

Conversing with an in-power Crystal should be a breeze. Crystals are bright and can carry on highly intelligent conversations. They are avid learners and are usually well read on a wide range of subjects, so they will be comfortable discussing almost any topic you find interesting.

Crystals appreciate people who are willing to build the relationship slowly — they tend to be guarded when it comes to developing intimate relationships. This doesn't refer to just their sexuality. They are naturally sensitive and trusting, but their life experiences may have taught them to become more guarded and mistrustful. Having the ability to connect deeply with people energetically, many of them have been hurt by others' lack of tact and decorum. Most people do not understand the fragile nature of these beings. And because Crystals are reclusive, few people take the time to really get to know them. Be sure you are serious about this Crystal before proceeding too far — if you become physically intimate too quickly, you risk damaging your Crystal. Crystals do not take relationships lightly. Be honest and real, but gentle.

These interesting creatures, however, do not always make it easy to get to know them. They tend to be aloof — not snobbish, but they can be perceived to be that way by those who do not understand their need for privacy. They fiercely guard their sacred rituals and can resent people invading their silence. Crystals are so used to being alone that they may not allow their partners to join them on their sacred journeys. They appreciate patient mates who allow them their own space. By being gentle and understanding, you may earn the trust of these guarded souls; trust is required before they will allow you into their inner sanctum.

Crystals are self-sufficient, intelligent, and self-confident enough to enjoy living alone. If they go to the trouble of getting involved with someone, or if they find the courage to let someone into their lives, they prefer partners who will be sensitive to their unusual needs and behaviors. Not everyone is comfortable being with such solitary individuals, or with those who consistently change their personalities to match others around them.

If you find yourself in love with an in-power, emotionally available Crystal, it can be a pleasant experience. In-power Crystals are wonderfully supportive, patient, and understanding. These spiritual companions will quietly sit by your side, lovingly listen to your dreams, and gently encourage you to follow your heart. They will remind you to look deep inside for your answers. They are equally content to be alone, to be with you, or to sit with a few close friends. They are easy to please.

Crystals can hold down stable jobs, provided they are in comfortable, stress-free environments with pleasant, polite people. In power, they are adept at managing their finances. They prefer to keep life simple by paying off their bills each month. Staying out of debt is important to them, because it gives them a sense of freedom and ease. There might not be much money left at the end of the month, but this does not worry them since they have simple needs. If you join with one of these Crystals, you probably will not have an extravagant or lavish lifestyle, but your life will be clean, simple, and debt-free.

On the subject of children, many Crystals cannot handle the rowdy, noisy energy of children or the ongoing, often stressful responsibility of raising children. Out-of-power Crystals are like lost children themselves, so they have very little to offer these young souls. Being around kids can drain them.

Most Crystals are not eager to have children, although there may be a few who can accept the idea. You may encounter in-power Crystals who are willing to raise well-behaved children. They may require the assistance of a nanny or other domestic help, however, so that they have the time and opportunity to retreat alone and unfettered into their quiet gardens. You may have to make sure you earn a good enough income to be able to afford this luxury.

Occasionally you can find these rare creatures hiding in the corner at the library while silently browsing through books about culture, history, spirituality, or other life-enhancing topics. Or you may find them sitting unnoticeably in the back row at a bookstore lecture. The mysteries of life fascinate Crystals, but typically they prefer quietly reading or watching television, exploring other countries and other worlds in the peaceful tranquility of their own homes. They love low-key simplicity.

Take heart, though, if you desire to travel. Eventually your chameleon partner will most likely absorb your qualities and characteristics and develop a desire for the same adventures. At this point, your Crystal will quietly travel by your side to almost anywhere you desire to go. Being sensitive creatures who prefer comfort and ease, however, Crystals may still prefer to go to lovely, peaceful, and safe locations, possibly spiritual, exotic, or sacred lands, rather than venture into dangerous, remote locations where survival could be an issue. Crystals are not fond of the harsh, dirty, or uncivilized elements of the world. They are not fond of bugs, filth, or unsavory characters. They are not that adventurous. Life is more of an inward journey for them, rather than a worldly quest.

If you fall in love with an out-of-power Crystal, your experience will be quite different. These individuals are often so afraid of life that they stay hidden inside their safe, familiar surroundings. They rarely venture from their own homes. (Out-of-power Crystals and Lavenders are very similar. Both are delicate and sensitive creatures who tend to retreat into their own private worlds. Frightened Crystals, however, will hide out in peaceful but nonetheless physical environments, while Lavenders will escape into fantasy worlds.)

Not only are these unusual Crystals difficult to figure out, but they also have a challenging time understanding themselves. They can be lost, frightened, and confused young souls. Looking into their eyes, either you see panic and desperation or you see emptiness. They do not seem to know why they are on the planet or what their life purpose is, and they look to other people to take care of them and guide them. They can frantically jump from teacher to teacher, one mentor to another, old friends to new friends, seeking guidance and direction. They try endlessly to find someone, anyone, who can tell them what to do, where to go, or who they are. If they cannot find answers, they lose faith in themselves and in life. Many out-of-power Crystals waste their entire lives pondering their reason for existence. They eventually lose hope and give up on ever finding their greater purpose in life. Intimidated by a cold, harsh world, these unstable beings can live tortured, lonely lives.

They often try to find love to fill the void. They desperately search for someone who will take care of them and handle all of life's difficulties for them. These terrified and lonely individuals become so anxious that they scare potential suitors away. Then they can become incredibly moody and sullen and isolate themselves, shutting out friends and all possibilities for love. These individuals can become forlorn and depressed.

Other out-of-power Crystals learn to cope with the uncertainties of life by becoming busybodies. Unsure of their own purpose and direction, they distract themselves by getting involved with everyone else's lives. To avoid facing their own fear, pain, and loneliness, they immerse themselves in other people's stories and dramas and can become irritating to their friends and family. Many people report feeling drained in the presence of these Crystals. Looking for connection, trying to fit in and to be loved by others, these lost individuals can unconsciously absorb the energy of those around them, which makes them a challenge to be around.

If you have gained the trust of a Crystal, you will have a loyal and faithful friend and partner. Crystals' desire to form meaningful relationships with those who will support them and accept them as they are is almost as important to them as their need to be alone.

Chapter 9

Creating Harmony
with Your Love Colors

If you have met and become involved with your love interest, you may want some ideas about how you can create and maintain a harmonious life together. Or if you have not yet gotten involved with a particular person, perhaps you want to know what it could take to create a wonderful balance in your relationship even before you begin a partnership. Do you want to know about the potential challenges you may be up against and what you can do to work through these challenges? This chapter discusses ways to fulfill each color's needs, and it suggests various solutions to the different difficulties that may arise.

Each of the Love Colors has a unique personality. Understanding and respecting your partner's individuality and honoring her or his special needs and desires can increase your ability to have a long-lasting and fulfilling partnership. So many people expect their partners to be just like themselves. Realizing that their companions have different styles and behaviors often leads to hurt, anger, or resentment between partners.

This chapter is designed to help you understand each Love Color's priorities, needs, and desires so that you have a better chance for happiness and harmony. What will make your partner happy? What is important to him or her? And what will you need to know to create peace and maintain mutual respect and admiration with this particular Love Color?

Reds

There are different Reds with different tastes and desires. If you want to create a compatible, harmonious relationship with a Red, knowing which type of Red you have in your life can be helpful. Some powerful Reds want fiery passion and excitement in their lives. Other, down-to-earth Reds want quieter, less demanding, more traditional companions. All Reds desire mates who are honest, trustworthy, hardworking, and appreciative.

Some Reds love having partners who can excite them with physical vitality and spirited energy. People who are intelligent, physically fit, sensuous, alluring, and sexually confident exhilarate these Reds. They demand loyalty and monogamy from their partners, however. If you betray them, they will leave.

Most Reds love to be mentally stimulated and inspired by their partners. If you want to be in a relationship with one of these individuals, be supportive of the Red's plans and ideas, but also be totally honest. These strong souls value candor, so question them if you think they could do better. Don't criticize or demean their ideas, however. Most Reds have fierce pride. Challenge them in a way that lets them know you expect more from them because they are so powerful and competent. Bring the best out in them by demanding the best from them. Then fully support and encourage their improved ideas.

Other Reds prefer dependable, faithful, unpretentious, and hardworking partners who will not challenge their authority. These Reds are loyal and responsible mates, but they do not want a lot of drama in their lives. They want to know they can trust their partners and that they can create a comfortable home together. They appreciate mates who are willing to quietly take care of their needs — cook dinner, clean the house, fix the kitchen faucet, or maintain their vehicle. To show their gratitude, they will make sure their partner's needs are met as well. Reds treasure strong moral support and respect those who have sound ethical values and do their work without complaining. Reds do not easily tolerate people with weak principles or those who whine about their lives. If something is wrong, they expect you to fix it or, if the task is beyond your capabilities, to respectfully ask for their help.

Reds need people to stay out of their way when they have something to do. They typically take their work seriously. Some love playing the role of the bold, courageous hero — braving the elements to prepare for the hurricane or rescuing trapped survivors. They take great pride in accomplishing tough tasks and don't always want to share the glory. If you have this type of Red, remember that they appreciate generous helpings of awe-inspired praise.

There may be other times, however, when you will earn their admiration by working alongside them to accomplish a project. Reds admire bravery and hard work, and they enjoy teamwork when their partners are doing their equal share. Of course, very few people can physically accomplish what a Red can. Not many match the physical stamina of these powerful personalities. But Reds will respect your attempts anyway.

Some Reds are bold and blunt, so you will know exactly what they want and when they want it. The quiet Reds, on the other hand, expect their mates to eventually learn and remember what they want from them at any given time. Many Reds, strong and in control at all times, do not share their thoughts and feelings. You will need to carefully observe their signals to know when to be a quiet, supportive companion standing firmly by their side, and when to leave the room. Learn when it's appropriate to accompany them on an adventure, and when to let them go alone. Reds want their mates to know when to stand up to their incredible power and when to back away. And they need partners who are always honest and trustworthy.

Reds need to know that their partners respect and appreciate all they have together. They are not happy when their partners demand more than what the Reds can earn or provide. You may insult them and wound their pride if they think you are dissatisfied with their performance, and you may frustrate them if you insist on having what they believe to be nonessential extravagances. They may perceive you as selfish, greedy, and ungrateful, which will not bode well for your relationship.

If you believe your Red is not providing enough wealth or abundance in your life, ask yourself why you feel this way before you place an unnecessary burden on your partner. Most Reds work as hard as they can. Why do you feel unfulfilled if your Red is offering you security and loyalty? If you truly believe you want a Red, and you want a relationship with this particular Red, you will either need to relax and expect fewer physical possessions, learn to value what you already have, or find a way to buy the creature comforts you desire on your own. If you are going to create your own wealth, do so without insulting or demeaning your Red partner.

If you have an out-of-power Red who can't seem to hold a job, or one who fights with every authority figure, then you are justified in being frustrated. Many out-of-power Reds become alcoholics in order to run farther from their problems or to physically punish and abuse themselves. These Reds are stubborn and usually will not go for therapy.

Changing the situation requires discovering their deeper reason for self-sabotage — finding why they have low self-esteem and are engaging in self-destructive behavior. If they won't tell you honestly what's bothering them, listen carefully between the lines or watch closely for clues in their behavior. Reds are typically guarded, but there will be signs if you pay attention. Or maybe you know them well enough to understand their history; possibly they have issues left from childhood. Once you discover their fears, strongly demand that they face their inner demons and get back on their feet.

If instead you coddle out-of-power Reds, they'll lose even more respect for themselves. If they sense you feel sorry for them, they'll feel even lower. Reds are happiest when they feel strong, competent, and productive. Sometimes what Reds need is a strong kick in their emotional backside. Get them to fight to believe in themselves again. Push them to face and overcome their fears.

Reds need their incredible power, strength, and stubbornness to work for them, not against them. They need to work, period. They need to feel a sense of accomplishment. If they can't find a job, you put them to work. Physical labor is the best therapy for Reds. Make them repair things or clean the house. Have them mow the lawn, water the garden, or change the oil in the car. Simultaneously, keep them searching for a job. Reds hate being told what to do, but when they fall out of power and lose faith in their abilities, you have to give them a push — a strong push. They may become angry with you, but they will also respect and appreciate your belief in them. Someone needs to believe in them. Who better than a loyal partner?

Wanting more emotional intimacy from your Red is a different matter. Understand that Reds are not comfortable expressing feelings or being emotionally vulnerable. You'll find them more willing to bring you physical gifts — like candy, flowers, tools, or appliances — or to build you something — like a house, a deck, or a fireplace — than to give you greater emotional intimacy. See this as their way of being close to you, of showing that they care. Didn't you want the strong silent partner, someone you could respect and count on, someone dependable? Have you changed your mind now, or can you find a way to appreciate the good, decent, and solid qualities of this mate?

Sometimes the passionate Reds will start arguments just to bring up heat and energy. Some become bored when life gets too quiet. You will need to know how to energetically spar with these Reds, like a bullfighter with a bull. Use the figurative red cape to engage and excite your bull, but also know to back away when tempers flare. Know when to stop. If they become frustrated and walk away, don't follow them or pursue the discussion. If your Red tells you the conversation is over, let it lie. Be self-confident enough to not be intimidated by the Reds' domineering personalities if you want to keep their respect, but do not taunt an angry Red. They enjoy fire but not constantly. If you push angry Reds, they can become hostile and even physically violent. Once they lose their temper, you may want to take cover.

If you were fighting over a real issue, and not just arguing because your partner was bored, it is better to let the situation calm down before you bring up the conversation again. Do not patronize Reds. And do not give up just to pacify them, because they will feel you do not respect their intelligence or competency. And whatever you do, do not say "I told you so" to Reds. It's not a good idea to humiliate them or damage their egos. If you hurt them, they will act much like wounded animals. They will strike out or shut down and walk away to sulk.

If the blunt and often tactless Reds have hurt you, insulted you, or behaved inappropriately, it will be very hard for them to apologize. If they feel bad and want to atone for their wrongdoings, they will probably bring you a gift, cook you a special dinner, or finally repair the fence you've been begging them to fix. See this behavior as their way of apologizing. Making them say the words will humiliate them. Once they show you they are remorseful, they will expect you to accept their apologetic action and then move on with life. Put the incident in the past and forget about it. It's in your best interest never to bring it up again. You'll earn their respect as well as their gratitude.

In order to maintain a peaceful existence with your Red, do your best to keep your discussions about feelings and your relationship to a minimum. Reds have little if any interest in such discussions. If you can be self-confident enough to know for yourself how your relationship is progressing, your Red will be happier. Reds don't want to emotionally coddle or constantly reassure their partners. They want their partners to be strong and self-assured.

Along these same lines, you may end up being the emotionally supportive parent for your children. Most Reds appreciate their partners' willingness to handle the children's emotional needs while they provide the physical necessities. If you really desire your Red to connect more fully with your children, encourage them to learn how. Since Reds are usually uncomfortable being open and communicative, help yours feel safe and supported. Coach them without making them feel foolish or insulted. Since Reds value strength and courage, show them how being open and available to the children is the more courageous act. Then learn not to push too hard. They will need time. Reds often become frustrated with impatience. Instead, give them encouraging feedback whenever they take a step toward emotional intimacy. These steps can be used to improve the quality of the emotional connections in your relationship as well.

Most Reds are also not interested in discussing spiritual philosophies. They usually prefer to focus on the three-dimensional world they can physically touch, taste, smell, hear, or see. If you want your Red to become involved in your faith or religion, accept that he or she may be generous enough to build something for your church but probably won't be interested in what the preacher has to say. Although many Reds will defend their country's religious beliefs and freedoms, it often has more to do with fighting for what they believe is right and just.

You may be involved with a high-maintenance, decadent Red. Many people find these Reds exciting and challenging. Your life will certainly not be boring. These Reds can be very strong-willed and demanding — they want the best, and they love all the physical pleasures that exist in life. If you have a Red that constantly lusts for new designer clothing, expensive jewelry, quality furniture, fine dining, and frequent trips to the spa, be prepared to make a lot of money to support those desires. These Reds love pampering. Or your Red may want the latest tools and gadgets, the most expensive and technologically advanced entertainment centers, or the fastest, most sought-after cars.

If one of you in the relationship is not making a great deal of money, overspending could be the topic of many of your arguments.

To create a fulfilling, compatible, and stress-free relationship with this type, the answer is simple: be a multimillionaire. Or earn your Red's respect by being strong enough to say no to the constant demands. The alternative could be spending your life in debt.

On the other hand, this type of Red could also bring out stronger, more powerful qualities in you. This partner may force you to become a greater and wealthier version of yourself than you thought possible. You may be stimulated to find better or more creative ways to make money. To paraphrase the philosopher Friedrich Nietzsche, "What doesn't destroy us, makes us stronger."

Reds are usually physically fit, so you'll rarely have to take care of an ailing Red. They don't enjoy being under the weather and typically will hide it if they do feel ill. They will press on. Your greater challenge may be getting them to the doctor once something is wrong with them. Reds are stubborn and they don't like admitting they have weaknesses. To keep harmony, respect their need to be in control of their own life. If they feel strong, they may just be powerful enough to heal their own bodies.

Are you getting the picture that you have a powerhouse on your hands? Reds typically run the show. They'll be loyal mates if they feel you respect them and appreciate what they bring to the relationship, whether this is money, sexual energy, intelligence, companionship, or an ability to bring ideas into physical form.

If you want to have a compatible, successful, and long-term relationship with these amazing creatures, appreciate their strengths, match their energy, and learn to allow or at least tolerate their moods. If they want to go places and have a good time, go out and play with them. If you have Reds who want to argue, spar with them. Help them release their frustrations. When they want to be alone, find other things to do. When they want to be passionate, be their sexual equal. Earn their admiration by maintaining your own self-worth and strength. If you treat your Red with respect, reverence and awe, like you would any force of nature — a hurricane, a tornado, or a tsunami — then you can have an exciting and rewarding relationship.

Reds respect partners who...

- are honest, loyal, and trustworthy.

- are self-confident.

- accept them as strong-willed, powerful partners.

- appreciate the lifestyle they have provided.

- allow them time to be alone.

- are healthy, physical, passionate, and sexually monogamous.

- support their desire to spend time with their friends.

- do not insist on having discussions about spirituality.

- are either traditional and agreeable, or strong and fiery.

- do not bother them with discussions about their relationship and their feelings.

- treat them with respect and never patronize them.

- offer them generous praise for their accomplishments.

Oranges

The independent Oranges prefer partners who are adventurous, self-confident, and self-reliant. They enjoy companions who will join them on their daring exploits, or who will not be ruffled or sulk if the Oranges choose to go off alone. Oranges need a lot of time to themselves. Realize that, if you have fallen in love with one, you will have to accept the consequences of living with an often-absent swashbuckler. Oranges are not homebodies. If you want harmony in your relationship, learn to respect and admire your Orange's strength and bravery.

If you have chosen an Orange, you probably wanted a strong, independent partner whom you could respect. You probably wanted someone you could not intimidate or control. Deep inside, you probably valued your freedom and preferred someone who would not be around all the time energetically suffocating you. You can be assured your Orange will not be home much. If you can accept this tradeoff and learn to appreciate the positive qualities this exciting soul can offer you, then you can have a fascinating life.

If security is important to you and you have found yourself involved with an Orange, perhaps you are fortunate enough to have a cunning Orange who is agile enough to dodge danger, or you have found yourself a very lucky Orange who has not yet used up all of her or his nine lives. You will quickly learn that worrying about these rebels does no good. And they certainly will not give up their adventures for you.

Many Oranges were suppressed and restricted as children. Their parents worked hard to control these little daredevils, trying to keep them from seriously injuring themselves and spending many nights in the emergency room with these young souls. Only as adults do some of the Oranges finally find their freedom. Now, no adult — and this includes you — can prevent them from jumping out of planes or from racing their motorcycles down mountains.

If you attempt to suppress your Orange partner or try to prohibit this soul from going on adventures, you will have an unhappy or rebellious companion on your hands. The most loving way to support Oranges is to allow them to explore life with daring, skill, and courage. If you can have faith that they know what they are doing, and trust that they are intelligent enough to escape or survive danger, then you have the potential to create a happy relationship.

It's best if you maintain your own life, your own independence, your own dreams and goals, and do not depend too heavily on an Orange to meet your needs. They aren't comfortable with partners who require a lot of emotional reassurance. Oranges flourish best in relationships with equals, with those who understand their need to live on the edge. Few people understand the desires and lifestyles of Oranges, so if you can be one of their cheerleaders, you will gain their trust and appreciation and they will enjoy your company.

If you are not one of these natural risk takers yourself, perhaps you can learn to incorporate some Orange qualities, attitudes, and behaviors into your life. If you can develop an appreciation for some of the same daring quests and travel alongside your mate, you could have a long-lasting union. Just train yourself to be safe. Oranges have had years to learn how to think and react quickly. Their extreme sports are nothing to mess with if you feel at all uncertain. If you do not feel as surefooted and adept, then wait patiently back at the tent or lodge until they return. There is no sense getting hurt or killed attempting to keep up with Oranges. They will probably appreciate your efforts, but stay safe. Something else to consider: Since Oranges can be very competitive people, it is probably better that you do not try to surpass them. This could get both of you seriously injured or worse.

If you agree to create a family together, be prepared to take charge of creating the home environment for yourself and your children. Don't expect your Orange partner to be home much, and certainly do not expect him or her to join in on the home decorating. It's rare to find Oranges who enjoy being in a traditional home environment, and most do not enjoy the responsibility of raising a family. However, these Oranges do exist. If you can allow them time for adventure, they may repay your understanding and patience by spending more time at home, at least until the children are older and on their own.

Once they actually have families, most Oranges are responsible enough to provide for them. It is common to find that Oranges who have families had them by accident or under pressure. Some of the more self-centered Oranges prefer to live dangerously and not use birth control. Others end up with children because they acquiesced to pressure from their partners. This does not mean Oranges are necessarily selfish, although when they are out of power this is one of their qualities. They just love their freedom and independence. Having children is a long-term commitment and can delay the Oranges' opportunities to travel and explore. It is rare to find Oranges who want to explore the Himalayas with a baby strapped to their backs.

If you can appreciate your Orange's willingness to earn an income and give you some or most of the money, and if you can accept your partner's need to go off on independent explorations, you have a better chance of creating a happy relationship. Oranges' jobs often take them away. Think of wild animals who prowl the jungle and then return to their prides days later. Some Oranges are wilderness guides who take groups on dangerous safaris and may be gone for days. Some take high-risk jobs working on fishing boats in the treacherous Arctic Sea. They may be gone for weeks or months at a time, and in cases like these, you'll need to learn self-reliance.

If you need a life partner who comes home every evening to enjoy a quiet evening with the family, then you'll probably be better off with a different Love Color. You will almost never have this type of life with an Orange. Oranges may not spend as much time connecting and bonding with you or the children as you would like, but most likely they will care about the family. You must be self-confident enough to know who you are, because your Orange partner will expect strength from you. Oranges are not good at showing their feelings, so if you can become adept at noticing the signs that yours does care, you will create more harmony between the two of you.

If you are involved with an out-of-power Orange, you probably know how very cold and self-centered Oranges can be. They are rarely interested in improving themselves to appease their partners. Do not expect your Orange to be introspective or enlightened. Oranges believe that exploring the physical world and challenging their physical skills are what is important.

You can attempt to show your Orange there is more to life than running from one dangerous situation to another. But you'll need to do this in a respectful, nonjudgmental, noninvasive way. If you feel brave enough to tackle the task of teaching your Orange how to become more introspective and more emotionally available, you might do so by showing that it is safe to talk, it is safe to be open and vulnerable. Realize that in the Oranges' world, however, vulnerability can lead to death. Show your Orange that being emotionally and psychologically accessible is not life threatening, and don't criticize the personal thoughts and feelings she or he finally shares with you. If you encounter stubborn resistance from your Orange, it is better to let it go. Live your life as an example of emotional availability, kindness, and spiritual awareness. If your Orange ever does develop an interest in these subjects, perhaps he or she will feel safe enough to ask you for guidance.

If you are determined to control or criticize one of these free spirits, if you try to stuff your Orange into a responsible and traditional lifestyle, you will probably see the stubborn and rebellious Orange nature emerge. Trying to cage a wild animal is never a good idea. It is easy for Oranges to walk away, to abandon any type of restrictive structure, rather then dealing with your controlling behavior. They are not prone to deep feelings of guilt, and they are not usually attached to having a home or a lot of possessions. Don't expect your Orange to look back. If Oranges are not afraid to face a raging river, they are not afraid to live alone — they actually relish it. They would rather face a dangerous mountain lion than live a suffocating life. They would rather take their chances in the outside world than feel buried alive in the suburbs. It you were attracted to the raw courage and ingenuity of Oranges in the first place, allow them to maintain their intriguing and adventurous personality.

Oranges appreciate partners who...

- are self-confident, self-reliant, and adventurous.

- understand their passion for danger and excitement.

- support their independence and need to be alone.

- love the outdoors.

- enjoy traveling and adventuring.

- admire their courage.

- never try to control or suppress them.

- maintain their own independence and self-respect.

- stay on track with their own personal life goals.

- trust that Oranges know what they are doing.

- trust they are safe and don't worry about them.

- don't compete with them.

- appreciate an exciting and untraditional life.

Magentas

So the idea of going down the rabbit hole fascinates you? You always loved *Alice in Wonderland* as a child? And you don't want or need a stable, traditional lifestyle? You don't need to be married...at least don't need to be in a long marriage? Are you prepared to live like an outcast, or at least live *with* one? If you want a zany, quirky, and unpredictable partner, then being with a Magenta should suit you just fine.

Magentas like to be around people who have fun and relish life. They enjoy partners who are free and easy. Be prepared to attend a wide variety of wild parties, strange art exhibits, or off-the-wall live performances. And understand that you probably will be keeping strange hours with this partner; you may start your evening late and continue well past sunrise. And you will probably meet all sorts of fascinating people — Magentas have a way of finding them. However, these fascinating people will end up being only fleeting acquaintances, since Magentas do not typically cultivate long-lasting relationships. They will eagerly learn about people, laugh, have fun with them, shock them, and then move on. Go with the flow. If you have a tendency to want to keep friends, you may be disappointed in this relationship. Magentas enjoy new things. They like variety.

Magentas like to figure people out, to see what turns them on. But they themselves do not like to be analyzed or figured out. They'll enjoy seeing you try but will keep you off guard with a good game of hide-and-seek. They like being unpredictable, so don't try to pin Magentas down. They love entertaining people, so be interested and be fascinated by them. This will help keep them intrigued by you.

Magentas love to be mentally and emotionally stimulated and surprised. They love to be kept on their toes. They like anticipation and not knowing what to expect from you — it keeps life interesting. It's better to approach them in a lighthearted and playful manner, not in a manipulative way. They do not like mean-spirited or malicious mind games. Magentas are not cruel, just fun and curious. Keep them fascinated by constantly reinventing yourself. Frequent wardrobe changes could also be fun.

Magentas are delighted by creativity, so it helps if you are a resourceful or inventive person yourself. If you're not a talented artist, take heart — even coming up with imaginative ideas enthralls Magentas. They enjoy all forms of creativity and innovation and prefer to have fascinating and intelligent conversations with you, rather than being serious or intense for long periods of time. Keep your playtime together light and entertaining, but still entrancing.

Magentas enjoy partners who are independent but available. Have your own life and your own projects, but stay accessible. You don't want your Magenta to become lonely. They've been rejected by people before and are used to being abandoned, but they don't like it. They'll find your commitment, and your willingness to tolerate their strange personality, captivating. Most people flee early on. Magentas do need their time and space to be alone. They need time to think of strange ways to bend reality into unusual forms and then create their amazing works of art; but don't go too far away for too long. Just be unpredictable. And don't be clingy or needy — they find that boring. Just find ways to be happy and entertain yourself.

These madcap characters will amuse you every day. They can come up with amazing and bizarre inventions and may astound you by actually developing their zany ideas into something real and physical. Some of their ideas may even make them rich.

Your Magenta may also surprise you one day by agreeing to marriage. But look carefully at the motives involved. He or she may love you but also may be focusing on the idea of having a fun and exciting wedding. After all, your Magenta will be the center of attention at the party. This may not be the best reason to get married. Then again, why not? Life is too short not to have fun. Magentas think we take it all too seriously anyway. Some Magentas believe in commitment because it's the best way to really become intimate with someone, to really learn all about that person. However, for most of these unusual souls, long-term, intense relationships are too confining. When the relationship turns into a responsibility or becomes hard work, they prefer to wander away.

Frequent and short marriages are common for these personalities. They want the freedom to explore and experiment and don't want to live with rules or expectations. Monogamy takes the variety out of life, so they usually prefer open marriages. Does this fit with your picture? Are you just as adventurous and experimental? Does the possibility of this lifestyle intrigue you or bother you? It's not always the case that Magentas resist monogamy. If you can remain beguiling, they may feel fulfilled with one partner. Realize that their sexual desires and styles could be just as wacky and unconventional as they are. Magentas appreciate companions who are willing to experiment with them.

If you want to have a long-term relationship with a Magenta, keep life fun, provocative, and ever changing. If you can continue to evolve in unpredictable ways yourself, there is less probability that your partner will become bored. This doesn't sound fair? It sounds as if you have to do all the work to keep the relationship alive? Well, realize that Magentas are not that attached to having long-term relationships, so you may be more invested in your union than your partner is. It's just as easy for a Magenta to go off on a different adventure. There are too many interesting people in the world to waste time being stuck and unhappy. They typically don't take life that seriously.

You do not need to work hard on this relationship, however. Just relax and be yourself. If you are laughing and enjoying each other's company, if you are exploring new ideas and projects together, and if you can handle your Magenta's unconventional lifestyle, your partnership can easily be compatible.

More often than not, Magentas prefer to live in cities where they can find extraordinary art, intriguing entertainment, and a variety of restaurants that are open late or all night and, most of all, where people will leave them alone so they can live their eccentric lifestyles. There is a good chance that if you live in a small town your Magenta will feel out of place and unaccepted. To be tolerated in such places, Magentas often have to lie low or suppress their true identities. Eventually this suppression could create depression or illness. Are you willing to live in a big city with your Magenta partner?

Are you comfortable with your home decor being avant-garde and unusual? If not, could you consider living in separate residences? Magentas do not like the mundane and ordinary. If you can see your home as a work of art and appreciate your partner's wild taste, your abode could be delightful   and different from anything you could have imagined. Certainly people will talk about it.

Will there be challenges related to money in this relationship? Most likely. Perhaps one of you — or both — is independently wealthy, or someone wonderful has set up a trust fund in your name, because Magentas are not known for their financial stability. They know how to work to earn money, but many of them just don't like the restrictions created by clocks, rules, and structures. Some of them are lucky enough to produce amazing works of art that sell tremendously well. A few of them have invented or written something out of the ordinary that is still bringing in residuals. Some may make a great living in costume or set design. But Magentas are rarely, if ever, found in standard, dependable, nine-to-five jobs. They do not usually keep regular working, or waking, hours. Magentas prefer to live irregular artists' hours — working when the creative muse inspires them and sleeping whenever they want. Jobs just get in their way. Freedom to be spontaneous and innovative is more important to them than money, certainly more important than worrying about humdrum financial security.

You might end up being the more responsible, reliable, and grounded partner in this relationship. Having your own separate and quiet sleeping accommodations might be beneficial, in case you work all day while your Magenta partner sleeps. You never know — that creative muse could strike in the middle of the night and wake up your artistic companion. Keeping different schedules like this could eventually put a strain on your relationship. Your relationship might survive better if you also had flexible hours and an unconventional career.

If financial security is important to you, and you pressure your Magenta into getting a stable job, you'll eventually have an unhappy and despondent mate. If you can support the free-spirited Magenta nature, encourage your partner to follow through on inventions and creative projects and then maybe even support her or him by finding ways to market these products, you'll have a much happier partner.

Be really sure you want life with a Magenta before you plan to have a family. Magentas are not the most responsible or stable souls, so you face the potential of being a single parent in the future. Magentas are overgrown children themselves. It's not hard for them to break commitments and go off in a different direction. If you can create a playful environment for both your children and your mate, you have a better chance of keeping your Magenta around.

Occasionally, people find themselves involved with Magentas who were pressured or raised to act like well-mannered, socially acceptable citizens. You too may have a suppressed Magenta in your life, in which case the outlandish behavior could be more subdued and controlled. Realize, however, that under the restrained demeanor still beats the heart of a mischievous and unusual soul. The true nature could emerge at any time. You may see signs that trouble you: your partner's otherwise normal behavior might be slowly turning more bizarre and unpredictable. Magentas who can no longer contain or suppress their natural desires have been known to suddenly walk away from their long-term relationships, careers, and homes.

To prevent a total meltdown of your relationship, maybe you can find ways to help your Magenta slowly regain the innate Magenta curiosity and creative abilities without disturbing or chasing away all your friends, or destroying everything you have already built.

If you have hooked up with an out-of-power Magenta, life can be an entirely different experience. The Magenta's biggest challenge is dealing with the loneliness of being misunderstood and socially unaccepted. Unfortunately, there are more wounded Magentas than healthy ones in the world. Most of them have been raised in narrow-minded societies, so they feel unappreciated, unwanted, and rejected.

If you have a sullen and depressed Magenta, chances are you are having problems in your relationship. One wonders how you ever encountered this person in the first place, since out-of-power Magentas do not usually let people near them. They hide out in their own strange worlds. They can be so depressed, confused, and lost that they have no interest in dealing with other people, no energy to face anything. They avoid life and rarely leave their apartments. (Most Magentas do not own homes. Owning is too confining and limiting. Renting makes it easier for them to spontaneously leave when they want a new adventure.)

If you do have a wounded Magenta, you have an unusual challenge. Most Magentas at this point do not care if others want to be near them. They are used to being alone. Magentas can become seriously depressed and question their reason for living, and their own bizarre way of look-ing at life can be their worst enemy. They can view themselves and all other human beings as mere objects in an indifferent, hostile, or illogi-cal universe where there is no meaning or purpose. Life becomes ab-solutely dark when they feel this alone.

The best way to reach them is to humorously remind them of the absurdity of life. Get them to laugh. If life really is that short, they might as well explore the world and enjoy the little time they have here. If you can find outrageous works of art or original literature that will show them that others perceive life in similarly unconventional ways — if you can help them see that they are not alone in their out-landish thinking — they are likely to come back to life. Then get them to work on their own art or zany inventions, so they that fill their mind with their own ingenuity and creative ideas. Or take them out to ob-serve all the other strange people in the world. Sit together in the park and laugh at others' strange behavior. Show them that no one has exactly the same thoughts or lifestyle as another, that everyone is unique and interesting.

Magentas like to experiment, so occasionally they try drugs just for fun, just to see if it takes them on a real-life trip into a strange new world. Some can outgrow this interest once they become bored with the experience. Or you can bring healthier alternatives to the table to stim-ulate their natural curiosity and playful personality.

However, if Magentas are deeply wounded and they begin drinking or taking drugs to numb themselves, if they have gone to extremes and become seriously addicted to unhealthy substances, you'll have to find a very special and understanding therapist. Be aware that many profes-sionals diagnose these bizarre Magentas inaccurately — claiming they are schizophrenic, psychotic, or bipolar. Magentas, however, are so out-landish and different that they just do not fit into any common, textbook formula.

It's tough for Magentas to find effective therapy. They don't always relate to some of the support groups or organizations, such as Alcoholics Anonymous, that emphasize connecting with a spiritual source, because many Magentas question the existence of a God. To support your troubled Magenta, work together to find an alternative, open-minded therapist, one who can encourage your Magenta to recover his or her natural, optimistic, but strange style once again. With any luck, this therapist will see clearly, will not judge or condemn, and will support and reinforce the Magenta's unique personality and peculiar modes of expression. If not, your Magenta will not accept the therapist's help and you could be facing a very lonely and isolated life with this wounded soul.

If you are truly concerned about your Magenta and want to try to help her or him change any negative or unhealthy behavior without the assistance of a therapist, your arguments, ideas, and suggestions will have to be very well thought out and accurate. Magentas are usually quick and intelligent. Make sure their actions really are self-destructive or life threatening before crying wolf. Then appeal to their natural zest for life. Show them that they will be missing out on a lot of fun if they damage or destroy themselves. Magentas do not want to be told what to do, but they certainly do not want to be bound to a wheelchair or hospital bed while others have all the fun.

For Magentas to stay happy in relationships, they must have partners who will allow them to stay true to their natures, who will appreciate and accept them as unique individuals, give them permission to be different, support their ability to see life from unusual perspectives, and allow them to act on their creative impulses. If you want to maintain a happy relationship with a Magenta, find ways to enjoy his or her eccentricities and to maintain the perspective that life is fun and not to be taken seriously. Trying to suppress, mold, or change the Magentas' habits and lifestyles is not the way to gain their love and appreciation. Many have tried. Most Magentas will just move on.

Please note: Magentas and Yellow/Violet combinations are often mistaken for one another. Many Yellow/Violet Love Color combinations think they are Magentas because they have so many similar qualities and experiences. Magentas, however, tend to focus on and enjoy the strangeness of the physical world. They are not usually concerned about spirituality or about humanitarian and environmental causes the way Yellow/Violets are. Make sure you know the difference between these different personalities, because they have dissimilar priorities and relationship needs.

Magentas enjoy partners who...

- laugh and enjoy a fun and strange life.
- will try new and creative things.
- are intriguing, intelligent, and stimulating.
- remain independent but also available.
- are self-confident and unaffected by others' opinions.
- can be flexible and open-minded.
- find ways to be resourceful and inventive.
- keep needy and clingy tendencies at bay.
- accept a life free of rules.
- enjoy sexual experimentation.
- prefer living in a city.
- enjoy continual change.
- embrace underground and unusual art, music, life.

Yellows

Yellows desire playmates. They prefer laughing and enjoying life with their best friends, their companions, and they need to know they make their loved ones happy. One of the best gifts you could give the

Yellows in your life is to let them know how happy they make you, and how much you like them. Laugh and smile around them, and watch your Yellows light up. It can be very easy to please them.

Have you found a Yellow that you really like? Do not chase Yellows — they don't like to be captured. Let the Yellow come to you. If you are light, fun, and easygoing, the Yellow could show up on your doorstep ready to respond in kind.

Imagine Yellows as little wild animals. If you hunt them or stalk them, they will run away from you. If they feel cornered or trapped, they will growl and snap at you. They will not answer the phone when you call and will avoid you or withdraw deep into themselves where you cannot reach them.

Yellows need to know they are safe around you. Once Yellows feel safe and not judged, controlled, or possessed by you, they will want to be near you, play with you, and please you. They will think of a variety of ways to entertain you. If they sense they have made you unhappy, they want to shut down or run away. If they cannot make you smile, they will not feel fulfilled in the relationship.

If you are going to create a lasting and fulfilling relationship with a Yellow, remember to be her or his best friend and find ways to make even the most mundane responsibilities fun and easy. If the dishes need to be done and the house needs to be cleaned, turn on music and dance through the chores together. If the car needs washing, sneak up on your Yellow beside the car and start a water fight.

Keep balance in your relationship. Take care of the responsibilities but make sure you find ways to play together. Plan some fun vacations. Surprise your Yellow with unusual adventures or trips to your mutual favorite places. The trips don't have to be costly, just amusing, entertaining, or relaxing.

A great place for Yellows to recharge is out in nature. Persuade yours to spend time outdoors, surrounded by sun, water, trees, and fresh air. If your Yellow is depressed or grumpy, gently encourage him or her to find some pleasurable outdoor activity or to do some hardy exercises to release stress. Yellows need exercise to feel sane and healthy. Sometimes you can accompany them; other times, it is best if they go alone. Observe your partner's current mood to know which is the best choice at any given time.

It will also help if you love your Yellow's dog. Most of these play-ful individuals have dogs, unless they are Blue/Yellows, in which case they may have cats instead, or they may have both. Yellow/Greens often have inner conflict about owning pets, since most Greens do not like the inconvenience of owning animals. For most Yellows, however, their dogs are their very best companions, their best buddies who accept them unconditionally. Accept that the dog will play a major role in your relationship. Your Yellow will appreciate it if you can avoid feeling jeal-ous of the dog. You will lose if you try to compete for your partner's attention, and this may make the Yellow feel guilty. But after all, the dog has stuck around through the bad times as well as the good times and does not complain or demand anything special from the Yellow. These playful pooches appreciate every moment they have with their Yellow owners. Can you make that same claim? On the other hand, if you can learn some tips from the fun-loving, easygoing canine companion, you may end up with a happy and dedicated human companion for life.

As much as Yellows love to play with friends — and perhaps you will be your Yellow's best friend — they also need time alone. Being around you all the time can feel suffocating, even if you usually have fun together. Yellows also need variety and time to play with others. Allow them to spend time with other people, and perhaps even be the one to suggest it. They will appreciate you even more when they sense your approval and your permission to be who they are. It is better to not take this occasional need for solitude and change personally. Stay trusting and self-confident. If you allow them to balance their energy by taking time to be alone, they'll return as the same cheerful, gener-ous, and optimistic companions they were before.

Some Yellows can be nervous and anxious about relationships. Watch out for the back-and-forth, yo-yo games of Yellows. They don't want to lose you, but they don't want to commit, either. If you desire an easygoing, carefree relationship, then this may be the perfect situation for you. If they will not commit, you won't need to either. However, if you want a loyal, devoted, and long-term partner to live with and marry, then you may have to look at shifting the dynamics in this relationship.

The best way to handle these insecure and elusive Yellows is to stay centered. Don't chase them, and don't run away. Stay firmly committed to your highest relationship ideal, and see if your frightened Yellow finally shows up. If this particular Yellow does not commit, someone else will. Trust and believe in yourself enough to feel calm, happy, and confident. This way you are comfortable and safe for others to be around. If you become desperate, people will run away. Even if you don't act anxious, people will still sense your fear. It's an uncomfortable energy for others to be around, especially the skittish Yellows.

If ultimately you find that you have one of the fear-based Yellows who cannot seem to decide about your relationship and make a commitment, you may be better off letting go so you can meet someone else who is ready for a relationship. Yellows are so charming that it can be challenging to let them go; however, you don't want to experience this same unreliable behavior from your Yellow throughout your entire time together, do you? If your Yellow has doubts about your relationship, be yourself, love yourself, and let the Yellow figure out his or her own life. If your Yellow cannot see your value, you don't want to have to work that hard.

A good way to make relationships work with Yellows is to allow them choices. Yellows do not like ultimatums but need to feel that they always have freedom to choose. If you make Yellows feel guilty or you complain about how much you are suffering in the relationship, they may choose to leave to avoid causing you any more unhappiness. They will also leave to get away from the guilt. If you want to go somewhere but your Yellow does not want to, then it's better to go with a friend. If you make Yellows feel wrong, if you pressure them into doing something with you, into feeling they're responsible for your happiness, then you'll get to experience the sad little face or the resentful eyes of the confined animals you just trapped in your cage. Either way, you'll know your Yellow is not happy. It is better to know people like you and therefore choose to be with you of their own accord than to feel like you've trapped them against their will. Manipulation, trickery, force, and ultimatums will always backfire on you. You may always feel insecure, because you'll never know if your Yellow truly loves you.

Healthy Yellows like sex, affection, touching, holding, and being playful. They enjoy physically connecting with their mates. So be comfortable with physical displays of affection. This is often how Yellows show their partners that they like them and are happy to be with them. Yellows can be strongly affected by other people's physical energy, so if they want to be near you, it means they like and trust your energy.

Yellows are happier with partners who do not frequently judge or criticize them. Of course, this is true for most people. However, Yellows tend to be more sensitive to criticism than others. "I like you," "You make me happy," and "I believe you" are the best words you can offer your Yellow. Yellows actually prefer "I like you" to "I love you." Love can feel too serious and intense for some Yellows. "I like you" is lighter and more playful.

With out-of-power Yellows, the kinder and more supportive you can be to them, the sooner they will learn to believe in themselves again. If they feel that someone believes in them, then they feel safe enough to grow up, to explore, and to find creative ways to live up to their full potential. Out-of-power Yellows can have serious problems with self-esteem and self-confidence. Their laziness or lack of drive can merely be a symptom of some deeper fears and insecurities. Many lack sufficient belief in themselves, so they tend to live their lives well beneath their potential. This is especially true of Yellows who have experienced harsh criticism from important people in their lives — parents, siblings, teachers, or partners.

A lot of people misunderstand the simple, childlike personalities of Yellows. Therefore, in an attempt to make them "grow up and do something with their lives," well-meaning but often hurtful and critical authority figures can damage the spirit of the sensitive Yellow. Many Yellows then turn to drugs or alcohol, become physically ill, or wander through life not knowing which way to turn. An addiction to porn can also be a way to hide out for the lonely, misunderstood, and highly sexual Yellows.

A major priority for Yellows is to make people happy. If they feel they have disappointed anyone — parents and partners are the most common candidates — they will often sabotage their own happiness and fulfillment. This is a typical way for Yellows to punish themselves for failing.

It is especially common for Yellows to have issues with their fathers. Yellows may even sabotage themselves with physical injuries and ailments because they feel guilty about disappointing their fathers. Their fathers may have rejected or abandoned them or may have been physically or emotionally unavailable. Their fathers may have slaved away in an office or factory to support the family. Watching the unhappy and trapped parent — an example of what it means to be a grown-up — can increase the Yellows' fear of marriage and responsibility. These childlike personalities do not want to live their lives working that hard or feeling trapped. But they feel they have no right to be free and happy when their fathers struggled so hard to provide.

If your Yellow appears to have self-worth issues or other related fears, there are ways to heal them. Most Yellows shy away from therapy because they are too uncomfortable and embarrassed to let others know of their failures. Most have to hit bottom or see that their lives are at stake before they will agree to go to therapy. And even then, it is hard for them to open up. If your Yellows resist therapy, encourage them to go somewhere quiet — outside in nature works best for them. Suggest that they use their imagination to envision a different scenario with the displeased, emotionally unavailable, or distant parent. Their life may improve if they can change their inner picture or memory of their childhood. Suggest that they imagine their parents no longer absent, disappointed, or critical, but happy, proud, supportive, and encouraging. Or suggest that they imagine the absent or emotionally distant parent close to them, hugging and praising them. Sensing a different, positive, and loving energy from that parent, Yellows may finally allow themselves to be happy. They may stop fearing life and running from relationships.

Yellows often feel ashamed of themselves for not wanting to commit to one job or career throughout their lives. They feel they are not like the "responsible adults" who stick to one occupation until they can respectably retire. Feeling like there must be something wrong with them, some Yellows again can subconsciously sabotage or punish themselves. They continuously create the circumstance of having no money, which keeps them from having fun. Or they create tension in their relationships to ensure they are rejected and punished.

If you are unhappy with your Yellow partner's financial situation and want it to change, realize that Yellows need work that they enjoy, or that at least gives them the freedom to be outdoors. They can become depressed if they are stuck in jobs they dislike. Yellows appreciate mates who understand this and encourage them to work in their desired vocations. If you absolutely need yours to work at a regular job to help pay bills, encourage them to do their creative projects on the side until their projects are successful and they can quit their job. Yellows need to know they are not doomed to work in an unfulfilling job for the rest of their lives. If someone believes in them and supports their desires, the Yellows have a better chance of accomplishing something and being happy.

If money has become a serious issue for you, and you have grown to resent your Yellow's casual attitude or lack of ambition, you may not really belong with a Yellow. Yellows just want to make people happy and live simple, easy, fun-filled lives — which is not usually valued in a work-until-you-drop world. If these playful creatures can learn to accept the fact that they are not here to live the workaholic lifestyle of many others, that they have a different life purpose, then they have a better chance of living happy and fulfilling lives — which can enable them to also have happy relationships.

Being in a relationship with one of the hurt and misunderstood Yellows can be sad, frustrating, or even painful. Damaged Yellows often will not let you help them. They can be rebellious, and if you attempt to tell them what to do, they will do the opposite just to prove you cannot control them. Sometimes when dealing with a Yellow, you will feel like you're dealing with a rebellious teenager or a child in the "terrible twos."

Having health problems is another sign that your Yellow is not happy with life. It can be challenging to live with someone who has chronic health issues. Yellows' typical problem areas are their backs, legs, knees, hips, liver, and prostate gland.

Because Yellows tend to avoid facing their issues, one way they get their own attention — one way they create a wake-up call — is by damaging their bodies. Sports injuries, illnesses, and even car accidents are all experiences that can show Yellows that something needs to be addressed and changed in their lives. Unless they finally deal with these issues, health problems will probably continue to haunt them.

So how do you handle being in a relationship with one of these wounded and resistant Yellows? How do you create a healthy relationship instead? One of the most important things Yellows need to hear is that you believe in them, that you like them, and that they make you happy. You can dislike their behavior — and let them know of your disapproval — but acknowledge that they are valuable and good souls. Once Yellows feel safe, understood, and accepted, they often begin to shift to healthier behavior. Yellows just want to be liked and to make others happy.

Maintain a balanced and healthy lifestyle alongside your Yellows. Natural foods are best for them. They can overeat at times, especially if they feel a need for emotional protection. In order for your Yellows to be healthy so they can do their part to create a healthy relationship, the most important thing they can do is get regular exercise, find the strength (or get support) to stay away from all negative addictions, and maintain their natural lightness and sense of humor.

If you want to be close to your Yellows, to share a long and happy life together, laugh with them, play with them, and tell them you believe in them. Give them space to be creative, to be with friends, or to just spend quiet time alone. Don't push them. Rather, support their natural abilities to develop creative ideas to make money so they can feel better about themselves.

Maintain an affectionate, easygoing, and playful physical connection with them. Knowing that they make you happy will please them. A contented Yellow can help you create a happy, fun-filled relationship.

Yellows like partners who...

- love to laugh, play, and enjoy life.

- express their happiness to them.

- don't chase or pressure them.

- enjoy being physically playful and affectionate.

- refrain from exhibiting demanding or possessive behavior.

- spend time playing or adventuring outdoors with them.

- exercise with them.

- happily allow them their time alone and with other friends.

- give them choices, not ultimatums.

- keep the relationship light, fun, and happy.

- appreciate their youthful and free behavior.

- eat healthy foods with them.
- support them in staying away from addictions.

Tans

Tans need companions who are down-to-earth, reliable, quietly loving, and sensible. If you want to create a harmonious relationship with a Tan, it's best if you keep a good head on your shoulders. Appreciate the security Tans offer you. They are happiest when they know they're sharing a comfortable home and lifestyle with their partners. If you desire a long-term, dependable life with a steadfast partner, a Tan can fulfill that desire.

Appreciate the fact that Tans are quietly unassuming, respectable, and responsible individuals who want to live harmoniously with the people they have dedicated their lives to. They want to be dependable and trustworthy companions. They look forward to living a long, faithful, and comfortable life with another person and will do everything in their power not to let down or disappoint their partners. When they make promises, they intend to keep them. If you have fallen in love with a Tan, you were most likely looking for these qualities in a mate. You probably wanted someone you could count on so you could feel safe and secure. Well, you have that and more in a Tan.

If you want to create a wonderful life with this soul, stay trustworthy, responsible, and respectful alongside your Tan. Use common sense — Tans respect calm, logical, and practical behavior. Financial security is a strong priority for a Tan, so make sure you do not overspend and you stick to the budget the two of you mutually agree on. If Tans feel they are working hard to provide a decent lifestyle or to contribute their share to your life plans, they could feel offended if they see you not treating their contribution with respect.

You'll need to trust that your Tan partner appreciates your love and companionship, because most likely your Tan won't tell you so very often. Observe the Tan's behavior. They are people of very few words most of the time, so be self-confident and create your own reassurance in this relationship. Realize that Tans consider their presence, loyalty, and financial support to be obvious signs that they are committed to the relationship.

You'll need to have friends — not so many friends that your Tan partner never sees you, but enough so that you have others with whom you can share your feelings. Since most Tans are not comfortable dealing with emotional subjects, and they are not always interested in deep conversations about your relationship, you'll need other friends who will listen to you. If you attempt to have a lot of such discussions with Tans, you will irritate them and eventually wear them out.

Tans also do not appreciate or understand emotional outbursts or hysteria. If you are prone to flare-ups, again, find friends. If you do become upset, your Tan may try to calm you down. If, however, you cry too much or too often, Tans will eventually withdraw into another room. They don't know how to handle this type of seemingly unreasonable, unexplainable, or illogical behavior.

You may be mildly successful at training your Tan not to avoid emotional discussions, but overall, Tans will never be completely comfortable or happy with deep, soul-searching talks with you or anyone else. Some can have simple, down-to-earth chats with their children, but many shy away from exploring too deeply even with them. You may be able to help your Tan learn how to be more open and communicative with the children. Otherwise, your kids could grow up not really knowing or understanding their Tan parent. There could be an emotional distance and disconnect between them. Be gentle and calm with your Tan as you logically explain the benefits of bonding with the children. If you can show them that they need not fear being vulnerable, that they will not be humiliated or teased, Tans may learn to express themselves more often. You may need to teach your children to be patient and tolerant of the Tan's uneasy or slow pace. Explain that their Tan parent is trying to show love for them by attempting to communicate and connect with them.

If you need Tans to make a decision, do not push or rush them — this will make them feel uncertain and uneasy. Be patient with their pace of processing information. They need to take life at their own tempo, slow and deliberate. Let them hear all the facts and look at all the information. When Tans are in power, they'll look at all sides of a discussion, walk away to think about it, then reappear when they have thoroughly analyzed the situation and made a decision. If you are consistently impatient with them, they'll fear they are standing on unsupportive, shaky ground, and that they cannot trust you as a partner. They will shut down and walk away from you or become irritated and snap at you.

Respect Tans enough to pay attention to their stories when they tell you the events of the day. Realize they are planning on telling you every detail, so get comfortable and don't be in a hurry. If you are one of the less patient Love Colors, don't show your frustration. Appreciate that they are opening up and sharing parts of their lives with you. If they see you are uninterested, they may feel hurt and disrespected. They may never share with you again. Calmly listen while they are speaking. If you find listening to all the details unbearable, you can quietly think about other things. Just make sure you are present and focused before they finish their story — if you understand the gist of the story, you can comment, congratulate, or commiscrate with them.

You may have to occasionally encourage your Tan to get out for some exercise. Tans are typically sedentary people. They sit behind desks and computers a lot. Some are rational enough to know they need exercise, but others are not interested in physically exerting themselves. Maybe go for walks together or work out beside your Tan. Find a way to make exercising easy and convenient. You could always buy him or her a treadmill or exercise machine as a birthday gift if you don't mind defending how much it cost. If Tans don't find a way to stay at least moderately active, they could reap the consequences sometime in the future with health problems.

Even though Tans are usually the calm, rational ones in the face of challenges or disasters, they prefer to have a consistent and stable foundation under them. Most don't like surprises. Allow yours to keep a regular schedule. They need to know that their lives are predictable, and that they have a say over what is going to happen to them today, tomorrow, and years into the future. Tans need this certainty in their relationships, their finances, and their work. They are realistic enough to know that life holds no guarantees, but they will work hard to set up the most protected and secure life that they can.

If you discover that your Tan's job or position may be threatened, realize that this is a serious event for a Tan. Tans who are about to be transferred or relocated can feel traumatized. Patiently reassure yours that life will work out fine. Your attempts to comfort and reassure your mate will need to include the supporting data to back up your claims, however; otherwise, these will be just empty words, and your Tan will not feel any more secure.

If you remind Tans of past challenges that they survived, they may calm down. Then follow up by researching the facts — find information about the city they are being transferred to, help them locate data about the new job, look into the school districts if you have children, research real estate in the new area, get every detail you can about what to expect in your new home. This will help quite a bit. Tans need to know the details. Understand, however, that ultimately, as long as their lives are up in the air and their futures are unknown, they will be apprehensive and unhappy. Calmly stand by them as the future is slowly revealed and they begin adjusting to their new lives.

You will probably encounter the Tans' aversion to change in many areas. It can be challenging to try new adventures with them. If you want to try a new concept, product, or activity with them, try to introduce it slowly and gradually. If you want, say, a new desk, it may be a better approach to first discuss it before actually buying it. Know the budgetary constraints, reveal the approximate cost of the desk, and be able to explain the reasons why this is a good or necessary time to buy. However, by letting them know your intended plans in advance, you risk hearing a flat "no" or "not interested." If you do hear objections, then you'll have to decide if you are going to go against their stubborn resistance to change and buy the desk anyway, or if you are going to keep peace in your relationship by not arguing with them. After all, it is just a desk. Is it worth disturbing your relationship for?

Occasionally, if you just surprise your Tans with a new item, they'll eventually and begrudgingly accept the purchase — provided you did not go to extremes with the cost. After all, it's a safe bet that you have better taste and better decorating sense than they do. Once they have time to become accustomed to the new desk, everything will be fine again. Just don't move it too often.

Sometimes it can be helpful to talk about attending an upcoming event or traveling to a new location well in advance, so your Tans can have time to adjust to the plan. Give as much information and describe as many details as you can before actually taking them to the event. Similarly, describe any new concept or product step-by-step, explaining every detail. Tans like to know everything they can expect when faced with something new or unfamiliar. They'll let you know when they've heard enough. Usually more information is better. (Again, if you have one of the more flexible Tan combinations, you could find them more willing to be spontaneous and accommodating.)

Tans do not need a lot of social interaction. They're content to stay in the comfort of their own homes. If there is a special event you want to attend, you will probably have to beg them to go along. Maintaining conversations with others that they find uninteresting is unpleasant and challenging work for Tans. While other colors will feign interest, Tans see no value in pretending or listening to idle talk. Your Tan may even sneak off into the other room to catch the latest scores of the ball game. An outsider can engage the Tan in a discussion if it involves practical things like the best place to get a car repaired or the safest place to invest.

Out of power, Tans can become very close-minded. There will be no discussions of different or unusual points of view with them. They'll stick with the same beliefs and behaviors that have worked for them in the past. They like to do what they have always done. When they find something that works, they rarely veer from it.

Tans need things to be just and fair. If yours feel you are being unreasonable, if you are not listening to logic, or if you criticize them for something they haven't done, they will become agitated. They'll either physically and emotionally shut you off or fiercely defend their position. Armed with facts and data, they will adamantly argue their position. If they think your position is not factual, they will claim it has no merit. Tans are stubborn and will stand firm on their positions. They often pull in science or news reports to support their arguments. Either learn how to gather the facts to support your ideas and perceptions, or let the disagreement go and stay out of arguments with Tans.

If you have a hard time tolerating this type of behavior, your relationship could suffer. If you can learn to let your Tan partners see life their own way, can accept that we all have different perspectives, and do not try to change them by force, pressure, or criticism, they may feel safe enough to someday consider other options. You might have better luck with the unwavering Tans by teaching through example. It may take years to teach old dogs new tricks, but they are trainable. Tans are just more stubborn than most and slower to change. In the meantime, learn to appreciate their good qualities rather than focusing on what bothers you.

Tans value partners who...

- are reliable, responsible, and loyal.

- appreciate a secure, committed relationship.

- appreciate a dependable life with a steadfast partner.

- behave calmly, logically, and practically.

- keep emotional outbursts and dramas to a minimum.

- look to others for deep conversations about relationships.

- encourage easy and fun exercise.

- are trusting and self-confident.

- are conservative and responsible with money.

- are patient and allow them time to think and process information.

- politely listen to every detail of their stories.

- allow them to keep a regular schedule to maintain predictability and comfort.

Greens

Greens love partners who are interesting, quick, and motivated. They respect people with sharp intellectual skills. A well-educated or well-read person has the best chance of stimulating the quick mind of a Green. They need to be with intelligent partners whom they admire and who treat them with respect in return. They also want to be acknowledged and appreciated for their accomplishments.

Greens need to be listened to, so to avoid reoccurring arguments in your relationship, pay close attention to your Green's discussions. Being strong-willed, these powerful personalities are determined to have their own way. Keep in mind, though, that if they are always allowed to run over you, or if you continuously walk away from a good "debate," your Green will eventually lose interest in you. This can be a challenging balance to maintain. People rarely win arguments with Greens because Greens hate to be wrong.

If you always win arguments, your Green will become frustrated, moody, and difficult to live with. But if you give in every time, Greens will feel unchallenged and disappointed. If you disagree with their point of view, be prepared to have facts and figures to back up your perspective. If you can stand strong, stay emotionally centered, maintain your self-confidence, and intellectually stimulate them, they will learn to respect you. And if you are going to discuss anything with Greens, get straight to the point. Greens are busy people and can become frustrated with those who share every insignificant detail of a story.

Greens respect people who make good money and who also appreciate the money the Greens have worked hard to earn. They expect their partners to have high regard for their work and gratitude for the money they bring to the relationship.

Unfortunately — and this does not seem fair, but you need to know the truth if you are going to be involved with one of these perfectionists — they usually want their partners to maintain high standards. Greens can quickly lose respect for partners who gain too much weight, become lazy and unmotivated, or live in a disorganized environment. Most Greens take great pride in keeping their own appearance immaculate. They like to be well dressed, well manicured, healthy, and fit. They expect the same from their partners. Greens do not tolerate being humiliated or shamed and want their partners to exhibit a respectable level of dignity and sophistication. They strive to attain and maintain the highest level of luxury, comfort, and ease possible. Even during times when they do not have much money, Greens like to retain an image of wealth and success.

This also applies to their home environment. Greens often appreciate fine art, luxurious furniture, and an atmosphere of sophistication. The challenge for you will be to not overindulge while you create a regal, tasteful environment. Greens appreciate it when you make them look good, but they will not appreciate going into debt to support any kind of impulsive or lavish spending habits you may have. Remember to respect their money.

If you have children and you want to maintain harmony in your home, teach the children respect and discipline. When Greens are in power, they provide abundantly for their families. They want the best education for their children, and they do their best to support their children's interests. They encourage their kids to reach their potential. Most children grow up respecting and appreciating this hardworking parent.

Greens do not want to just be at-home parents, however. They want mental stimulation. If your Green partner needs to stay at home with the children, support your Green's desire to start a home-based business. Greens may try to do it all, and they may be busy entrepreneurs, soccer parents, and home managers. Help yours maintain balance in life so they don't become stressed, anxious, or unhealthy.

On the downside, out-of-power Green parents can be sharp, demanding, and impatient, often intimidating their children. Greens are so busy working on their businesses they are not always physically or emotionally available to their offspring. You may need to play mediator at times, referee at other times. You may have to reassure your children that their Green parent does in fact care for them, because they may not always be able to see signs of that. To prevent your children and your Green partner from misunderstanding, resenting, or pulling away from one another, encourage your Green to patiently listen to her or his children and to support their hobbies and activities. Remind them that writing a check to pay for the sports uniform is not enough to create a connection with the children — Greens usually try to fix a problem by throwing money at it. Green parents are usually happy, though, when the children are well fed, studying hard, setting goals, planning their future, and staying out of trouble.

The subject of spirituality may or may not arise in your relationship. Each Green is different. Some Greens find many spiritual concepts intriguing and thought provoking. The idea that one can or cannot prove the existence of a God can be mentally stimulating to them. They may even find some of the spiritual teachings comforting. Other Greens, however, are not interested in topics that cannot be discussed in an intelligent and scholarly manner. They see religion and spirituality as nonsensical fairy tales for the weak-minded. They find no logical rationale behind such ideas.

When Greens are out of power, they can be incredibly challenging to live with. They are typically intense and serious, especially when working toward their goals. They push themselves, always appearing to be in a hurry. Greens can become anxious and irritable when they feel blocked or unable to attain their goals. If they cannot find a solution to a problem, they often build emotional walls around themselves. They can become incredibly bitter, argumentative, and cruel and tend to blame everyone and everything in their way. Out of power, a Green can have a sharp tongue. Greens can be the most verbally abusive of all the Love Colors.

The best way to handle explosive or frustrated Greens is, first, to stay out of their way. Once they have regained some composure and rationality, it may be possible to reason with them. Never patronize them, however. Greens hate being talked down to. They also dislike being told what to do. It is in your best interest to know that no one but themselves can actually suppress or block the incredibly powerful Greens. They are often their own worst enemies. But they will not always accept this notion — they typically look for someone or something else to blame. However, by blaming others, Greens give away their power, and if you can help yours realize this, encourage them to regain a sense of control and mastery over their thoughts and energy, and remind them to focus on finding solutions rather than staying stuck in blame and misery, they can begin to move through their challenges. If your Greens don't regain their sense of power, you could be sucked into their angry world of frustration, cynicism, and resentment. Greens will always be harder on themselves than anyone around them, but it may not appear that way.

Sometimes it can be hard to know what Greens are truly feeling if they have buried their feelings of self-hatred deep inside. The signs are easy to see, however. If Greens are unhappy and impatient, somewhere they are disappointed with their own progress and dislike themselves. Greens expect a lot from themselves.

Remind your Greens that the quickest method for them to regain their center, their sense of power and control, is to take responsibility for their life, to remember their incredible intelligence and quick problem-solving skills. Greens feel more powerful and in control when they write down a list of clearly defined goals and then develop a plan to achieve those goals. They continue to thrive if they take action. They must believe they can take action. If they think there are obstacles beyond their control, changing their thinking will move them forward again. If they remain stuck in their own mental quagmire of anger and disgust, if they continue to beat themselves up over their failures, their lives will not change.

Encourage them to find other ways to reach their goals — to overcome the obstacle, find a way around it, or take a different approach. If you can walk that fine line between supporting and encouraging them without sounding demeaning, you will gain their appreciation. It helps them to know you respect and believe in them. They will come up with solutions far more quickly. When Greens are back in power, they become so vital and energetic that they do not have the time or the desire to blame anyone else for their problems. Once you see them smiling again, know they have taken stock of their lives and are satisfied with, even proud of, their own accomplishments.

Many Greens prefer to be the boss and own their own businesses. You may find yourself being asked to be a partner or assistant to yours. Be careful with this arrangement if you want to maintain harmony in your relationship. Maintain self-respect and control of your own separate department, or be comfortable taking a supportive role. Greens like to be in charge and usually try to control everything. If you can keep their trust and respect by being efficient and self-directed, and learn to avoid arguments, then your business could thrive. Greens can often create phenomenal businesses, but often at the expense of their intimate relationships. If you and your partner maintain mutual respect and healthy boundaries, you can survive combining business and an intimate partnership.

One of the best ways to contribute to your Green partner's quality of life is to help him or her stay healthy. Greens tend to be type A, workaholic personalities. They commonly develop stress-related health problems: ulcers, digestive ailments, migraines, high blood pressure, and heart disease. Convincing them not to take their work so seriously is almost impossible. They often believe their identity is in their work. It's better to help them find a balance between their "extremely important work" and their personal lives. Help them keep a rational perspective.

Because they like to stay mentally stimulated and alert, one of their main addictions is caffeine. This substance often exacerbates their condition. They would probably argue this point, however. Most Greens think caffeine helps them rather than hurts them. If you can find healthy, nonabrasive, and less physically irritating substances as a substitute, your Green will probably live a longer and healthier life. Your challenge will be to convince your partner to change the caffeine habit.

Greens are so focused on achieving their goals that often exercise and relaxation are deleted from their schedules, or at least banished to the bottom of the priority list. Even if Greens take time out of their busy work schedules to exercise, there is usually a constantly ringing cell phone attached to their ears. And no vacation would be complete without their computers and electronic organizers.

Since Greens do not like being told what to do, trying to convince them to slow down or take better care of themselves can seem hopeless. It often takes a doctor or, worse yet, a serious health scare to get them to wake up. Before yours reaches that point, find ways to ensure that they get regular, healthy meals, schedule some brief vacations (if it's in their calendar, you have a better chance of getting away), treat them to massages or other healing work on a regular basis, and practice taking deep breaths around them to help them remember to breathe. Of course, you cannot arrange any of these things without their permission. Greens will not be treated like children. Present your ideas in a rational way. Explain that if they are forced to take time off work for medical reasons, they will lose much more time and be that much less productive than if they were to take small, preventative measures now. If your Green argues with you on this point, then you have a frightened partner. Your mate is far more concerned about failing in the future than you realize.

Again, if you find your Greens are struggling with work or losing confidence in their abilities, they will appreciate your support and encouragement. Facing their fear of failure is the Greens' greatest issue. You could always remind them how intelligent they are, remind them of their past achievements, reassure them that their current projects will be successful, and that if not they can always try again. This will help to calm them down and give them a better perspective. It's best to learn to trust these risk takers and believe in the potential success of their projects, because if you don't, you will both have many sleepless nights. Greens need to pursue bigger and riskier projects or they become bored. Just remind them that the alternative to success is falling back into boring and mundane work. This should reinspire them to succeed and will make them appreciate their venturesome choices all the more.

Above all, Greens need to feel self-respect and a sense of accomplishment. If you can find ways to let yours know they are respected and appreciated for all the things they have already achieved, you will give them a great gift. Certainly you can find something. Or mention how brave they are for going beyond their comfort zone and trying to achieve greater things. Even if they have tried and failed, point out the fact that few people are courageous enough to even try. Treat them with respect and admiration, and remain faithful to them: these are the best ways to show your love.

Greens admire partners who...

- are intelligent, interesting, and stimulating.

- are well educated or well read.

- have healthy self-esteem.

- appreciate their accomplishments.

- treat them with respect and as equals.

- support their ideas and goals.

- respect money.

- are willing to work hard to financially contribute.

- keep a nice, respectable, manicured appearance.

- are faithful.

- support their desire to be entrepreneurs.

- help reduce their stress.

- maintain their own opinions and ideas.

Blues

Blues desire life partners who are devoted, loyal, caring, thoughtful, monogamous, trustworthy, and committed to them forever. Loving a Blue can be a wonderful experience. Blues will return your love and devotion tenfold. They are deliciously happy when they are in love, so give yours reasons to stay in love with you.

Maintaining a happy and healthy relationship with a Blue is very simple. Blues appreciate knowing how much you love and appreciate them. They desire partners who are faithful, monogamous, and true.

They need to feel emotionally connected to their significant other. Be kind and considerate with yours; they will be uncomfortable with anger, aggression, and rude behavior. See if you can get them to lighten up and laugh, though. Blues can become serious worriers at times. They worry about and take care of everyone.

Blues need partners who share feelings openly and who are willing to discuss the relationship. So if you want to make Blues happy, don't run away when they start talking about the things that matter most to them.

Most Blues will not pamper themselves, so it can be very easy to show them that you care. You can treat them to a relaxing day at a spa so they can rest and be pampered, or take them out to a special romantic dinner. Or you could simply take them to a movie — a romantic comedy is usually the best choice. If money is an issue for you, Blues may melt when you lovingly and sincerely look into their eyes, hand them a single rose, and tell them how deeply you love them. It's the simple gestures that matter. Most Blues do not need objects; they value genuine expressions of love the most.

Your biggest challenge could be convincing your Blues to accept gifts — they are not always good receivers. They feel guilty. If you show them how delighted you feel when you are able to give them something, they may accept your gift. They will do it to make you happy.

Actually, if you can learn to read their minds so you know exactly what they want and when, you will garner even more of their love and devotion. Blues are intuitive enough to sense what others need, and they do their best to quickly fill those needs. They would love it if someone else could do the same for them — because they will rarely tell people what they want or need. They expect their loved ones to just know, especially those who have known them for a long time, the same way they intuitively know what others need. Your best bet is to develop strong intuition yourself so you are ready to fill their needs when you sense their signals.

Blues are self-sufficient and capable of fulfilling their own needs, but they typically focus the majority of their attention on the needs of others. They are so busy taking care of everyone else that they often do not take care of themselves. Because they typically do not want to burden others with their responsibilities or problems, they will carry everything themselves. Expect to see the sympathetic Blues on the phone listening to their friends' problems, patiently counseling them through breakups and heart-wrenching woes. Understand that you may end up sharing your time or home with many stray animals or emotionally wounded people.

If one of your Blue's friends is going through a tough divorce, you will most likely see that friend staying in your spare bedroom. If you have not yet married this Blue, but are dating, that distraught friend may be invited to join the two of you on your date. The softhearted Blues do not want anyone to feel left out or unloved. They are extremely caring souls and can be taken in by almost any sob story. If you protest, they will be torn. You will be putting them in a very tough position. They will want to be with you and not want to upset you, but they also do not want to hurt or abandon a friend. You will earn points with Blues if you will support their desire to help a friend. After all, it is just one date. You will have other dates with them if you are kind and supportive this time. Blues feel that hurting a loved one could leave a scar on that person forever. They value kindness and loyalty. Keep this in mind if you have long-term plans for your Blue.

Be prepared to listen to Blues when they get intuitive hits. Blues are the most psychic of all the Love Colors. If you trust Blues, they can be beneficial in helping you make decisions. They can give intuitive advice about your business, money, relationships, or family dynamics. If your Blues are highly intuitive, and you go against their guidance, you will most likely regret not listening to them. Most of the information that Blues give is highly accurate. The infrequent times when they are incorrect probably occur when their desire to please you gets in the way.

Encourage your Blues to trust their intuition and follow their own advice. When Blues listen to their own intuition their lives are generally happier. It's when they lose touch with or doubt their feelings that they become lost and unhappy. In power, the loving Blues typically choose to focus on people's positive qualities. They prefer to see the good in others. Sometimes their blind faith in others is detrimental to their own well-being, however. Their tendency to forgive easily, make excuses for behaviors, and accept people's shortcomings shows that they will tolerate and love almost anyone.

It can be easy to take the loyal and sacrificing Blues for granted, therefore, so make sure you keep your senses about you. Blues are such loving and forgiving individuals that they make it easy for others to treat them like doormats. If you slip into this type of behavior, your hurt Blues could eventually grow to resent you. And their supportive friends will also help them by pointing out to them that they are being treated poorly.

It takes a serious betrayal, a constantly negative attitude, or repetitive destructive behavior for Blues to lose faith in someone. Once someone has finally crossed that line, hurt the Blues too severely, or betrayed them too often, it is challenging to regain their trust. If you have seriously hurt or betrayed your Blues and they have lost confidence in you, your relationship could be in serious jeopardy. Counseling may be the best approach to repair your relationship. If they see that you are willing to go to therapy to discuss issues, they may regain faith in you. They may believe that you still love them and want the relationship to survive. They will need to see honest attempts to change, however, or the relationship will still be doomed.

Blues have only two motivations: one is to give love; the other is to be loved. When you see unhappy Blues, you can be certain they are feeling unfulfilled in one or both of these areas. Out of power, Blues often doubt themselves and their self-worth. Until they know for themselves that they are lovable and wonderful, you may have to reassure them over and over again how valuable they are. When Blues are out of power, it can be challenging to let them know you care about them without feeling you are being manipulated or controlled by guilt and their self-pity. But be compassionate and patient with yours until they regain their center and sense of self-worth.

It may be easier to be sympathetic if you can understand that when they are feeling sorry for themselves, it just means they are feeling insecure, unloved, and invalidated. It may be that they are just tired — they have given too much, worked too hard, and become exhausted. Even though it is the Blues' responsibility to find ways to feel better, to find self-love and take care of themselves, they will appreciate your love and support. You can remind them of all the wonderful projects they have accomplished. Showing sincere gratitude for all their loving deeds will also help bring a smile back to their face.

Because Blues are so spiritual and such strong believers in God or a Higher Power, an effective way to help them realize they are loved is to remind them how deeply that Higher Power loves them. If they can learn to believe and accept that, they will be on the road to healing, which, in turn, will allow them to develop healthy relationships.

If your Blues have really lost their way, if self-pity consumes them, the best approach to take is to encourage them to help others. If you cannot locate one of their troubled friends for them to help, take your Blues to an animal shelter so they can comfort the poor abandoned animals. Once Blues focus on the plights of others, they move beyond their own pain and self-pity. They can then remember that their greatest strength and their deepest fulfillment lie in loving service to others.

Blues are typically loyal and protective of their children. In power, the devoted Blues often sacrifice their own needs and desires to ensure that their children are happy. Blues appreciate partners who love and cherish their children as well. Unfortunately, Blues often believe that sacrificing for others shows they love them, which only increases their tendency to sacrifice. They expect their partners to show the same dedicated expression of love for their family. If you are interested in a Blue who is a single parent, it is important that you adore her or his children as well or there will be small chance for happiness in your relationship.

If Blues, who have a deep need to bond emotionally with others, had parents who were emotionally or physically unavailable in childhood, they may carry feelings of abandonment into their adult life. It is very common for this type of Blue to fall in love with someone who is unavailable — someone who is married, lives far away, or is emotionally distant. Yours may recreate in you the parent who abandoned them by somehow forcing you also to abandon them. They may test you, push you away, and make you leave, thus making you "unavailable." Blues can unwittingly create their own self-fulfilling prophecy, their greatest fear, that of being alone and unloved. Keep watch for this type of sabotaging behavior. If and when it occurs, stay strong and aware or you may end up believing you really are the culprit, the mean and hurtful partner who abandoned them when all along it was they who pushed you out and made you leave. If you can gently point out their self-sabotaging behavior without offending them or hurting their feelings, they may change their behavior or possibly seek professional therapy. If they don't deal with their sabotaging behavior, the two of you could be doomed to riding an emotional roller coaster for years.

Many times Blues do not allow themselves to enjoy their lives. Subconsciously they can feel guilty if they have everything they desire while others suffer, so they don't always allow themselves to be completely happy. They will struggle so that others do not feel alone, abandoned, or inferior — especially if they know their mothers do not or did not have happy lives.

While Yellows frequently have challenges related to their fathers, it is very common for Blues to have issues with their mothers. Deep down most Blues love their mothers, but there can also be pain or feelings of guilt between them. Blues often sabotage their own enjoyment and fulfillment to avoid hurting their mothers or making them feel inferior.

Because Blues value long-term, happy, and monogamous relationships, if they sense in any way that their mothers were not as happy or fulfilled in their marriages, the sacrificing Blues often diminish their own happiness in order to avoid making their mothers feel like failures. Or, if Blues are happy in marriage, they may subconsciously create difficulties in their career or health instead. If the Blues have wonderful careers, they are financially prosperous, and they have great friends, they may subconsciously create struggles in their relationships so that their mothers or friends are not jealous. If you find yourself in a relationship with Blues like this, you may be able to help them realize that suffering will not improve their mothers' or friends' lives. Nor will it change their circumstances. Explain to them that by living a joyful, happy, successful life instead, they can show their mother and friends what is possible. Rather than suppressing their own potential, they can live their dreams and, at the same time, may actually encourage others to live up to their potential too.

If your Blues still feel guilty about improving their own lives, gently point out that they obviously do not believe in their mothers' (or other people's) ability to figure out their own lives. By carrying others' problems for them, they are basically revealing that they do not believe in those other people. If Blues can trust that people's souls know what they are doing, even if outwardly it appears that they do not, they may allow themselves to be happy. But if instead they continue to sacrifice for these other people, no one's life will improve. Their unhappy mothers and friends might feel that their own poor choices must have been unavoidable, since even the sensitive Blues cannot do any better — but ultimately no one wins.

Your Blue may eventually realize that another loving way to help others is to teach by example. Even though Blues tend to be rescuers, you may be able to convince them that inspiring others to live their greatest dreams may be a more powerful way to help people. Realize, though, that your Blue's motives always involve love.

Blues love partners who...

- are loving, compassionate, and considerate.

- show their sincere devotion and love for them.

- understand and allow them to be emotional.

- share deep feelings with them.

- are loyal and monogamous.

- support their desire to help and comfort others.

- embrace and love their children.

- put love and people before work and money.

- encourage them to spend time with supportive friends.

- trust and believe in their intuition.

- support and share their spiritual values.

- are willing to discuss and improve the relationship they share.

Violets

Violets desire partners who are inspirational equals, who share their lofty dreams and optimistic goals, who support them in achieving their ideals, or at least who allow them the freedom to pursue their visions. If you want to create a happy, healthy, and long-lasting relationship with a Violet, listen when Violets describe their visions. Be a motivating, enthusiastic partner. Be open, honest, and communicative with them. Violets want to be with mates who have integrity, who are honest and real with them — real, but not discouraging. It is best not to tear their dreams apart. Instead, encourage them to develop ideas about how to achieve those dreams. Live authentically, and live up to your own full potential. Violets admire people who do so.

Most Violets are like mighty eagles, hawks, or other powerful animals in the wild. They enjoy having a home base, a sanctuary, but not a cage. Violets cherish partners who are passionate, who will fly with them, and who will, occasionally, give them the space to soar alone. Violets are inspired by partners who are visionaries and who can match their great energy. Most Violets also desire passionate lovemaking — to be able to connect emotionally, spiritually, and physically so deeply with their partner that they completely lose themselves in the experience. To keep a dynamic relationship with your Violet partner, you will want to maintain this passionate connection. Being highly visual creatures, Violets also need to be with partners who are visually appealing to them.

Violets love beautiful homes and fine things, but they do not want to be owned by their possessions. Freedom is their most valued asset. They will embark on projects and journeys because this is their way. If your need for security gets in the way of your Violet's need for growth and exploration and desire to expand and create new projects, you will have an imprisoned, unhappy Violet on your hands. Clip the Violets' wings and they can easily become despondent. While hawks mate for life, they do need to be with other hawks, not chickens. You may think you will feel more secure having your Violet on a leash, turning him or her into a well-behaved, predictable partner, but is this really what drew you to your Violet in the first place? Didn't you love your partner's dynamic enthusiasm and ability to dream and envision great ideas? Didn't you admire the Violet passion?

If you create a family together, your Violet will go out into the world while allowing you the time to take care of the family at home, if that is your desire. Be careful not to become too domesticated, however, for once the children are old enough to fly on their own, your Violet will want you flying beside him or her again.

Your Violet does need to be the center of attention, to feel important, to be the king or queen of your life. If your admiration disappears, then trouble can develop. Once Violets lose passion for their partners, their relationships may never recover. If they feel uninspired or taken for granted, their eyes can quickly spot another. Violets are so charismatic that they typically attract many admirers. There could be many waiting on the sidelines to take your place. On the other hand, partners who maintain their dynamic personalities, high self-esteem, and supportive presence thrill and captivate these Violets.

The visions that Violets have are so huge that they are often intimidated by them. Full of questioning and self-doubt, they wonder if their dreams are too grandiose or if they will appear arrogant. They worry others will reject or criticize them. Violets already feel alone in the world — they feel different from those around them. Typically, they cannot walk into a room without being noticed, so to fit in and blend with others, they often suppress their own power. They often put on extra pounds as emotional protection or become extremely slender so no one can see them.

When Violets are too afraid to move toward their future, they often generate intense drama or distractions in their lives. They can fashion overwhelmingly busy and chaotic lives for themselves — this can include having affairs or developing other relationship problems. They create these distractions so they do not have to feel their sadness, frustration, loneliness, or lack of fulfillment. These Violets sense something is missing in their lives. When Violets are surrounded by drama, they cannot see clearly. If they can stand back, see the bigger picture, and realize that they may have created this drama because they are afraid to move toward their future, things can begin to change.

If you find your Violets have lost their way and can no longer envision a future, ask them what they see. Ask them not what they *think*, but rather what they *see*. Using visionary words like *envision*, *imagine*, or *see* will get them back in touch with their inner visions. Encourage them to keep track of their dreams at night. If Violets are not in touch with their visions while they are awake, they will receive insights and inspiration at night while they sleep.

Encourage your Violets to meditate, especially if they are overwhelmed with everything going on in their lives. Violets need quiet time alone to get in touch with their inner guidance. If your Violet can stay connected to this greater guidance, and then act on it, you will have a happier, more centered partner and, therefore, a healthier, more fulfilling relationship. Buy a journal for Violets so they can write down their visions and the intuitive words of wisdom they receive in their meditations. This will enable them to remember, keep track of, organize, validate, and eventually actualize their visions. Ideas written down become that much clearer and closer to becoming physical reality. Otherwise, their visions float in and out of their consciousness like clouds, and they do not sense that these visions are possible.

Encourage your Violets to design a dream board filled with pictures of projects they want to create, places they want to travel to, people they want to meet, and ideas they want to manifest. This board will be a tremendously helpful tool for them. Violets can create anything that they get a strong visual image of. Even if they are not always consciously aware of looking at these images every day, their subconscious mind will see them and find a way to bring them into physical form.

Violets need to have dreams and goals, to be moving toward ideals, always expanding, and constantly creating, or they become lost. If they are not accomplishing what they sense they are here to do, they develop serious self-doubts. Violets are so emotionally deep and passionate that, when they lose their way, they can become incredibly depressed and sullen. Often Violets outgrow their dreams before they even begin to bring them into reality, which also causes the Violets to become scattered and to question themselves. Help them to stay focused and to continue to listen to their inner voice. Reassure them that another dream will arise that will inspire them. Encourage them to take action on that next dream so they don't become discouraged by their own inactivity. Violets can have many dreams, but some of these dreams must eventually take form or these visionaries will lose faith in themselves and give up.

Because Violets are here to help save the planet, or to touch, inspire, and educate the masses, they often sense the pain and sadness of others around the globe — which further complicates their lives. Most Violets are deeply affected by any and all traumatic events that occur in the world. They usually do not realize that part of their depression results from feeling the pain and sorrow of the masses. Violets mistake this pain and sadness for their own.

They do have their own pain and sorrow, of course. In the midst of people, Violets can still feel alone. If Violets were suppressed or discouraged in childhood, if they felt "unseen" or discredited by those around them, they may have lost their belief in themselves, their vision, which would cause them to become scattered and confused. Some become so discouraged, fearing that they will never achieve their dreams, that they give up, believing that they must live small, ordinary lives.

If you have depressed Violets whom you cannot inspire to reconnect with their spirit and greater purpose, then therapy is an option. Help them find a highly intelligent and deeply intuitive therapist whom they can trust to guide them. Seeking psychological help for Violets may present a challenge, however, since typically they know more than the therapists — at least they believe they do. Violets are naturally intuitive therapists themselves, and they pick up impressions very quickly. They tend to be impatient, so therapy sessions must move rapidly and produce results quickly. Unless the therapist is powerful and amazingly perceptive and can get to the source of the problem immediately, Violets can become disappointed and bored. They doubt that the counselor will ever reach the deeper source of their problems and, therefore, will not be able to help.

Many Violets, if they would take the time, can actually be their own best counselors. Since typically they give insightful advice, they just need to learn to listen to their own words of wisdom. If Violets can sit somewhere quietly and meditate, if they can imagine talking to themselves as children, they may be able to get to the bottom of their own problems. Again, encourage your Violets to pay attention to their dreams at night, because they are likely to receive guidance in them.

A helpful visualization exercise for Violets is to imagine a client, patient, or friend coming to them with the same problem, challenge, or dilemma that they themselves are facing. The Violet can give advice to this imaginary person and see what information comes through. Violets can naturally channel higher information and advice from a deeper part of their souls — a part of themselves that they may not have been in touch with lately, which is ultimately the cause of the problem. If your troubled Violets can listen intently to the advice they hear within and follow that advice, they will most likely be back on their path and back in power.

The truth is that many of the Violets' problems will not disappear until they finally become fully engaged in what they are passionate about. Unfortunately, if they have not been on a fulfilling path, making the required change could seem to require a much bigger leap than is comfortable. Once Violets have gotten too far off track, it's hard for them to imagine they can live their lives any other way. Their original dreams appear too unrealistic to pursue at that point. But their lives come alive again if they return to their original passion or find something equally exciting and idealistic to replace it. Violets need to feel passion, or life is not worth living. Whether they get involved in charitable work, teaching, music, film, or some other form of creative expression, all Violets need to live large lives. They need to do more than just immerse themselves in ordinary life.

Another side, a darker side, to Violets can emerge when they are out of power. Some can become intensely bossy, controlling, impatient, and irritable. Out-of-power, tyrannical Violets can become ruthless dictators. Everything must be done their way, and they need to be right. They tend to be very dramatic and intense then. These arrogant individuals want to be worshipped. They tend to believe and therefore act like they are royalty, so they expect their subjects — those around them

— to revere and obey them. Some of these Violets have been pampered or raised to believe they can do no wrong, that they are God's gift to the world. The masses, or their fans, can feed their visions of grandeur. If you have become involved with these self-important Violets, you may not be able to trust them. They will believe that their needs come first, and you could find it a huge challenge to convince them otherwise.

Attempting to have calm and rational discussions with this type of Violet can be difficult. You could gather up your courage and stand your ground. You could explain to them how rude their behavior is and try to persuade them to change their ways. But they will probably refuse to listen or admit to any faults. Sometimes it's best to just give them room and hope they figure it out. Or perhaps someone, somewhere, will give them a taste of their own medicine. Violets often learn the hard way.

If these Violets can finally realize that we are all in this together, if they can see the bigger picture and recognize their small piece in the cosmic scheme of things, they may regain proper perspective and begin to treat others with respect and kindness. If not, it will probably take a bigger force than you, or a more dramatic wake-up call than your complaining, to set them straight. Usually these arrogant Violets need to fall off, or be pushed off, their pedestals before they will open their eyes and change their self-righteous behavior.

Violets in power are accepting: they give people room to follow their own paths. They enjoy their lives and believe in their missions, and they make wonderful, dedicated partners.

Violets admire partners who...

- support them in achieving their visions.

- are honest and communicative.

- are enthusiastic and motivated.

- allow them freedom.

- admire and respect them.

- treat them as equals and give them focused attention.

- motivate them.

- are passionate, interesting, and exciting.

- maintain their own identity, independence, and self-confidence.

- join them in their desire to make a difference on the planet.

- love to travel.

- maintain high integrity.

- possess compassionate and humanitarian values.

Indigos

If you find yourself in a relationship with one of these advanced souls, you are probably a very loving, understanding, and spiritually aware person. Indigos, as accepting as they are, will not be with just anyone. They have high standards when it comes to their personal intimate relationships. They would just as soon spend their time with friends as be in an unhealthy or unfulfilling relationship. In power, Indigos can sense people's souls. It takes an open, honest, and spiritual person to gain the trust of and create a deep connection with one — unless you have found an out-of-power, troubled Indigo, in which case you are probably taking care of a very sensitive and frightened soul. Because these Indigos need someone to help them through life, you may feel you are babysitting a wounded or temperamental child.

You will find that in-power Indigos are loving and kind. Yours may encourage you to become a greater, more fulfilled person and may teach you by example how to live with integrity and higher levels of awareness — Indigos may inspire the best in you to emerge. Most Indigos are strong, self-confident, and self-aware. They calmly follow their intuition and will not be swayed by the faulty, fear-based beliefs of others. If you have one of these balanced Indigos, your life will be interesting and joyful. To develop a healthy, long-lasting relationship with an Indigo, be open and honest. You have the best chance of gaining the Indigo's trust and respect if you are authentic — your Indigo must be able to trust you.

Actually, one of the best things about a relationship with an Indigo is that she or he will expect and encourage total honesty from you, which can be very freeing. It allows you to be real not only with your life partner but also with yourself. You will not have to play games, try to make your Indigo jealous, or trick her or him into cooperating with you. These particular behaviors are both unnecessary and distasteful to Indigos. Total honesty can be too intense, too intimidating, for some of the other Love Colors, but Indigos thrive on it. The more truthful you can be with your Indigo partner, the more you will have her or his devotion and appreciation.

This in no way gives you permission to be judgmental or cruel toward Indigos, however. If you do lash out at them or at someone else, they will expect you to realize that blaming or criticizing others is a sign that your own fears have been stimulated, and that your unhappiness has nothing to do with other people. They will expect you to look inside and face your fears. Once you do, your relationship will be back on track. Most in-power Indigos will wait patiently nearby while their partners work things out.

If you are hoping for a partner who will be a reliable and responsible provider, then an Indigo is a good match. Indigos will lovingly do their share to contribute resources for the home. They will not sell their soul for money, however; their work must reflect their belief system. They will not do anything that exploits people, harms the environment, endangers animals, or otherwise goes against their beliefs. Indigos do not understand greed.

If you pressure Indigos to take just any old job, if security and a desire for money become more important to you than their need to honor their ideals, you can expect to encounter serious resistance. They will leave the relationship before they will give in to pressure on this account. If you want to create a harmonious union with them, support their need to live with integrity. Living in accord with their beliefs is not merely something Indigos desire to do: it is an actual requirement. If they disregard their instinctive knowledge of what is right and wrong, what is ethical and unethical, they can become depressed and even ill. When that happens, your Indigo will withdraw from you and life in general. Is money worth sabotaging your relationship and the health of your beloved for?

If you are concerned about money, allow Indigos time to find other solutions. Let them find a method to make money that doesn't involve ignoring their values. In power, Indigos can be amazing entrepreneurs. They can come up with creative ideas that may be ahead of their time. They also tend to believe that the universe will provide for them as long as they stay true to themselves and their ideals. Just support the Indigos' standards and believe in their unusual abilities. Or if money is that important to you, and you fear your Indigo will let you down, find a way to earn sufficient money yourself.

Indigos do not need a lot of money, so if you are hoping for an ambitious partner who will provide a luxurious style of living for you, you may be better off with a Green, Red, or Violet. Indigos see money as merely an energy form that facilitates their acquiring certain necessities to live in a physical world — nothing more. They know money is not the source of happiness, and that spiritual experiences and love for other souls are what really matter. Once these are in place, everything else in the world is easy to enjoy and appreciate. They know there are many other adventures to experience, and that money is only one small part of life. They prefer to be with companions who see life this way too.

If you value spirituality and want your partner to join you on the same journey, you will likely have a willing partner in an Indigo. However, in-power Indigos feel they already know higher truths, so most trust their own inner guidance. Indigos may accompany you to spiritual conferences or meetings led by enlightened teachers, but they will do so just to be reminded of what they already know. If they feel the teacher has integrity and is offering something in alignment with their own beliefs, they will continue to attend. Indigos love to be in the presence of individuals with like minds. They love to feel supported by others on a spiritual path. These intelligent personalities enjoy having deep, philosophical discussions with people.

Indigos lose faith, however, in teachers who allow their egos to interfere with their teachings, and they will quickly abandon such teachers. They trust their own inner voices on the matter and will not be persuaded to return. Your Indigo partner will not criticize you if you choose to continue following a teacher such as this, but you could soon find the two of you traveling in different directions. Look carefully to see if your companion has observed the situation correctly. Your Indigo may be ahead of you intuitively.

Although spiritual Indigos love to meditate and connect with their higher Source, they also find life fun and fascinating. They like to play and explore all that life has to offer and will sometimes want you by their side to enjoy life's adventures with them. Yours will need you to be their best friend and trustworthy confidant, someone who will fully support them in their creative endeavors and their inner spiritual journeys. If you can find a balance between spontaneity and responsibility, the two of you can have an expansive and fulfilling life. Following the rules all the time bores Indigos, but they will always treat their loved ones with sincere respect and follow through on their obligations.

Occasionally they need time to journey off on their own. Although they love people, Indigos seem content to be alone. If you can be understanding and support their special need for solitude, if you can accept their independent nature and allow them time to fully explore life, you will have happy and healthy life partners. They will appreciate you for not taking their behavior personally, and for being self-sufficient enough to take care of your own needs. Some people feel uncomfortable or threatened by these unconventional souls. They see Indigos as strange and out of touch with reality, at least the reality they see. If you are in a relationship with an Indigo, the reactions he or she may elicit from others could be challenging for you to handle, especially if you have one of the psychic Indigos. Because many people do not understand psychic abilities or have been taught these are evil, you could be exposed to severe judgments or fearful reactions from others. Fortunately, most Indigos are aware of the world's level of consciousness and do not take the criticisms to heart. Hopefully, you can do the same.

Even your well-meaning, protective friends could become terribly upset if they see your partner going off on a "vacation" without you. Not knowing your Indigo is really on a journey of self-discovery or a vision quest, which ultimately could greatly benefit your relationship, your friends may assume your wandering partner is just being selfish and inconsiderate, possibly even off having an affair. You may be tempted to defend your loved one's reputation, or at least explain the odd behavior, but in this case that will not be necessary. Indigos are not interested in defending their beliefs or actions, so ideally, you too will learn how to be unaffected by others' opinions and judgments. In-power Indigos can take care of themselves. Just stand by them and support their decisions. They, in return, will support you.

Indigos typically do not have affairs, by the way. They see sex as a deeply spiritual, bonding experience between two souls, not merely a physical function. They do not take their encounters lightly. Sex is a cosmic union in which they can become emotionally and spiritually absorbed with another. Betraying their partners, taking advantage of someone else, and dishonoring a loved one's trust in them in order to fulfill some selfish physical desire is not their style. It goes completely against their principles. If you want a harmonious relationship, it is best to give your Indigo partner the benefit of the doubt. Indigos appreciate partners who trust them. And they appreciate partners who are trustworthy and faithful. While some of the other Love Colors may not be devastated by indiscretions, Indigos are. Indigos take their commitments seriously.

Indigos can become extremely disturbed and discouraged by intolerance and injustice and can be as easily upset by cruel and inconsiderate behavior from friends and family as they can be by devastating world events. They do not understand why certain conditions still exist — war, poverty, starvation, and destruction. Nor do they comprehend unconscious and hurtful behavior from their loved ones.

When you see them distressed by the world or by their own personal life, lovingly encourage them to go deep within themselves, to connect with a greater knowing, one that can potentially explain reasons behind the circumstances. This inner knowledge may help them see things from a different perspective. Indigos know that appearances can be deceiving. Help yours realize that there may be a greater plan behind the current events. Once Indigos truly connect with Source and their own inner knowing, they tend to regain their balance.

If, however, they remain upset by the circumstances, discuss their feelings with them and do your best to find solutions together. See if there is anything the two of you can do to change the circumstances. Since Indigos are intelligent and intuitive, the answers you uncover could be highly beneficial for the two of you as well as for the world, and possibly the solutions will be ahead of their time. Knowing that you sincerely care enough to help them, to stand beside them while they ponder life's dilemmas, they will come to deeply trust and appreciate you.

Many of the Love Colors prefer to shut themselves off from others while they look for solutions, and sometimes Indigos do the same. But when Indigos become completely lost, they are not able to find answers, and there are few people they can trust and turn to for guidance. Very few people understand the way Indigos think. They will not accept pat answers just because these have been the traditional answers in the past. The solutions must feel like the truth, or they will reject them and continue to search.

When Indigos become seriously lost and out of power, their behavior typically takes one of two forms. They may become scared, confused, and childlike, or they may become hostile, out of control, and self-destructive. It is common for Indigos to be diagnosed with attention deficit disorder, attention deficit/hyperactivity disorder, or other learning or behavioral disorders.

If you have one of the frightened Indigos, you can expect to be the caretaker in this relationship. They tend to attract people who are rescuers, those who love to take care of others. Indigos become cautious and mistrusting of the world if they have grown up feeling unsupported. Most people do not understand the depth and sensitivity of these amazing creatures, so they do not know how to treat them. When Indigos feel lost, it is difficult to create a healthy connection with them. They tend to run away or hide like injured animals.

If you are an emotional rescuer, you may feel comfortable or even safer connecting with this type of person, one who is so afraid of the world that they need you and cling to you. On the other hand, this may not be what you desire at all. You could quickly become frustrated with a partner who will not face life and be a responsible equal. Either way, this will not be the most fulfilling or happiest relationship for either of you over time.

Indigos heal faster when they are encouraged to regain their connection with their inner guidance, to remember who they are and become empowered again. Find quiet time to meditate by their side. Retreat into nature or create a quiet, safe place where they can be still. Because sometimes even their physical senses can be too acute for them, Indigos can be highly sensitive to foods, light, and sounds. They may become overwhelmed and may fearfully withdraw inside, become stubborn, or become hyperactive. Share healthy, pure foods that are organically grown to restore physical balance in their bodies. Create a quiet, serene environment, then gradually introduce different sounds and light into the rooms to help them become acclimated to the intensity of the outer world. Otherwise, you could find yourself held hostage by their ailments, reduced to living in a highly guarded and sterile environment aimed at protecting the sensitive Indigos, but which becomes your prison as well.

Out of power, Indigos can become extremely depressed, feeling that they do not belong on this planet. They can feel so lost, frightened, or grief stricken that all the love in the world will not comfort them or help them feel safe. To avoid feeling their pain, confusion, and fear, Indigos often turn to drugs or alcohol, or they hide behind their computers, often becoming compulsive with computer games. Isolating themselves this way causes them to sink even further into alienation, confusion, and despair.

You can seek professional help for such a mate. But you will need a therapist who is intuitive and insightful, one who can understand the unusual personality of Indigos and who can find solutions that match their highly spiritual qualities.

The solution to the Indigos' problems will always be the same, whether they are experiencing relationship difficulties, health challenges, drug and alcohol addictions, money and career challenges, or just difficulty relating to the world. They must become still to reconnect with their soul and their Source. Remembering that they came to the planet with all the knowledge they need in order to live with joy, grace, and ease will save them. They are already capable of living a fulfilled and harmonious life, and if you, as their soul partner, can help them remember this, the two of you can have a wonderful, dedicated, and happy relationship.

Indigos trust partners who...

- are open and honest.

- live with high integrity and authenticity.

- have strong moral, ethical, humanitarian, and spiritual values.

- treat them and others with love and compassion.

- are loyal and trustworthy.

- support their unusual and advanced spiritual beliefs and intuitive knowledge.

- accept their unusual psychic, intuitive, creative, and mental abilities.

- allow them to live according to their independent, strong-willed nature.

- have strong self-worth and self-confidence.

- understand their unusual physical sensitivities and provide a healthy environment.

- understand, support, and share their need for meditation and spiritual connection.

- are mentally, emotionally, and spiritually stimulating.

Lavenders

If they are treated with kindness, Lavenders are loyal and grateful partners. If you create a nurturing environment, these delicate songbirds will feel safe enough to sing, to gladly offer you their natural, creative gifts, and to live according to their highest ideals. In power, these appreciative souls try to do everything and anything to make people happy.

Lavenders can be fascinating partners, provided you are kind, gentle, and patient with them. They want to be with people who are trusting and trustworthy, people who do not expect them to live by normal everyday rules and standards but will allow them to be the gentle free spirits they are.

Living with one of these creative beings could be interesting. Lavenders could enrich your life and take you places that most of your friends will never enjoy. Their stories may be entertaining — your life could be a perpetual wonderland of fairy tales. On the positive side, you could have a lot of fun together.

If you intend to have a relationship with one of these loving souls, you must treat Lavenders differently than most people do. People frequently become impatient and frustrated and then sharply criticize the ethereal, ungrounded, and often irresponsible Lavenders.

It takes very special and patient people to understand and maintain relationships with the unusual Lavenders. Because they are not always focused on physical reality, Lavenders have a hard time maintaining stability in a relationship. Yours may be so naïve and childlike that you may at times feel more like a parent than a partner. However, if treated with respect and kindness, Lavenders can feel safe enough to become equally contributing partners in their relationships.

Lavenders thrive with partners who are so aware, so in touch with their own inner selves, so secure and self-accepting that they can easily allow these sensitive beings to live their own unusual lifestyle. Lavenders just want to be free to use their imagination and enjoy life. It is extremely helpful if you are so self-realized that you do not feel a need to change them or take away their dreams.

What your Lavender wants most of all from you is patience, support, and understanding. Imagine living with tiny, delicate songbirds. Before they will sing, they need to feel safe in their environment. When they feel secure and happy, their songs can be breathtaking. Let your Lavenders know they please you. Feeling your loyalty and love, they will repay your kindness with sensitivity, loyalty, and appreciation. Your love could inspire their creativity.

If you have found in-power Lavenders, most likely they are successfully creating wonderful works of art or expressing themselves in a way that is making them money. But if they do not feel safe in the physical world and haven't learned how to create abundance, then you may have to bring in enough money to support both of you.

If you are in a relationship with a Lavender who is completely out of power, then most likely you have discovered that these Lavenders cannot hold down a job or otherwise make any money. Lavenders do not relate to regular jobs; they have difficulty sticking to schedules, budgets, or any sort of financial plans.

Lavenders' ultimate joy is to be financially supported so they have the freedom to be creative dreamers. They want partners who are willing, able, and happy to provide for them in exchange for the benefits and rare gifts that Lavenders offer in return. Although other colors, such as Greens, prefer to work, to be mentally challenged, and to accomplish, Lavenders prefer the opposite. They enjoy relaxing so that they are free to dream.

If you are willing and prepared to act like the parent in this relationship, if you can be patient, kind, and financially supportive, this relationship can be rewarding. Many of the Love Colors are natural nurturers and caretakers. Maybe you are one of them. However, if economically this is not possible or is unacceptable to you, and you have decided your Lavender is "the one," then know that Lavenders can grow if their companions slowly and patiently teach them how to become financially responsible.

In fact, unless they find caretakers who will watch over them their entire lives, or they are trust fund babies who never have to worry about money, it is beneficial for Lavenders to learn how to function in this world. As tempting as it can be to worry about these young souls, to take care of them so they do not aimlessly wander, lost and alone, through life, sometimes rescuing them and providing for them is a disservice to them. If someone is always rescuing them, they never learn. If they can learn to rely on themselves, they may become happier and more self-confident. Rather than allowing your childlike Lavenders to remain irresponsible and ungrounded, you may help them more if you gently but firmly guide them into a viable career or dependable job. This is a wonderful gift to give.

If people become overly demanding, though, these timid beings will retreat into their inner worlds, possibly never to emerge again. When Lavenders see a disapproving or angry look on a person's face, their first response is to withdraw and hide. Yelling at them only increases their fear. These hypersensitive personalities began this way in youth — if their frustrated parents yelled at them, many Lavenders learned to cope by withdrawing into a fantasy world and hiding from the dangerous adults.

Remember to maintain balance with yours. If you are too accepting, your Lavenders may take this as a sign that all is well just the way it is, and that there's no need for them to change and become more reliable.

No matter how much you may try to talk to them, to explain the harsh realities of your financial circumstances or living conditions, you may find your Lavenders are not always listening — they have drifted off into another world. They can be adept at making it look like they are listening when in fact they're not. If you can learn to recognize when they are doing this, you can find ways to gently coax your escape artists back into physical reality. Remind them that they can explore their inner worlds but must also become mature and dependable contributors. Escaping into other realities is fine, but Lavenders' lives are better if they can learn how to feel safe in this world too.

Be supportive and optimistic so they are encouraged to believe in themselves. Point out all their positive and exceptional qualities. Show them why their unique imagination is an asset and could benefit them. They can access places in their minds that others cannot or do not, which can enable them to develop one-of-a-kind products and previously unimagined projects. They may finally allow themselves to treasure their own unique personality and creative style. Finding people who value, understand, and appreciate them is undeniably beneficial to Lavenders. They then become more creative and productive.

Creating a peaceful and serene environment for your Lavender is also helpful. These fantasy-oriented personalities enjoy soft music, wind chimes, candles, incense, meditation, and the rhythmic sounds of chanting. They enjoy any sound, color, or texture that can inspire their imagination and take them into natural but altered states of consciousness.

Once they have come up with ideas, you could assist them in finding ways to bring them into existence and to sell them. Lavenders are artists and idea people, not typically astute businesspeople. You may, however, be able to encourage them to imagine and develop an unusual approach to marketing their products.

Teaching by example is another good method to use with Lavenders. Live your life in a way that helps them understand this world. Help them enjoy this dimension by letting them see how much you relish it and how fun and easy it is to function here.

If you have found yourself with one of the consistently sick Lavenders, then you may have one who is afraid of life. Once they feel safe and secure here, once they trust life, they can begin their natural healing process. Convincing these frail individuals that their fears are causing or adding to their physical ailments can be challenging, however. Often, as soon as a healer helps a Lavender in one area, another health problem develops.

If they focus their powerful imagination on healing, Lavenders can effectively cure their diseases or disorders. To stay healthy, Lavenders should be encouraged to remember that they have physical bodies, and that it is beneficial if they take realistic, tangible steps to care for them. Eating healthy foods and exercising are good beginning steps. But most of all, Lavenders must feel safe in a physical body in order to heal.

If you are in a relationship with a Lavender who has become addicted to mind-altering substances, you probably realize that this is a form of escape. Many of the chronically ill Lavenders can also become addicted to their medications but sincerely believe they do not have a problem. Some convince themselves that various substances help them go into their favorite altered worlds and dimensions, but usually this is just an excuse, a form of denial that enables them not to look at what they fear.

Lavenders' bodies are usually so fragile and sensitive that abusing drugs or alcohol could damage or destroy them much faster than it would the average person. If you cannot convince them to look at the seriousness of their self-destructive behavior, therapy may be needed. Find a therapist who can understand and accept the eccentricities of a Lavender. Since Lavenders prefer to escape the intellect, hypnotherapy may be a good option. Using logic and reason with Lavenders could be less effective than helping them use their imagination to overcome their fears.

One of the challenges you could face being in relationship with Lavenders is dealing with the other people around them. More than likely, people will be impatient with and intolerant of them. Less understanding people can become easily frustrated by the Lavenders' irresponsible behavior. It may be difficult for you to defend the Lavenders' behavior, since by all normal standards they are usually inattentive, unreliable, and immature.

If you can educate people to see the value in these precious individuals, then you have provided a kind and helpful service for Lavenders. Everyone is different, and all people have their place and purpose for being here. Not everyone is strongly motivated, not everyone has a desire to accomplish great projects or to succeed in business. If you teach by example, if others see you being loving, kind, and tolerant of a Lavender, they may be inspired to do the same. Although some may accuse you of exhibiting codependent behavior, since you will seem to be tolerating irresponsibility, others may have enough vision to see that you are living with unusual circumstances — you are in a relationship with a sensitive Lavender. They may learn to accept and get along with these uncommon and sensitive creatures too.

If you can appreciate the Lavenders' innocence and creative imagination, if you can see them as an endearing and lovable souls, you can have a wonderful adventure in your relationship. Lavenders are gracious, sensitive, pleasant, and dedicated mates.

Lavenders appreciate partners who...

- are kind and gentle.

- accept their need for quiet and serenity.

- are patient with and tolerant of their childlike nature.

- support them emotionally as well as financially.

- create a safe and comfortable environment for them.

- understand and allow their desire to daydream and fantasize.

- appreciate their sensitive nature.

- do not make harsh demands on them.

- encourage their creativity.

- allow them to live an unusual carefree life with no strict rules and boundaries.

- listen to their stories and share their curiosity about other worlds and dimensions.

- encourage them to stay healthy by helping them feel safe in their bodies.

Crystals

Crystals desire partners who are quietly supportive, who understand and respect their need for solitude and self-reflection, and who help them create a calm, pleasant home atmosphere. One of the nicest gifts you can bestow on these introspective beings is to create a safe and tranquil setting as a personal sanctuary for them. Consider creating a beautiful Japanese garden, complete with benches where they can sit quietly, surrounded by flowers and gentle waterfalls or fountains. Or plant an English tea garden with a lavender-scented gazebo for their personal retreat. They will treasure either of these gifts from you.

Crystals love what is pretty, restful, and serene. Because they like simplicity and cleanliness, their homes tend to be tidy and orderly. Be comfortable with this if you want harmony with these partners. An unkempt environment will upset and disorient them.

Crystals are not fond of loud, obnoxious people. Hopefully you won't bring any of these people into your home. Being sensitive and easily overwhelmed, Crystals typically feel uncomfortable in crowds. They can easily become disoriented and even frightened. Outside the home, too, they tend to be repelled by people or environments that are noisy, harsh, or dirty, so be sensitive enough to avoid these when you are with your Crystal. The world often seems cold, heartless, and insensitive to them, and they can become easily disillusioned with the people around them. So if you can be warm, loving, and trustworthy, you may counteract their negative experiences and help them regain optimism and a belief in humanity.

You will make the best mate for a Crystal if you yourself have little or no need for excitement or drama. Crystals prefer partners who are content to be quiet and love to stay at home, who do not require a lot of extra attention, and who are independent and have a strong but unassuming self-confidence. They enjoy having companions; they just do not need someone to be by their side or in their presence at all times. They actually prefer to have time and space alone. They don't mind if you are at the far side of the house entertaining yourself; they can be quite satisfied just knowing their beloved is nearby.

Crystals often physically and emotionally detach from the world, which could make you feel isolated and disconnected from them. They may appear not to care about you or the relationship, and this may leave you wondering what you did wrong and why they have abandoned you. Crystals don't withdraw to be cruel or inconsiderate. They just need to have some quiet time to cleanse their auras and reclaim their energy. They can become easily fragmented and overwhelmed by the dizzy and hectic pace of other people. Maybe you can show them how to retreat in a kind and respectful way. Better yet, learning to recognize their signals and realizing this is their pattern could help you get used to their behavior. Be understanding and gracious enough to allow your Crystal time alone without being personally hurt or offended. If you are one who needs a lot of emotional reassurance and quality time with your partner, a Crystal may not be the most fulfilling companion for you.

If you enjoy mental stimulation and interesting conversations, Crystals will not disappoint you. They are intelligent, well-read people. When they grace you with their presence, you can have wonderful discussions.

If you like to be in the world accomplishing important tasks, find ways to be comfortable in the world without this particular partner. When you go out into the world, learn, gather information, be stimulated, and accomplish your goals, then return home to share your knowledge and experiences with this reclusive soul. If you are hoping for a companion who will explore the world with you, typically Crystals are not your best choice. However, they will be excited to hear about your exploits and will support your going back out into the world the next day. Their strength lies in providing a loving and peaceful home and welcoming your return.

If you desire a loyal, dedicated, and serene companion who is content to sit quietly at home with you, this is the perfect Love Color. Crystals will not demand great things from you or push you to climb the social or financial ladder. They will be easy to please — money and possessions are not major priorities for Crystals. They want to feel secure, but connecting with their spirituality is their primary focus. If you have the ability to support the two of you on your own, your Crystal partner will be even happier and more grateful. If you require your partner to contribute financially, your Crystal will graciously bring home a basic paycheck — Crystals will not shirk their responsibilities. In-power Crystals are responsible partners. They are not really interested, however, in learning how to invest or how to amass a fortune, so if having long-term financial security is important to you, you will need to be the one who sets up the retirement funds and the life insurance policies.

At the same time, Crystals feel safest with partners who are providing their share or more. These people do not tolerate instability or debt well. If you have difficulty holding down a job or bringing in a steady income, they could become insecure and learn to mistrust you — and could eventually close off from you. Usually Crystals do not stay with people they mistrust. To help them trust you, provide a wonderful haven for them, make sure all your financial obligations are covered so they don't have to worry, and generally enable them to live a peaceful, easy life.

Since Crystals don't need their partners to be around them all the time, you will have plenty of freedom. They enjoy their independence and solitude, so you won't need to feel guilty if you are a workaholic or enjoy spending time away. However, if you're being sexually indiscreet, know that your Crystal partner will not entertain a physical relationship with you. Crystals may be hurt and insulted that you have betrayed them, but even more, they'll be afraid of contracting some disease from you. Crystals value and protect their sensitive physical bodies.

Disrespecting their sacred practices, dishonoring their spiritual beliefs, or obstructing them from following their inner path can all be more offensive and unforgivable to Crystals than any worldly or sexual infidelities. They are less bothered by human foibles and take spiritual disloyalty far more seriously. They know people are "human" and make mistakes. Their understanding of the human condition and human nature is one reason why they prefer to separate themselves from civilization so often. This by no means gives you carte blanche to behave any way you like. The more Crystals grow to mistrust you, the further they will withdraw from you. If you want to develop a healthy relationship with one of these sensitive beings, know that Crystals value respect, trustworthiness, and integrity.

When Crystals are out of power, they seem to forget why they came to the planet. They have no idea what they are supposed to do or what is expected of them. They tend to watch others to see what is socially acceptable and appropriate. When they lose touch with their natural intuition, they don't act according to what they know to be true and instead constantly look for reassurance and guidance. They are often insecure about making decisions and can become dependent on others to run their lives.

Keeping this in mind, you may find that the best way to help out-of-power Crystals who are racing around in circles trying to find themselves may be to teach by example. Remember, Crystals pick up on the energy of those around them. If you are self-confident, you can help these Crystals become self-confident. If you are calm, they will feel safe enough around you to be calm and centered. If you become upset and angry, if you yell at Crystals, they will either withdraw and run away from you or shoot that anger right back at you. This will just create perpetual tension, hurt feelings, and mistrust in your relationship.

Another important way to help Crystals through their insecurity and confusion is to encourage them to meditate, to quietly go within to reconnect with their Source and find answers to their questions. They will need to feel safe enough to let go of the chaotic outside world that they have been trying to cope with or control. They will need to trust that things will not fall apart while they retreat inside their sanctuary and become still enough to regain their center.

If they don't seem to be able to become secure and quiet enough to go within, then encourage them to spend time in nature. Crystals appreciate the beauty and wonder of nature, which is why it is best for them to retreat into gardens or lush forests. It gives them a chance to connect with their spirituality.

If they are still incapable of finding solace, of reconnecting with their gentle and trusting nature, it may be time to find a kind but understanding therapist. Crystals are usually good at finding their own solutions, but when they have veered so far away from their intuitive nature, getting guidance from other insightful people may help. Therapists must be patient, calm listeners in order not to frighten these sensitive souls. If you have spent any time at all with out-of-power Crystals, you know how challenging it can be to get them to come out of their shells.

If they are so lost that you see them becoming interfering busybodies, if they have become more interested in other people's lives than in their own, it's a safe bet they do not know who they are or what they could be doing to fulfill their own potential. You may want to find a tactful way to bring inappropriate behavior to their attention, to let them know what you see. Before they alienate and lose all their friends, see if you can support them in becoming happier and healthier. Be careful, though. Crystals are sensitive beings, and you don't want to hurt their feelings so badly that they withdraw permanently from you.

This may be a good time to encourage your Crystals to go to school to discover a direction, to see which vocations they may find appealing. Out of power, Crystals become so scattered that they are not sure what type of job or career they want. They may lose not only their direction but also their belief in themselves. Crystals love to learn, however, so this may be a good approach to get yours back on track. Allowing them the time and space to study different topics to see which ones stimulate them is a loving way to support them.

If you are involved with Crystals who want to become healers — healing is one of their natural gifts — being emotionally and financially supportive while they pursue this endeavor will earn you their undying gratitude. Or if one of these highly introspective beings decides to become a writer, artist, or spiritual advisor, again, receiving your support and encouragement will be invaluable to this person's health and happiness.

If you desire a partner who will devote himself or herself to being in a loving, reliable partnership, then a Crystal can be a good match for you. If you are happy going out into the world, making a living, being mentally stimulated and challenged, and then are content to come home to a quiet, restful environment, then you'll find a Crystal is a good partner. This will be an ideal situation for the Crystal too.

Crystals appreciate partners who...

- love quiet and serenity.
- create a simple, calm, and peaceful home environment.
- remain kind and gentle.
- are independent, self-sufficient, and self-confident.
- are intelligent and mentally stimulating.
- share their spiritual beliefs and ideals.
- allow them their quiet time alone.
- understand and accept their unusual shifting qualities and changing personalities.
- are patient and supportive when the Crystals become confused and lost.
- support their healing and creative abilities.
- help them create a natural outdoor sanctuary where they can meditate.
- support them in staying healthy with natural foods and a loving, safe home.

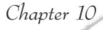

Chapter 10

Challenges and When to Let Go

How do you know if you have the best partner for you? How do you know if you're giving up on someone too soon and are running away from a potentially great relationship? Or how do you know if you've worked on your relationship long enough and it's time to let it go?

The answer is always: Be still and go deep inside yourself; listen to your own inner voice. Ask yourself these questions: Does your partner exhibit behaviors that annoy or disturb you? If these behaviors are merely annoying, can you focus on your partner's good qualities so that the bad habits don't bother you? Or is your partner doing something so seriously disturbing that it is diminishing your happiness, well-being, peace of mind, or health? Will this person ever change? Does she or he want to change? In choosing this partner, did you create a mirror for yourself? Are you the one who needs to change — are the problems in this relationship really your own issues? Or did you recreate an old, self-defeating pattern from your childhood? Do you sense that the relationship is unhealthy or unrewarding for you? Are you afraid to be alone? Are you afraid you cannot create something better — something more fulfilling for you?

Deep inside, we all know whether our relationship is healthy, whether our issues with our partner are ever going to improve, and whether this relationship is the best one for us. If a relationship is unfulfilling and we are confused about what steps to take, it may be because we are afraid to face what we are sensing. Perhaps we are afraid to change our own lives, our own behavior, or our own relationship status. As long as we focus our confusion or annoyance on someone else's flaws, we do not have to face our own fears. And we will stay stuck until we are honest enough and brave enough to dive into our own fears and deal with them.

Ultimately, though, when there are more negative, unfulfilling experiences in a relationship than positive, loving experiences, when there is little improvement, progress, or growth, then it may be time to let go. If you recognize any of the following situations in your own relationship, consider the option of moving on. If your partner has a Red Overlay, described below, maintaining a healthy partnership can be even more difficult.

Red Overlays

This element is different from a Red Love Color. People are not born with Red Overlays. The Red is usually added during childhood because a person feels unsafe or has a life-threatening experience. Usually a Red Overlay develops in people who feel physically, mentally, or emotionally abandoned, rejected, or abused. This also applies to people who had birth complications or almost died at some time. Life feels unsafe, so the person adds the denser Red to their aura for protection.

People with Red Overlays usually exhibit intensely angry behavior or are perpetually sabotaging their lives. If your partner has a Red Overlay, he or she will probably not allow the relationship to be harmonious or easy. Each of the different Love Colors displays the behavior of the Red Overlay in a unique way, depending on whether the Love Color is more physical, mental, or emotional.

A partner with a Red Overlay has issues that must be worked out if the relationship is to survive. Therapy is one solution and may enable the relationship to become healthy and long lasting. If you feel that you or your partner may have this overlay and would like to know how to release it, please read the chapter on Red Overlays in the book *Life Colors* for more in-depth information.

If you are uncertain about whether to leave your partner, here is more information about each of the Love Colors to help you decide.

Reds

When to Disengage from Your Red

There are typically four main reasons why people leave Reds: their Red partners are explosive and physically abusive, they become unavailable emotionally or physically or both, they have serious addiction problems, or they are so self-centered that they care about only their own needs and immediate gratification.

Even though the dynamic Reds can be exciting to be around, if you feel you are not having the emotional or spiritual connection you desire with your partner, it may be time to let go. Reds are not always open, and they can stubbornly refuse to change their behavior. If you find your Red spending more time alone or partying with friends without you, or spending all the money on clothes or other possessions regardless of your feelings on the matter, realize you have a partner who is not interested in your needs. These Reds can even have affairs and justify them as fulfilling their own physical needs. If you are feeling forsaken and your partner is not interested in discussing it, it could be time for you to move on to someone who is emotionally more available, more loyal, and more interested in your mutual happiness and fulfillment.

Reds are typically too stubborn to change, and they do not mind being alone. So unless you are willing to also be alone, to spend the rest of your life feeling like you are not a priority, it's better to find a more compatible and willing partner.

You may have a Red who has a substance abuse problem. Reds can get so focused on their own physical addictions, so obsessed with satisfying their own desires, that they overindulge. Satisfying their cravings takes precedence over anything and anyone else. Some of these Reds are too lazy and unmotivated to get a job. They can lie around all day feeding their addictions. Substance abuse, sexual addictions, laziness, and even overspending are common for out-of-power Reds. Any of these can put a strain on a relationship.

You may have a physically violent Red, one who gets into fights too often or, worse yet, one who is abusive with you. Or you may be tired of picking these Reds up from bars late at night because they are too drunk to find their way home. Maybe you have had to bail them out of jail once too often. These are all legitimate reasons to separate from your Red. Unless you enjoy the drama and unpredictability of this type of relationship, you may want to consider the fact that there are healthier partners in the world.

Getting away from your Red may not be that simple, however. Often Reds are so controlling and ego driven that they will not let their partners go. While other Love Colors will use guilt, shame, or other mental and emotional manipulations to keep a partner nearby, Reds tend to use physical force or threats to maintain control. They may threaten to take all the money away, which leaves their partners feeling trapped and helpless. More often than not, these Reds become physically threatening and may frighten their partners so much that they fear for their lives.

If you are with a physically abusive or controlling Red, seek professional help or find an organization that can assist you in making the break from this partner.

Reds with Red Overlays

A Red with a Red Overlay is without a doubt the most dangerous of all the combinations. Most Reds are hot tempered as it is, but when you add the wounded quality of a Red Overlay, the anger grows exponentially. Imagine this Red as an injured and cornered ferocious wild animal.

If an argument escalates and tempers reach a critical level, Reds can become extremely hostile and threatening. They are the most physically violent of the colors, and their outbursts can be unpredictable and uncontrollable. They can become blind with rage, making it impossible to reason with them. The problem is exacerbated if the Red has a drinking or substance-abuse problem, which many of them do. Reds with Red Overlays are also prone to being sexually abusive. Unfortunately, many battered partners are forced to flee for their lives when their out-of-power Red loses control. You are advised to leave this type of Red before your relationship reaches such an intense level.

There are many Reds with Red Overlays in prisons, most of them for committing murder or other violent crimes.

Oranges

When to Detach from Your Orange

Living with an Orange could be the greatest challenge you ever take on. There are two main reasons why people end their relationships with Oranges. First, they feel physically and emotionally abandoned by their Orange partners. Second, they cannot handle the stress. Most ordinary and sane people cannot handle the strain of being in a relationship with an Orange — and Oranges know this. Partners end up spending most of their time waiting, worrying, and wondering how long their Oranges will live. If you have a tendency to be anxious anyway, living with an Orange could give you ulcers — or possibly a heart attack.

Often, partners feel emotionally disconnected from Oranges because not only are Oranges gone most of the time, but they also don't feel a need to discuss relationship issues or emotionally bond with their partners — which creates another type of loneliness for their loved ones. Out of power, Oranges tend to be self-centered. They can be egotistical and sometimes even cold and distant. They are more interested in experiencing excitement and thrills for their own pleasure than in committing themselves to working on any long-term relationships. Facing life-threatening challenges is their pleasure, and they typically don't care how it may affect others. They are not willing to give up their exciting lifestyle for the sake of family or friends.

Moreover, out-of-power Oranges have no problem having multiple sexual encounters with a wide variety of people. Selfishly, they see it as just another form of challenge and conquest.

Because Oranges are so independent and self-sufficient, when they disagree with their partners, when there is more struggle in the relationship than fun, it is simpler for them to just turn and go their own way. It is easier to become angry with their mates and leave rather than facing themselves and finding out they may be part of the problem. Most Oranges have no desire to change. They are not interested in emotional therapy or discussing ways to improve the relationship.

If you find yourself alone and miserable too often, realize this pattern will probably not change — not while the Orange is young and vibrant. Possibly, one day these Oranges will be too old to go on the adventures and will need someone to take care of them — if they live that long. Expect to be alone in the meantime.

It can be tough to let go of these exhilarating people. They are usually vigorous, exciting, healthy, and sexy. But be honest — did you really have them in the first place? Or have they just been humoring you or spending time with you in between their "real" life episodes — the life that is apparently more important to them than you?

There are other powerful and stimulating Love Colors that may be more emotionally available to you. If you no longer wish to be alone and you realize your Orange partner will never change, believe in yourself enough to let go and find another partner. Allow the two of you to experience the lives that you truly desire, the lives that bring each of you fulfillment and pleasure.

Oranges with Red Overlays

Because people often add Red Overlays to their auras if they have life-threatening experiences and believe they are going to die, it is easy to see how the natural personality of the thrill-seeking Oranges could get them into perilous situations. Many Oranges faced death in their youth. Many others added Red Overlays because they felt suppressed or mis-understood as children.

If you have an out-of-power Orange with a Red Overlay, it could be exceptionally challenging to stay with her or him. These Oranges can exhibit intensely self-destructive behavior. They can put themselves in extremely perilous situations — beyond what even their most daring Orange friends would venture to do. These angry individuals appear intent on harming themselves and can become reckless and even dare life to come at them. For example, a police officer, hunter, military leader, or some other Orange with a Red Overlay in a position of authority may exhibit extremely aggressive and out-of-control behavior. These Oranges may risk not only their own lives but also the lives of those around them.

Since Oranges are natural loners, they will not turn to others for help. Instead they will angrily push people away. If you tend to be an emotional rescuer, it can be tempting to try to save these souls, to stay patiently by their side when no one else will — but these Oranges will not let you near them, nor will they be emotionally available for you to rescue.

Because Oranges are highly physical, they can also become physi-cally violent and abusive. More often than not, they tend to remove themselves from society and stray off into the wilderness alone. But occasionally, if they think they need to stay put and make money, they can become volatile people — often feeling trapped. They can be highly unpredictable too, like caged animals. One minute they are aloof, de-pressed, and sullen; the next they are explosive and ferocious.

Oranges are brave enough to face every challenge except going inside to face themselves. In this case, if they are to live healthy lives, they need to learn to face their inner issues. You will not be able to do that for your Orange. If Oranges are to heal, they must be willing to get to the bottom of their self-destructive and abusive behavior. If they don't, no one is safe near them. As much as they resist therapy, it may be their best method of finding a solution. Until they do, it is better to leave them alone to face themselves. If you tolerate their self-destructive behavior, you allow them to continue with it. If you truly desire a healthy and happy relationship, let go and move on. Let them face the consequences of their actions so they can see for themselves what they need to change.

Magentas

When to Say Good-Bye to Your Magenta

There is usually one main reason people leave their Magenta partners. Magentas may be interesting, quick, unpredictable, and energetic, but their eccentric ways of living can eventually become tiring for their mates. And Magentas do not usually go out of their way to help anyone keep up with them — not even when they have committed themselves to a relationship. They enjoy marching to the beat of their own drummer and do not want to be kept back by anyone. Their behavior often comes across as self-centered — they do what they want to do and will not listen to anyone who tries to tell them to behave differently. They will create their own separate world if they need to; they will do anything to live the way they desire.

If your lifestyle has become too unhealthy, your sleeping hours too erratic, and your eating habits atrocious, and this has made you physically ill, it may be time to save yourself. If, in addition to the strange and unwholesome tendencies your Magenta may have had to begin with, he or she has become addicted to drugs or alcohol, you could be pulled down even further. Take care of yourself. If you feel worn-out and overwhelmed, if you feel unimportant and your needs are not being met by your partner, it may be time to move on.

Magentas will not be manipulated or controlled, so there is very little chance you can change yours. They will have to want you in their life badly enough to change their ways. If it was easy for Magentas to alter their behavior to please others, they would not be such outcasts. It is far easier for them to live alone than to go against their independent and unconventional nature. They probably had plenty of practice being rejected and abandoned long before they met you. They know how to live on their own.

Oddly enough, though, it is usually the Magentas who leave their partners. These independent and quirky personalities can become bored and restless very quickly. Remember, many Magentas consider monogamy restrictive and limiting. Your Magenta's inability to be monogamous may be another reason you choose to leave.

In power, Magentas are not malicious. They are kind enough not to hurt their mates when they leave, and in fact they usually remain very good friends. Their exits are usually made with tact and grace.

Magentas with Red Overlays

When wounded, out-of-power Magentas add a Red Overlay, their already bizarre behavior often takes a darker turn. They become sullen, depressed, withdrawn, or emotionally unavailable. Anyone involved with this kind of Magenta will tell you life is lonely. These Magentas typically won't discuss the problem and they reject therapy, which means life with them will probably never improve. They can create such dark and depressing environments that their partners feel pulled down and swallowed by them.

Usually, threatening to leave Magentas will not induce them to change. Many of your friends may have left long ago because they could not handle your Magenta's morose, morbid behavior. You may have become secluded yourself while trying to fit into your partner's world.

It may feel as if you are all alone, but don't stay trapped there. There is an entire world outside waiting for you to rejoin it. Most people are not the isolationists that Magentas are, so go meet some different types of people. Learn to live again.

You probably hoped your Magenta would be the fun, creative person you saw inside her or him, but it didn't work out that way. It may seem sad to abandon such a pitiful loner, but your Magenta must choose to face the issues, not withdraw into a different world or create strange distractions to avoid feeling pain.

Yellows

When to Move Beyond Your Yellow

Yellows are among the most fun and endearing partners to have. They can melt your heart with their charm, innocence, and generosity — when they are in power. Even during times when their immature, irresponsible, or stubborn behavior frustrates you the most, they can be hard to abandon. The truth is, however, that when Yellows are out of power, having a relationship with them can be very challenging.

If you have been waiting forever for your Yellows to grow up and make a commitment, but they do not seem to be in any hurry, or they change their mind daily, you have a few choices. If your dream is to get married and have children, you could wait an eternity for your partner to choose to marry. Many Yellows see marriage as a trap. They fear becoming bored, getting old, and then inevitably dying. If you have one of these Yellows, moving on to love another will probably be the quickest route to achieve your dreams.

If you have no desire to marry and you can learn to enjoy the space Yellows will give you, then living an alternative type of relationship with them may be a good option. Possibly living in separate homes, enjoying time alone, taking the opportunity to go out with your other friends, and then occasionally getting together to play with your Yellow will work for you. This arrangement will probably suit your Yellow just fine.

If your Yellow lover just cannot seem to make a choice between you and another person, or refuses to finally leave an unhappy marriage, and if you find yourself spending all the holidays alone and this is not what you want, then moving your life forward is your best option.

You don't necessarily need to slam all the doors shut on your Yellow, if this seems too painful or difficult to do. If you become clear about your true desires, envision your highest dreams for yourself, and then move in that direction, the energy around your relationship will begin to shift. Shifting the energy and changing your behavior could even wake up these Yellows. It may help them realize you will not wait forever for them, and this may prompt them to change their lives too. But if they remain indecisive or remain in some other, unhealthy relationship instead of choosing you, then at least you will be free to find a more fulfilling relationship. If you just wait and wait and wait, you allow your Yellow to remain stuck too.

Be warned, however, that when Yellows sense you pulling away, they may panic. They may quickly show up on your doorstep more charming and affectionate than ever. Once you seem to be hooked again, they will feel safe going back to their old ways.

Yellows are pleasers. They do not necessarily want a commitment; they just want to make sure you still like them. The only way to stop this game is to stay firmly committed to your own dreams, stay focused on your own life, believing you can have a wonderful relationship with someone. Either your Yellow will grow up and show up, or someone else will. At least you can open yourself up to other possibilities.

Another common reason people leave Yellows is that their negative addictions become too much of an issue and interfere with the Yellows' ability to have emotional connections with their partners. Often their addictions rob them of all their money as well as their self-respect and

health. If you are tired of dealing with the Yellows' out-of-control behavior when the drugs and alcohol take over, if you are tired of being
destitute or struggling financially because of their problems, it is time to
leave this relationship. These Yellows need to face their issues, and you
cannot do that for them. Besides, knowing they are disappointing you is
making matters worse. Yellows like to make their loved ones happy. If
they see you unhappy, they can become even more unhappy and self-
destructive.

Yellows with Red Overlays

Because Yellows are so sensitive, they are easily affected by others'
anger or disapproval. They are highly susceptible to tension in their
environment. Oddly, Yellows are among those most likely to have been
sexually or physically abused as children, possibly because Yellows are
such innocent pleasers. They are also more easily controlled by physical force. Many energetic and curious Yellows felt the harsh hand of a
frustrated, overwhelmed parent trying to control them. Fearing physical pain, Yellows will subconsciously add the denser and stronger Red
to their aura for protection.

Because Yellows tend to be so physical, adding a Red Overlay to
their aura increases their tendency to become physically or sexually
abusive themselves. And with a Red Overlay, Yellows can be far more
aggressive and self-destructive with their addictions. Self-loathing Yellows are typically too afraid to deliberately commit suicide, so their best
escape is to overdose on drugs, smoke until they die, or drink themselves into oblivion.

If you have tried over and over again to rescue self-destructive Yellows, but they seem hell-bent on destroying themselves, you may want
to reconsider your options. If you have tried to convince them to seek
professional help but they refuse, then, as sad as it seems, it is better to
walk away from them than to be sucked into the bottomless abyss
alongside them.

Tans

When to Move Away from Your Tan

The most common reason people leave Tans is that they cannot emotionally connect with them. If you have found yourself in a relationship with a Tan who is closed off from the relationship physically, mentally, or emotionally, and your deepest desire is to be with someone who is communicative and connected, it is best to move on. Out-of-power Tans are stubborn and see no reason to change.

You have the choice of either tolerating this unavailability for the rest of your life or believing in yourself enough to know that you can find a different, more fulfilling partner. Many people are living in unhappy relationships with emotionally unavailable Tans. Their relationships are so disconnected and lacking in passion that they feel more like roommates than romantic partners.

Possibly by moving forward and creating your own separate life, you may actually help your Tan change too. By leaving, and therefore upsetting the safe, predictable, and comfortable world they created, you may give them a wake-up call. Not much else is likely to change their habitual behavior. Wake-up calls are usually shocking. They serve as tools to help people look at what is not working in their lives so they can change. Tans do not like to look at emotional issues, so they usually require a strong and upsetting reason to change. This kind of wake-up call could be better and less severe for your Tans than contracting a serious or life-threatening illness. You may be doing them a favor.

If the Tans feel you are leaving for no apparent reason, if they feel your actions are illogical, they will probably blame the relationship's failure entirely on you. If, however, you have spent years expressing to them your feelings of loneliness and dissatisfaction, if you have patiently tolerated their emotional abandonment, and then you finally leave in frustration and exasperation, Tans will logically know that blame for the failure of the relationship rests with them. Even if they do not admit it out loud, they will know it deep inside.

This may or may not prompt change within them. They may suddenly realize that, even though they have provided a secure living for the family, they have never been emotionally available to anyone. They may then make a desperate attempt to get closer to you or the children. It may be too late, however.

If you have remained faithful but unfulfilled for years in this relationship, if you feel you have suffered long enough, and you have finally reached the stage where you have decided to leave, most likely there will be no turning back. It usually takes a long time for people to leave the reliable Tans. Tans are typically not bad people, just inaccessible emotionally. At this late stage, you most likely have given up believing you can retrain your Tan mate or rekindle any romance that may have existed in the beginning of your relationship. So find a fair and practical way to divide the assets and move on.

Tans will certainly not see the fairness in any divorce settlement that gives you half of their hard-earned money — especially if you stayed home to care for the children while they worked day after day to earn the money. But in-power Tans will be fair and just and will want you to be adequately provided for. They will also want their children to see them in a good light.

Most Tans see the rationale of negotiating through mediators rather than hiring expensive attorneys and will prefer this route. They see more logic in keeping what they can, rather than doling it out to attorneys. Out of power, Tans will hold a grudge for the rest of their lives if you leave them in a financial situation that requires them to start over, one where they cannot live in comfort despite all their years of hard work. Once Tans lose financial security, they become severely unhappy and depressed.

Because emotional, intimate relationships can be tough for Tans to figure out, they may decide to give up on them. They may try to find a way to continue to live some semblance of their familiar lifestyle, continuing to plan for their retirement, but remaining alone and distant their entire life. If it comes to this, realize that this was their choice — this is how they felt safest, this is their decision about how best to survive life. Rest assured, there was nothing more you could have done. Sometimes it takes Tans a long time to learn how to change. So realize that the best thing you can do is to move forward and teach by example. Teach your Tan about living life to the fullest, with gusto, hope, and an optimistic belief in love. Maybe slowly but surely your Tan will change and become more emotionally available.

Because Tans want companionship and security, your Tans may go out and find other companions or caretakers to be with them. Most likely they will not be any more emotionally available to the new person than they were with you. It may be the case, however, that your leaving serves as such a serious wake-up call that it becomes just the jump-start they need. They may change more quickly than is common for the methodical, slow-moving Tans. You may, at that point, wonder why they couldn't have changed while they were with you. Just bless them and realize that your actions almost certainly brought about the change. Know that you are probably better off finding a different relationship or being on your own. Your Tans still could easily revert back to their old behavior, and then you would be right back where you started — unhappy and unfulfilled. Most likely, however, depending on their age, your Tans will stay alone and isolated for the rest of their lives.

Tans with Red Overlays

As with all people who have added Red Overlays, Tans can display extreme anger. They can be very mean. Although most Tans tend to be mentally disciplined enough not to be physically abusive, when they have Red Overlays they can become extremely emotionally and verbally abusive. They demand that their authority be respected and their rules followed.

Tans with Red Overlays also withhold from people emotionally, physically, and financially. They withdraw so deep into their own heads that there is no reaching them. At this point, even their disapproving silence can be deafening. They shut down, close off, and express themselves only when they are pushed so far that their anger explodes.

They can also be so miserly and tightfisted that, if they control the money, their partners are lucky if they get a meager allowance. These controlling Tans demand to know where their partners spent every penny of their money and even demand to see all the receipts.

The most difficult quality in Tans with Red Overlays is their intolerable behavior toward others. They become extremely critical. They judge everyone else's behavior and beliefs as being inferior to their own. They justify their offensive behavior by simply stating that they are correct and that other people are out of line. They will not listen to any arguments. These Tans can become so shortsighted that they become cynical, seeing only the negative qualities of others and of life. If you are in a relationship with one of these Tans, you will most likely find this behavior extremely uncomfortable or disturbing.

Greens

When to Leave Your Green

If you discover that you and your Green have different priorities, or if either of you has lost respect for the other, staying in the relationship is senseless. Greens can become cold and unfeeling if they are no longer interested in their partners. If you find that you cannot emotionally connect with your Green, that he or she has become physically, mentally, or emotionally unavailable, it may be time to let go. Greens often withdraw into their own minds or immerse themselves in their own interests so completely that family and friends are squeezed out. If your partner is spending too much time making money or working on projects and not enough quality time with you, and this feels unfulfilling to you, then by all means move on to someone who will make your relationship a priority.

If you have a healthy and balanced Green, you can separate amicably. When Greens are in power, they can be reasonable in assessing the situation and can see that it is not meeting the needs of either of you. Greens can be fair in dividing up joint assets. Intelligent Greens can even remain friends with you, provided they have not felt humiliated by the experience.

If Greens are out of power, however, dealing with them can be much more difficult. They can be extremely self-centered, controlling, and verbally abusive. Intense arguing and yelling is common behavior — they often feel that the world owes them, so they become demanding, impatient, and bitterly hostile toward others. They are also severely critical and judgmental. When Greens are out of power, there is no pleasing them. Nothing anyone else does is right. They demand attention and respect from others, then they turn around and push those same people away.

These Greens can also become possessive and want to control your every move. They may accuse you of betraying them, when in fact you have done nothing wrong. Greens are highly suspicious, and in severe cases they can become so obsessed that they will even hire detectives to spy on their partners.

If you find you cannot trust your Green, that she or he has become verbally abusive or unreasonably controlling, it may be time to seek out a highly skilled attorney to handle your affairs. Be sure that you hire the best attorney you can afford, however, because you can be certain your Green will do the same. Greens want attorneys who have a sharklike approach to divorce settlements. If you have reached that point in your relationship, they will feel that their money is more important than you are.

Greens are frequently serious gamblers, which may be causing you additional concern. These risk takers can lose control and get their families into overwhelming debt. Some lose their money, their homes, and their possessions on this particular addiction. If your Green is not willing to get help to give up this addiction, it's best to move on.

Greens with Red Overlays

The added anger of a Red Overlay makes Greens even more mentally, emotionally, and financially dangerous to tangle with. These Greens can be so ruthless and vindictive that they will think nothing of destroying or damaging anyone they feel has betrayed them. Their usual way of harming others is to financially bankrupt them.

Their selfish nature can cause them to lie, cheat, and hide money for their own gain. Greens are verbally proficient and so manipulative that they can be very convincing when they defend their innocence. Many people have suspected but had no proof, or found out too late, that their Green partners had lied and hidden money in secret bank accounts. While it is usually Reds who go to jail for physical-abuse crimes, it is Greens who tend to be indicted for embezzlement or other white-collar crimes. Greens with a Red Overlay can be so self-serving and deceitful that they care little for others' well-being. They will do anything to ensure their own wealth, security, and selfish pleasures.

Because they are keenly aware of their own dishonest behavior, they are often suspicious of others' motives and behaviors as well. Their fear and mistrust of others can evolve into such serious paranoia that it can cause them to isolate themselves even more. Maintaining any sort of reasonable relationship at this point is nearly impossible.

Blues

When to Separate from Your Blue

Unhappy Blues can create such drama, misery, and woes in their lives that most people feel suffocated by its weight. This is the reason most people leave their Blues. It is a shame, though, since Blues ordinarily have such a great capacity to experience genuine love. The heaviness can show up even in the Blues' physical bodies. These Blues frequently use food or sweets as a replacement for the love they so desperately desire. They can develop serious eating disorders, or they can put on excessive weight to protect themselves from others.

If your Blue has become too emotionally heavy, and nothing you do, short of sacrificing your own happiness, seems to change his or her attitude, it may be time to move on. If guilt is holding you back, realize that suffering with someone else never empowers that person, and it rarely makes anyone happy.

When Blues are out of power, they get lost in their own loneliness and then feel sorry for themselves. Because Blues are sensitive to others' needs and they help those who are suffering, they expect people they love to offer the same courtesy in return. When people do not want to rescue these Blues, or they don't know how to comfort these hurt souls, it just increases the Blues' pain. They feel even more neglected and unloved.

Blues often use guilt to try to influence others to be there for them. The brokenhearted Blues do not try to manipulate others because they are bad people. They are just hurt and lonely, and they don't know how else to get people to pay attention to them. Pointing out this behavior to the Blues usually makes them feel worse about themselves. But if they are allowed to manipulate others through guilt, they still may never be completely happy, because they may always wonder if people are with them out of pity rather than love.

People are often repelled by the Blues' forlorn behavior. Their desperate cry for love feels too demanding and overwhelming. How could anyone possibly fill such a huge emptiness? The desperate Blues typically scare people away, thus fulfilling their greatest fear — abandonment. These Blues come across as victims and martyrs. No matter how much one may try to console these Blues or shower them with love and compassion, the Blues cannot accept it. Their low self-worth causes them to reject the heartfelt offers. These Blues usually have a hard time even accepting compliments.

The trouble may have started when they were young. Many of these wounded Blues felt abandoned and neglected as children. A parent may have left when the Blue was just a child, or a parent may have been emotionally unavailable. If this is the case, the sensitive Blues were probably emotionally traumatized — whether they consciously remember the events or not. Blues tend to take these situations very personally. A parent's departure will make Blues feel unlovable and unwanted. Of course, it probably had nothing to do with them, but they do not perceive it that way.

Blues have a stronger and deeper need to connect emotionally than most people. Other Love Colors are more independent and rebellious. One can see examples of these differences in divorced families — one child can be extremely affected by the divorce, while a sibling seems to take it all in stride. It is not the age of the children that accounts for the difference in their reactions; it is the variation in their personalities and temperaments.

If Blues felt neglected or abandoned in childhood, they may repeat that pattern in relationships. They may subconsciously be drawn to people who are unavailable so they can feel abandoned and neglected all over again. The people could be physically unavailable — they live far away or they are married — or they could be emotionally unavailable. Or your Blue may subconsciously push you away, then make you feel guilty for abandoning her or him — and then draw you back through pity. If this yo-yo behavior is occurring in your relationship, it is not healthy for either of you.

The Blues' hardest lesson and greatest challenge is learning to love themselves. If they refuse to take responsibility for their lives, to re-examine and change their low opinion of themselves and let go of their feelings of despair, then it is best not to drown with them. If they cannot learn to love themselves, they will probably never trust others to love them, either. If you walk away, the Blues may wake up and save themselves. Facing their fears could make them stronger. If not, they may just find another rescuer. Either way, you are free to find a healthier, more joyful partner.

Blues with Red Overlays

Blues are so sensitive, and they so deeply want to be loved, that when they feel abused, neglected, or abandoned as children, it is common for them to add the protective Red Overlay. Any of the Love Colors can remove or heal a Red Overlay, and at least Blues are open to therapy, so there is hope for those willing to take this route. However, if the Blues have become so stuck in depression, self-pity, or self-loathing that they cannot seem to find their way out, moving away from them may trigger their search for deeper answers and healing.

These Blues can become so despondent that they have thoughts of dying, of going back home to God, where life can be easier and where maybe someone will finally love them. Take heart in knowing that, typically, although not always, Blues will not commit suicide, because they do not want to hurt others. Some Blues, however, especially Blues with Red Overlays, can become so desperate for love and attention that they will actually attempt to take their lives. They usually fail. They did not really want to die; they only wanted to know that someone cared enough to come to their rescue. One hopes these Blues will seek out serious therapy.

If staying with your Blue is destroying your happiness, if he or she is holding you hostage by threatening suicide, get professional help so you can find a way to change the dynamics. Otherwise, you could stay stuck in this codependent, painful, and dysfunctional relationship to the detriment of you both.

Violets

When to Venture Away from Your Violet

The most common reason for separating from a Violet is that your plans, visions, and desires have gone in opposite directions. Violets must be true to their dreams. If you cannot agree on common goals, if you see different paths and cannot find a way to connect the paths, then it is usually best to part ways. If you talk Violets out of their ideal visions, you will eventually have a frustrated partner. Other colors can tolerate altering their plans better than Violets can. They are the visionaries and really are happiest when they are supported in living their dreams.

You may be frustrated with out-of-power Violets because they are not accomplishing anything or living up to their potential. Many such Violets become so lost, scattered, and confused that they are challenging to live with. If Violets were not taught to believe in themselves, they typically do not know how to accomplish their dreams or goals. It is common for partners to lose respect for these lost souls. They can watch helplessly as their Violets wander through life unfulfilled, their dreams unrealized. Most people cannot tolerate being with these sad dreamers. Attempting to solve the problem, they try to convince their Violets to give up their dreams of becoming famous actors or musicians or something equally "unrealistic" and find regular, secure jobs. Since Violets are not really cut out to be regular employees, conflict can arise in the relationship.

If you have lost faith in your Violet, if having a partner who can provide a stable income is a priority, then it may be best to let your Violet idealist continue on her or his way. One never wants to crush the spirits and schemes of Violets, so rather than make your Violets feel even worse, let them go their own way. Maybe they will learn to believe in themselves and eventually fulfill their dreams.

It's common for wounded Violets to become so depressed and despondent that they will not let anyone reach them. It is challenging for Violets to go to counseling, because they usually feel they know more than the therapists. Violets have such deep inner wisdom, they fear no one can understand them or relate to their complex issues. If therapists cannot get to the source of their problems in a quick and direct way, Violets become bored and disappointed, and they shut down even more. They then feel hopeless, like they are a lost cause. They often wander off feeling alone and disillusioned. Violets have to reconnect with their vision and sense of purpose; they need to live their dreams or they will not be emotionally available partners.

Some out-of-power Violets are too self-absorbed to be in relationships. Because many Violets sense that they are royalty, they treat their partners like servants rather than partners. They prefer people who will stroke their egos, those who will make them feel important and wait on them hand and foot. These Violets can become controlling, obsessive, and self-centered. For some, this type of strong-willed, domineering partner is ideal. However, be clear on your true desires before becoming involved with these Violets. They are not easily changed. They see no need to change. They are too narcissistic to consider putting another's needs or desires before their own. These Violets, if uninspired in the relationship, will see no reason not to satisfy their needs elsewhere. They can have numerous affairs and be fully convinced there is nothing wrong with their behavior. Their egos, however, will not tolerate the same behavior from you. They are too proud and would be seriously offended if you made them look bad to the outside world.

These particular out-of-power Violets can be charming and convincing. They are masters at deception and manipulation. They are grand storytellers. They can effortlessly have you thinking you are paranoid, mistrusting, or ungrateful — especially since they have given you so much in life. They will convince you that it is you who has the problem.

Be aware that if you finally decide to move away from these self-important Violets, they may become even more controlling. If they are concerned about their reputation and status in the world, or, just as likely, if they fear losing their money and possessions, then be prepared to face a potentially dramatic power struggle. A Violet such as this will think nothing of spending time and money fighting you in court and then will blame you for all the trouble. Out-of-power Violets have very strong egos. It is best to obtain powerful legal help from someone who is not intimidated by your Violet's intensity. Of course, it is always better to prevent this level of drama by learning to recognize the signs well in advance; then you can avoid this type of Violet altogether or at least leave earlier in the relationship.

Violets with Red Overlays

Because Violets are among those most commonly abused as children, especially sexually abused, more Violets have Red Overlays than any of the other Love Colors. Violets can be very beautiful and charismatic, even when they are young, which can attract sexual predators. Also, because Violets are here to help save the planet and aid those in need, troubled people are intuitively drawn to them. Simultaneously, those same people can be intimidated by the wisdom that shows in Violets' eyes. Threatened by the Violets' advanced awareness, people often mistreat them.

Communicators that they are, Violets can become verbally hostile if they have red in their auras. In addition, trapping the freedom-loving, eaglelike Violets inside the cage of a Red Overlay can cause them to sink into a deep depression. Unless Violets get therapy to undo the damage done in childhood, they are certain to struggle and face more drama in their lives than most of their peers.

Indigos

When to Move Away from Your Indigo

There are a few reasons you may want to leave Indigos: they have become depressed and emotionally unavailable, or they have become disturbed and self-destructive, or both. Any of these behaviors can be wearing on your relationship. You may be struggling to improve the situation, but when Indigos do not want to cooperate with people, there is nothing you can do to mend that. Unless Indigos want to transform, they will not change.

When Indigos are out of power, they feel like aliens in a frightening and unsupportive land. They withdraw from the world. They go into their own secret inner hiding places and become unreachable. Many of them turn to drugs to further distance themselves from people. Because Indigos cannot be changed, coerced, or manipulated by pleading, rationalizing, threats of punishment, or even physical force, people often become frustrated when trying to reach them. Very few counselors understand Indigos, although some therapists are becoming better educated about them and recognize how to deal with these very special souls. Regardless, the depressed Indigos are difficult to reach, especially by their untrained partners.

These sensitive and misunderstood souls often end up in hospitals, where professionals try to analyze them, alter their behavior, and mold them into socially acceptable people. Some of these unhappy, out-of-power Indigos are institutionalized. Many have been misdiagnosed as psychotic, obsessive-compulsive, bipolar, or even autistic. It can be challenging to maintain a relationship with one of these troubled Indigos, and if you remain dedicated to the attempt despite the prognosis, your life's work will be struggling to understand your Indigo while you try to find professional help for him or her. If you feel you want to devote your life to your Indigo anyway, sensing that no one else will stand by him or her, realize your own needs and happiness will most likely go unfulfilled. Dealing with the Indigo's problems will take every bit of strength and stamina you can muster.

As sad as it is to think about abandoning these sensitive, unusual beings, it can also be hard feeling so alone in this type of relationship. These Indigos can become so depressed and sullen that they can negatively affect the lives of everyone around them.

Even though Indigos seem advanced and have such a great potential to teach us a new and evolved way of thinking, you may still need to move away from yours. If you have tried your best to reach a self-destructive Indigo, but to no avail, then you may want to look at letting go. These Indigos need to face the consequences of their own choices and behavior. They have an inner awareness of the difference between right and wrong, so if they are acting out, it is with their own full knowledge. Indigos will not be forced into changing their ways if they have decided on a particular course of action. They need to correct their behavior, their thoughts, and their beliefs on their own.

Indigos with Red Overlays

Indigos are often rejected or abused as children. Because they can be sensitive and sometimes psychic, and because they cannot be controlled by traditional methods, these children often frighten or intimidate their less-aware parents. Many adults do not know how to deal with these special souls. In an attempt to control them, parents can become physically or mentally abusive. When Indigos add Red Overlays to protect themselves, their already odd behavior intensifies.

If you have become involved with an out-of-control and self-destructive Indigo, you can expect to have a difficult challenge on your hands. Many Indigos are angry that they are here. They feel as if they were abandoned on a dysfunctional planet. There are few teachers or healers who can give them answers or help them find solutions to coping with the pain and loneliness they feel here. Their behavior often becomes highly antisocial. They can lash out, sometimes violently. They often reject becoming a functioning member of society, refusing to make money, choose a career, or even find a life direction.

If you have one of these Indigos, you may have already thrown your hands up in despair. These Indigos will not let you in, will not accept your help or guidance, and will not let others influence them. They seem tormented inside and determined to take it out on others. Their anger and despair can reach such serious levels that it becomes obvious they don't want to be on the planet. This can be a frightening time for you. Because Indigos rarely accept professional help, you could become emotionally tormented, fearing they could take their own lives. These Indigos can unwittingly take their loved ones down with them. Their behavior can destroy families — a very good reason to stay away from them.

Lavenders

When to Depart from Your Lavender

The most common reason people give for leaving a Lavender is that they can no longer tolerate the irresponsible, irrational behavior. People become tired of financially supporting this little fairyland creature. Cute as Lavenders can be at times, their unwillingness to grow up, to mature into responsible adults, can be exhausting for their partners.

Lavenders do not always hold up their end of the relationship by providing emotional stability, meaningful communication, or financial dependability. They mean well, which can make it more difficult for people to leave these innocent and sensitive children, but having good intentions does not put food on the table or pay the bills.

If your desire was to be with a strong, equal partner, to have a secure life, and to enjoy some physical pleasures in life, you may now realize that Lavenders are not very capable at providing these things. Their lifestyle is anything but stable and grounded. They are usually monogamous, but they are not always physically present. Many withdraw into their own personal fantasy worlds, becoming emotionally and physically unreachable. Lavenders can even become so hypersensitive that they recoil from physical touch, becoming physically and sexually unavailable to their partners. These strange souls can become so bizarre that it is hard to maintain a semblance of normalcy in the relationship. They can become paranoid or neurotic, living in such a strange, fear-based world that they seem to lose touch with reality.

People can also become weary of the Lavenders' persistent health problems. The constant stream of medical expenses can create a severe financial hardship, as well as taking an emotional toll on everyone around them. If Lavenders feel unsafe on the planet, they can develop such a wide variety of illnesses and diseases that it can seem like one trip to the doctor after another. Their pale bodies cannot tolerate much. It's true that Lavenders are typically more sensitive and fragile than most of the other Love Colors, but still it can be challenging to know whether the Lavender's ailments are real or imaginary. This can apply to almost every area of Lavenders' lives: they can easily blur fact and fiction, reality and fantasy.

Lavenders with Red Overlays

When these highly sensitive creatures are abused or abandoned as children, and as a result they add the protective Red Overlay, their already uncomfortable world becomes a frightening nightmare. Many Lavenders with Red Overlays develop such intense fears of life and other people that they withdraw deeply into a world of their own and stay there. These souls rarely reemerge into the light of day. Some of them develop multiple personalities, schizophrenia, or autistic behavior.

Most Lavenders with Red Overlays have been so damaged that they rarely allow others near them emotionally. Chances are these Lavenders are not in a relationship. However, you may have been able to develop a relationship early on with one of these sensitive Lavenders, at a point when there were no obvious signs of the Red Overlay. If you are starting to notice a change in your Lavender, a steady deterioration in his or her behavior, the childhood issues may just now be starting to emerge.

Out-of-power Lavenders have many challenges facing life as it is. The overactive imaginations of Lavenders with Red Overlays can further intensify the fearful images they hold. These Lavenders need therapy. If you can find a therapist who can understand, comfort, reassure, and educate one of these unusual beings, then do your best to get your Lavender some help.

However, many of these tortured souls become so adept at finding other worlds and realities to hide in that they will not let anyone pull them out. Why would they want to live in this world, where people hurt and abandon them, when they can stay "safe" in a world where people cannot affect them? Many of these Lavenders become institutionalized. Sadly, unless they are willing to accept help and face their inner demons, you may have to move on and find a healthier and more available partner. Your other choice is watching helplessly or riding the out-of-control roller coaster with them.

Crystals

When to Release Your Crystal

If your Crystals have gotten lost in their own inner world, if they have isolated themselves from everything and everyone, including you, then there is probably very little relationship left for you to extricate yourself from. You may be tired of walking on eggshells in your own home. You may be weary of waiting for them to regain a sense of self so you can have a life together. The out-of-power Crystals can become so aloof that you can feel alone even in their presence. There will be no sense of connection or emotional availability, and staying in this type of relationship is not only unfulfilling; it can also be painful.

On the extreme side, these fragile souls can become so paranoid and phobic that they do not feel safe coming out of their homes. They tend to be so reclusive that no one can touch them. If they have become frightened even of you, or have shut down so much that they will not talk to you, then it may be time to let these Crystals live a solitary life. If they are no longer physically, mentally, or emotionally available, your relationship may have become too empty or too painful for you to continue. Hiding from the world can become an out-of-power Crystal's way of life. Many of these terrified souls retreat into monastic lives, turning inward to their spirituality for solace and comfort. They often become celibate. In and of itself, celibacy is not a bad thing, but it does not necessarily lend itself to creating a close or intimate relationship with another.

It may be that you have just become bored with your life with a Crystal. After all, Crystals don't need much stimulation. They are often so content to sit alone in meditation and contemplate other spiritual worlds that they have very little interest in anything the physical world has to offer. They feel they do not require anything or anyone else to be in their lives.

You may desire a partner who is willing to have more fun, someone who is not so easily affected or traumatized by everyone and everything around them. Maybe your needs have changed. You may have wanted the security and quiet serenity that your Crystal portrayed, but now you desire to be with someone who can be more adventurous or more outgoing.

If you can leave Crystals with grace and respect, if you can leave without criticizing or making them feel inadequate or wrong, then they will heal quickly. Crystals can be hypersensitive, but they can also be content to live alone. Most likely, they have felt your restlessness and discontent, which may have caused them to feel anxious. They may have begun to doubt they can trust you. Crystals need a steady, calm, and peaceful environment, so if you have become fidgety, you probably have begun to irritate or unsettle them. Removing yourself from their sanctuary may be a blessing to them.

Abandoning a troubled and frightened Crystal, on the other hand, can be a different matter. People can become quite concerned for these sensitive and lost individuals. Many out-of-power Crystals can feel vulnerable and out of place in this world, and they develop a strong pull to return to spirit. If they feel totally alone and abandoned, they may become so depressed and despondent that they consider taking their own lives. If you have one of these highly damaged Crystals, you are strongly advised to seek professional guidance. Because out-of-power

Crystals can withdraw so deeply into their own inner worlds, they may not agree to get counseling. It may fall upon you to get help for yourself. You may feel very helpless in this situation, and therapy may help you know how to handle leaving this dysfunctional and disruptive relationship.

Crystals with Red Overlays

If these fragile souls were abandoned or abused as children, their already unusual behavior could become even more bizarre. Because Crystals are so affected by those around them and can take on the patterns and personalities of others in their lives, if they were exposed to people who were angry or abusive, they may unknowingly have absorbed that energy as their own. Because these sensitive souls are so quiet, they can be easily taken advantage of as children. They do not want to cause any trouble, so they keep their feelings and traumas buried deep inside.

Damaged Crystals, in an attempt to figure out who they are and why they are here, and in an attempt to connect and feel loved, may take on the personalities of all those around them, potentially creating severe inner chaos and confusion, and, on the extreme end, even developing multiple personalities.

Most people with Red Overlays are either extremely angry or self-sabotaging. Crystals are no exception. Because most Crystals are not outwardly expressive or demonstrative, and they are intimidated by the intensity of rage, their hurt and fear turns inward and takes the form of self-destructive and self-sabotaging behavior. Their self-loathing and self-deprecating tendency is to shut off from everything in the outside world, isolating themselves and becoming so reclusive that people are no longer aware they exist. They can become seriously anorexic and try to starve themselves to death in an attempt to disappear.

Crystals do not usually physically harm others, only themselves. Their self-abusive behavior, however, can be emotionally taxing and mentally exhausting for their friends and families. Usually Crystals are open to therapy, but when they are severely distraught they reject help from everyone. They usually choose to isolate themselves and waste away. Feeling completely alone and unloved, they long for a different life — a life that is beyond this one.

If you are in a relationship with one of these wounded souls, and you realize that despite all your best efforts you are not able to reach or save this person, it may be time to move on. As with all souls, Crystals need to choose life and choose to be healed. If they don't, it can be nearly impossible to reach them.

Summary

If you realize your current relationship has too many problems, and you have decided to move on, you now have tools to help you on your voyage toward a more compatible partner. Be courageous and optimistic. If you remain positive and realize that each new encounter helps you learn more about yourself, and that each relationship can be a stimulus for personal growth, then your journey will be beneficial and you won't be afraid to be adventurous in relationships.

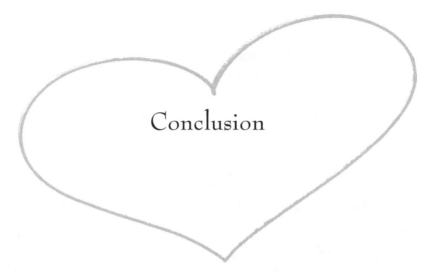

Conclusion

You now have a new perspective from which to explore your personal experiences of love and create your most fulfilling partnership. You may be anxious to find your one true love, the one with whom you can happily spend the rest of your life. Possibly this book helped you realize which Love Colors are most compatible with you, or maybe it helped you uncover reasons why you have not created this relationship so far. Or if you are already involved with the love of your dreams, you may better understand your current relationship now and know ways to strengthen your bond.

If you are going through challenging experiences on your way to love, the material in this book may have provided you with ways to work out these issues so you can be with your ideal partner. Remember, you can change your life and your circumstances. You need not suffer loneliness or be trapped in unhappy circumstances any longer than you choose. You are a wonderful, powerful soul who can create anything you desire. You now have information that can help you accomplish this.

The most important point to remember is to be authentic and true to yourself. You are a special soul deserving of love. Appreciating, respecting, and cherishing yourself ultimately enables you to accept true love into your life and then to share this love with your beloved.

Trust yourself. Don't doubt your heartfelt desires or criticize yourself for past choices and experiences. If you judge yourself, you could prevent yourself from finding or accepting real love. Regardless of which path you take, which Love Color you choose, or how long it seems to take, be kind and patient with yourself.

Keep in mind that there really are no right or wrong ways to experience love. Each Love Color has their own unique style and different desires for different experiences. Your relationship may never look like anyone else's. Your life adventures may be entirely different from your friends'. You have free will and can create, choose, and experience any type of relationship you desire.

The wonderful relationship you create could become a shining example of true love and an inspiration to others. Believe in yourself. Smile. Keep your heart open and optimistic. Enjoy the wonderful adventures along the way as you explore love.

About the Author

Pamala Oslie became interested in psychic work in 1983 after attending a psychic development class taught by the English shaman Michael Bromley, and she discovered that she was able to receive information about people clairvoyantly. Then, after attending numerous aura workshops led by Dr. Barbara Bowers, who was able to see the aura physically, Pamala noticed that she was receiving psychic information about people that corresponded with Bowers's descriptions and data on the various aura colors.

Eventually, Pamala also developed the ability to see aura colors herself and, through her psychic work, uncovered even more about the personality traits that coincided with each color. There are many valuable clues about a person hidden in the aura. The various aura colors reveal people's life purpose; their goals and priorities; their relationship compatibility; their most fulfilling careers and occupations; their attitude toward money, family, and sex; and their potential health challenges.

Being able to perceive the aura and understand the meaning behind each color helps Pamala better understand and have compassion for herself as well as for those around her. Her purpose in writing about the aura is to bring this knowledge to others, to enable them to understand how and why they process life in a particular way, to help them become more accepting of themselves and others, and to teach them effective ways to change their unwanted behaviors and attitudes.

For more information on Pamala's books, CDs, DVDs, and future workshops, contact Pamala at:

P.O. Box 30035
Santa Barbara, CA 93130-0035
Telephone and fax: 805-687-6604
Websites: www.auracolors.com and www.pamoslie.com
Email: auracolors@auracolors.com